DATE DUE

OCT 1 8 1993	

BRODART.

D1124655

Cat. No. 23-221

VISAYAN
VIGNETTES

INAUGURATION
SOUVENIR
Program

Siquijor, Siquijor

Jan. 8, 1972

VISAYAN VIGNETTES

Ethnographic Traces of a Philippine Island

Jean-Paul Dumont

The University of Chicago Press

Chicago and London

Jean-Paul Dumont is the Clarence J. Robinson Professor
of Anthropology at George Mason University.

The University of Chicago Press, Chicago 60637
The University of Chicago Press, Ltd., London
© 1992 by The University of Chicago
All rights reserved. Published 1992
Printed in the United States of America

01 00 99 98 97 96 95 94 93 92   5 4 3 2 1

ISBN (cloth): 0-226-16954-5
ISBN (paper): 0-226-16955-3

Library of Congress Cataloging-in-Publication Data

Dumont, Jean Paul, 1940–
    Visayan vignettes : ethnographic traces of a Philippine
island / Jean Paul Dumont.
        p.   cm.
    Includes bibliographical references and index.
    1. Ethnology—Philippines—Siquijor Island.   2. Cibuano
(Philippine people)   3. Dumont, Jean Paul, 1940–   .
    4. Ethnologists—Philippines—Siquijor Island.   I. Title.
GN671.P5D86   1992
305.8'009599'5—dc20   91-37573
                                                            CIP

This book is printed on acid-free paper.

For

RESIL B. MOJARES,

in grateful acknowledgment of

his contagious enthusiasm

about the Visayas

CONTENTS

ILLUSTRATIONS

Photographs follow page 138

ACKNOWLEDGMENTS

Many—perhaps too many—years have elapsed since I originally thought of looking at the Philippine archipelago with ethnographic eyes. For as many years I have been intrigued, attracted, and even seduced, first by the name of one of its islands—Siquijor—and subsequently by the social and cultural reality of its inhabitants, the *Siquihodnon,* who live almost in the middle, in what is known as the Visayas. "Visayas" is a term that refers to the central part of the archipelago, an area roughly circumscribed by the northern island of Luzon, the southern island of Mindanao, and the western island of Palawan.

Toward the *Siquihodnon,* and to the inhabitants of the municipality of Lazi in particular, I feel I have the greatest debt, a debt that can never be repaid, an *utang sa kabubuton,* as they say, a "debt of the inside." I cannot mention everyone here. Indeed, if their privacy is to be maintained, I cannot mention any of them. But I hope that the actual persons who, in the following pages, hide behind the characters of Auntie Diding, Tropio Quilicot, and Ned Pasco will recognize themselves.

My initial field research in the Philippines that launched this study was conducted on the island of Bohol in 1979 thanks to a summer grant from the Graduate School Research Fund of the University of Washington (Seattle). The bulk of my fieldwork on the island of Siquijor was done during a lengthier sojourn in the Philippines in 1980 and 1981, made possible by a Fulbright-Hays Fellowship administered by the Philippine-American Educational Foundation (Manila) while I was affiliated with the Department of Sociology and Anthropology at Silliman University (Dumaguete) and with the Cebuano Studies Center at University of San Carlos (Cebu City).

I was able to revisit the Visayas and the island of Siquijor briefly during the summers of 1983 and 1986, on the occasion of my participation in conferences that the Joint Committee on Southeast Asia of the Social Science Research Council held respectively in Penang (Malaysia) and in Cebu City (Philippines).

Ethnohistorical research in the archives of Spain, the Vatican, and the Philippines was supported in 1982–83 by two consecutive grants from the Social Science Research Council and the Spanish-American Friendship Treaty, as well as by a leave of absence with pay from the University of Washington. Consistent, gracious, and precious help was provided, in the Philippines, by the staff of all the parish and municipal archives on the island of Siquijor, the episcopal archives in Dumaguete, the Cebuano Studies Center at the University of San Carlos, the Lopez Memorial Museum, the National Archives (Bureau of Records Management), and the National Library; in Spain, by the Archivo General de Indias, Archivo Histórico-Nacional, the Biblioteca Nacional de Madrid, the Museo Naval, the Archivo Histórico Militar, and the Archivo de la Provincia de Filipinas de los Agustinos Recoletos; in Italy, by the Archivio Segreto Vaticano and the Archivum Generale Ordinis Augustinianorum Recollectorum; and in France, by the Bibliothèque Nationale.

A substantial part of this book was written while I was a member of the School of Social Science at the Institute for Advanced Study in Princeton under a fellowship from the National Endowment for the Humanities.

To all these institutions, I am grateful.

Within the long list of individuals who—whether here or there, whether by the warmth of their hospitality or by the sharpness of their intellectual stimulation, if not a combination of both—have contributed to this project, I can only make an unfair selection, even though my gratitude toward each and everyone is no less heartfelt.

First of all, I wish to thank Elli, my companion and partner in life, for sharing at once the excitement and boredom of fieldwork, for her sustained help in the writing process, for her critical, uncompromising, and unflagging support, for her love. And I also wish to thank my parents, Geneviève and Paul-Ursin Dumont, for slightly more than a half-century of sustained and supportive encouragement.

In addition, I am specially grateful to Alexander Spoehr, who, as one of my teachers at the University of Pittsburgh, initiated me over a quarter of a century ago into the complexities of Southeast Asian ethnography and who, much later, generously and patiently encouraged and guided my first hesitant steps towards the Visayas.

While I was on the faculty of the University of Washington, I owed much, intellectually as well as emotionally, to the enlightened collegiality and stimulating friendship of E. Valentine Daniel.

I also wish to recognize with gratitude the warm hospitality as well as the energizing intellectual contributions in France of Georges Condominas and Charles Macdonald, in Italy of Father Angel Martínez Cuesta, in Spain of Carmelo Lisón Tolosana, in the Philippines of Oscar and Susan Evangelista, Loy Maturan, and Father Theodore Murnane.

Many friends and colleagues were kind enough to read, comment, criticize, and otherwise help improve part or all of one or another draft of this book: Lila Abu-Lughod, Jon Anderson, Valérie Chaussonnet, Michael Cullinane, E. Valentine Daniel, Prasenjit Duara, Elinor Dumont, Clifford Geertz, Susan Go, Donna Haraway, Reynaldo C. Ileto, Evelyn Fox Keller, Dorinne Kondo, Charles F. Keyes, Resil B. Mojares, Sally A. Ness, Vicente L. Rafael, Joanne Rappaport, Paul Stoller, David Szanton, Toby Volkman, Pierre-Etienne Will. Lucille Alsen, Judith Hudson, and Priscilla Coit-Murphy graced my text with their editorial skills. Peter G. Roe and Egon Verheyen, each with admirable patience, provided their artistic talent and computing expertise for the maps and figures. And without T. David Brent's gentle and firm prodding at the University of Chicago Press, this work might still be in progress.

Finally, I was privileged to encounter Resil B. Mojares, Director of the Cebuano Studies Center at the University of San Carlos, to whom this book is dedicated. For his total generosity with his time and energy coupled with his encyclopedic knowledge and interests when it came to the Philippines, for his extraordinary patience with me, for his ability to solve any problem whether logistical or theoretical, for his stimulating companionship and his constant readiness to engage in any serious debate, for his voracious reading appetite, for his ability to explain, restate, and rephrase, for his capacity to accommodate my every request, in short for having made me love the Visayas, he had no match, no match whatsoever. I relish today, as I did then, his friendship and the sort of refuge within/without the field that he provided me throughout and beyond my fieldwork experience in the Visayas.

NOTE ON LANGUAGE

Throughout this book, material originally written in a foreign language has been translated into English by the author, unless otherwise specified. Cebuano—the Visayan language spoken on the island of Siquijor—is written with the alphabet that Spaniards imposed, and consequently there are a great number of spelling inconsistencies in the language. For instance, Cebuano has only three vocalic phonemes (/a/, /i/, /u/), but the writing system uses the full gamut of five vowels inherited from Spanish orthography (a, e, i, o, u), leading to inconsistencies. In Cebuano publications, the relevant glottal stop is used only sparsely; for the sake of simplicity, I have not transcribed it. I have generally followed the spelling that Wolff (1972) used in his *Dictionary* despite the departure it represents from common everyday usage. It is not perfect, but it uses one character per phoneme in all but three cases: (1) the palatal voiceless affricate "ts" (as in *tsismis*, "gossip") uses two characters; (2) so does the palatal voiced affricate "dy" (as in *dyulin*, "marbles"); and (3) so does the dorsal nasal stop "ng" (as in *ngawngaw*, "to cry loudly"). The following is thus an approximation of the pronunciation:

   i as in b*ee* or in b*ay*
   a as in f*a*ther
   u as in d*oo*m or in d*o*me
   w as in *w*et
   y as in *y*et
   l as in *l*ust if slightly rolled and not retroflex
   r as in Spanish pe*r*o, a flapped *r*.
   h as in *h*it
  ts as in gu*ts*
  dy as in *j*eep or in d*u*ty

p

t

k

b

d

g　as in *g*orge (never as in *G*eorge)

m

n

ng　as in the velar nasal si*ng*i*ng*

Note. Contrary to English, none of the consonants *p* to *n* is ever aspirated.

DRAMATIS PERSONAE

This list is meant to help the reader keep track of the different actors in the social drama represented in the text that follows. For the sake of greater clarity and ease of use, I have restricted the list to main characters, leaving out others whose names appear merely in a kinship chart or who are mentioned only in passing.

In order to preserve the anonymity of my informants, a number of place names (all *sitio* and *barangay*) have been changed, although I have kept the actual name of municipalities. With the exception of historical characters without known living descendants in the municipality of Lazi, all personal names have been changed. All the pseudonyms, however, have been drawn from the pool of actual names in use on the island of Siquijor. Married women are always referred to by the last names they had prior to their marriage. In the list itself, last names are in boldface while first names and nicknames are in regular type.

Auntie Diding—A sixtyish resident of *sitio* Camingawan, born **Quilicot**, the widow of Pedro **Dagatan** and mother of Virgie, Berto, and Oyo **Dagatan**.

Bato, Santas—Deceased wife of Tropio **Quilicot**.

Dagatan, Berto—Son of Auntie Diding, married to Milia **Palongpalong**.

Dagatan, Oyo—Son of Auntie Diding, married to Cording **Jaictin**.

Dagatan, Luis—Brother of Tibay **Dagatan** and father of Pedro **Dagatan**.

Dagatan, Pedro—Deceased husband of Auntie Diding.

Dagatan, Tasing—A resident of Camingawan, unmarried daughter of Tiyong **Dagatan** and one of Virgie **Dagatan**'s father's brother's daughter.

Dagatan, Teofista—Wife of Loloy **Tundag**, and first cousin of Pedro **Dagatan**.

Dagatan (*manang*) Tibay a.k.a. Primitiva—A Camingawan resident, wife of Bonifacio **Quilicot** and mother of Ramon, Tropio, and Aurelia **Quilicot**.

Dagatan, Tiyong—Brother of Pedro **Dagatan** and father of Tasing **Dagatan**.

Dagatan, Trina—Daughter of Berto **Dagatan** and of Milia, living at Auntie Diding's.

Dagatan, Tiyong—Auntie Diding's brother-in-law and husband of Angela **Villaros**.

Dagatan, Virgie—Auntie Diding's youngest daughter.

Dalugdug, Minay—A health professional married to Ned **Pasco**.

Duhaylungsod, Soy—Teenaged grandson of Auntie Diding.

Isoy, Leon—A resident of Camingawan, one of Ned **Pasco**'s fishermen, and one of Virgie **Dagatan**'s first cousins.

Jaictin, Cording—Wife of Oyo **Dagatan**.

Lapinig, Filemon—An eligible bachelor, resident of Camingawan and one of Ned Pasco's fishermen.

Larot, Daniel—a young eligible bachelor from Camingawan.

Mahinay, Fidel—a mature resident of Camingawan married to Hermenegilda **Pasco**, and one of Ned **Pasco**'s fishermen.

Mahinay (*manang*) Iyay—First cousin of *manang* Tibay **Dagatan**, sister-in-law of Andres **Sumagang** and one of the eldest women of Camingawan.

Palongpalong, Milia—Wife of Berto **Dagatan**.

Pasco, Hermenegilda—Daughter of Leoncio **Pasco**, married to Fidel **Mahinay**.

Pasco, Jesus—Resident of Camingawan, brother of Leoncio **Pasco**, and distant relative of Ned **Pasco**.

Pasco, Leoncio—Resident of Lapyahan, brother of Jesus **Pasco**, and distant relative of Ned **Pasco**.

Pasco, Ned—A town resident and entrepreneur, married to Minay **Dalugdug**.

Pasco, Saturio—Father of Ned **Pasco** and town resident.

Pasco, Victoriano—Former mayor of Lazi and first cousin of Saturio **Pasco**.

Quilicot, Aurelia—Youngest sister of Tropio **Quilicot**.

Quilicot, Bonifacio—Deceased husband of Primitiva **Dagatan**, brother of Auntie Diding, father of Ramon **Quilicot**, Tropio **Quilicot**, and Aurelia **Quilicot**.

Quilicot, Dadoy—Eldest son in Camingawan of Feliza **Taracarol** and Ramon **Quilicot**.

Quilicot, Diding—see Auntie Diding.

Quilicot, Linda—Daughter of Tropio **Quilicot**.

Quilicot, Lisa—Daughter of Ramon **Quilicot**.

Quilicot, Ramon—Tropio **Quilicot**'s elder brother, married to Feliza **Taracarol**; father of, among others, Dadoy and Lisa **Quilicot**; and one of Ned **Pasco**'s fishermen.

Quilicot, Tropio—A middle aged widower at Camingawan, son of Primitiva **Dagatan** and Bonifacio **Quilicot**, brother of Ramon and Aurelia **Quilicot**.

Saplot, Victor—*Barangay* captain, distant relative of the **Quilicot**s.

Sumagang, Andres—The oldest male resident of Lapyahan, father of Cristita **Sumagang** and grandfather of Zosing **Yano**.

Sumagang, Cristita—Resident of Camingawan, daughter of Andres **Sumagang**, and mother of Zosing **Yano**.

Taracarol, Feliza—Wife of Ramon **Quilicot** and mother of Dadoy **Quilicot** and nine other children.

Tundag, Loloy—A fisherman of Camingawan, married to Teofista **Dagatan**.

Villaros, Angela—Resident of Camingawan and wife of Tiyong **Dagatan**.

Yano, Zosing—A young fisherman at Camingawan, son of Cristita **Sumagang**, and already married.

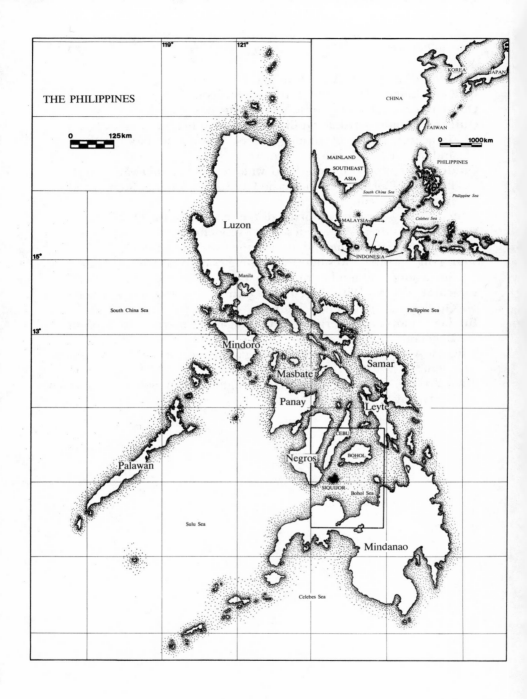

MAP 1. The Philippines and Southeast Asia

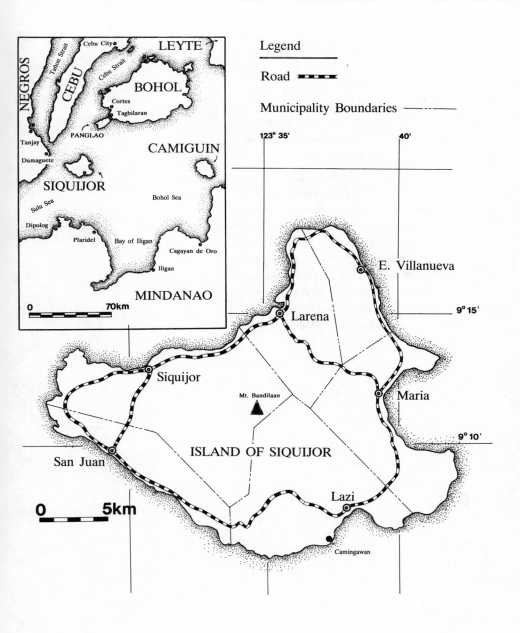

MAP 2. Siquijor and the Central Visayas

Je t'avais promis à mon
départ de t'envoyer cette île:
la voici. Tu seras sans doute
un peu déçue. . . .

Je désirais te faire le
récit le plus simple, et le
plus vrai, sans rien y ajouter d'imaginaire,
bien que tu saches que tout ce que nous
voyons est aussi bien éclairé
par notre regard que par le soleil,
et que d'autre part les petites
retouches mensongères font mieux
apparaître la vérité.
GEORGES LIMBOUR,
Soleils Bas

1

Prologue:
Ang mga hulagway sa kabisaya-an
or
Visayan Vignettes

F|ROM THE OUTSET, I have consistently
thought this to be a book about the Visayas, the islands of the central
Philippines, and particularly about Siquijor, which lent its expanse to
our shared interpretive enterprise. But wishing for greater accuracy,
I must state that my text is less about the island itself than about its
inhabitants, or at least about the handful of people whom my wife
and I came to know as we shared their lives in 1980 and 1981 and
whom I revisited in 1983 and 1986. I may even have to qualify this
statement further and recognize that, really, my text is about our mutual interaction as I am able to represent it in the following pages.

As the title intends to convey, this book contains no definitive
truth; nor is it a work of fiction either. It contends with some fragmented realities, gathered in the Visayas, in the concrete, historical,
social and cultural context of our mutual interaction. In an effort
at representing such realities, I propose a plurality of images—
vignettes—that superimpose themselves upon each other to create an
out-of-focus ensemble, since cultural contours are never sharp and
stories never straight, neither those I heard nor those I tell.

Like the small vines from which the word derives, "vignettes" reflect such fragmentation in the Visayan world, in its interpretation
and in their respective representations. *The Concise Oxford Dictionary
of Current English* (Fowler and Fowler 1956:1429), my faithful writing
companion since my high school days, defines "vignette," first, as an
architectural "ornament of leaves & tendrils" and, in a metaphorical
sense, as a "photograph or portrait showing only head & shoulders
with background gradually shaded off; (fig.) character sketch."

To designate a small but precious scene or portrait, to mention
what in fine arts or in literature would be called a vignette, a Cebuano

speaker would use the term *hulagway,* which refers at once to a picture, a portrait, a description, or even a mental picture. This phrase results from the collision of two other words: *hulad,* which means "to describe," "to depict," but also "to publish," as well as "to copy according to a pattern," even to "translate"; and *dagway,* which corresponds to nouns for the "human face," for the "looks," for the "appearance," but also to the adverbs "perhaps" or even "probably." I have a rather formidable task in front of me if I am to do justice to the complexities of such *ang mga hulagway sa kabisaya-an.*

──────────── *Transforming Voices:* ────────────
Anthropological Writing

Here are my concerns. Books written by anthropologists, including the present one, are "always already"—to borrow Derrida's (1976 [1967]: *passim*) fashionable phrase—suspicious. And so they should be, necessarily and immediately; for they are not evoking eternal truth, but localized, situated, partial, special, little, ephemeral realities, which would lose their entire content if deprived of the context from which they emerge.

If, as is usually the case, anthropologists "speak" through an ethnography, all too often they mask (see Rabinow 1979) the conditions of emergence of their text for the sake of a wishful but fallacious coherence. I am not referring exclusively to the place of the anthropologist in the fieldworking enterprise, since an effort toward self-reflexivity (see for instance Rabinow 1977, Dumont 1992 [1978]) has now become part and parcel of the trade. Here I am mainly concerned with the writing process, which has been the object of much, perhaps even too much, attention since the publication a few years ago of *Writing Culture* (Clifford and Marcus 1986).

With a few notable exceptions, however, among which John Dorst's *The Written Suburb* (1989), Dorinne Kondo's *Crafting Selves* (1990), and Paul Stoller's *Fusion of the Worlds* (1989) definitely stand out, most ethnographers have had a great deal of difficulty in operationalizing the programmatic statements of the theorists. In this respect, the bibliographies of even the most recent books by "textualists" (e.g., Tyler 1987, Manganaro 1990), despite their otherwise stimulating insights, remain long on theoretical promise and short on ethnographic performance.

The passage from any specific ethnographic experience to its discursive representation, from actuality to textuality, remains problematic. Hence, the recent bewildered fascination of anthropologists with their own production (see for instance Carrithers et al. 1990; Manganaro 1990; Richardson 1990; Roth 1989a, 1989b). Otherwise ethnographers would have as little trouble writing up their material as they have had writing down their fieldnotes.

Fieldwork is a social encounter in which ethnographic reality offers itself—whether it is taken without asking makes no difference in the present context—in quite contingent ways. No matter how careful and indeed prudent the ethnographers' planning, cultural realities are bound to trample expectations, shatter assumptions, and shuffle the fragments of experience in such a way that everything may eventually make sense, although little does on the spot. This is why anthropologists feel compelled to "write everything down" as fieldnotes.[1] They never know when anything might become useful, enlightening some aspect of the cultural picture. And they have no difficulty taking notes because they cannot perceive the people they study other than in the confusing thickness and confused commonality of their shared experience. As a matter of fact, anthropologists revel in these difficulties, since they have chosen to meddle in social milieux in which they are by definition particularly ignorant. Trapped in that fragmentation, they live in a domain of endless potentialities.

When anthropologists come back from the field, however, they take a completely different tack and painstakingly, if not painfully, construct ethnographies that sacrifice most narrative demands at the altar of discursive coherence. To use Toulmin's felicitous vocabulary (1990:198–201), here too the "rational" triumphs over the "reasonable."

Coherence—and it always creeps into ethnographic texts—is generally forced upon the gathered data and witnessed events ex post facto. All happens as if—the die of fieldwork having been cast—the odd bits and pieces, the undigestible morsels, the weird fragments, and everything else, all fall in place at once. And yet, at the moment when one is confronted with a specific ritual or hears a specific story, one is unlikely and often unable to grasp what is going on. Testimonies from many different fieldworkers may well concur, at least the oral ones sometimes given off the record in unguarded moments of candor. But in the writing process, the meanings of cultural things can be brought about inexorably by the ethnographer. "It is I who will describe them," said Malinowski (1967:140). In other words, the apparent coherence of an ethnographic situation is always the result of a writing, not to say rhetorical, effort, achieved at the cost of doing violence to the evidence. At best, it repackages ethnographic situa-

1. With the notable exception of the contributors to a recent book specifically dedicated to that subject (Sanjek 1990), ethnographers have been so far extremely discreet about their fieldnotes and whatever turns around the process of generating them.

tions into the rationality du jour; at worst, it becomes an ideological fabrication that takes the light pretext of a frustrated ethnographic encounter to spin its tale.

The origins of this problem, provided it be identified as such, are to be found in the fundamental contradiction(s) that subvert ethnographic praxis. In the field, anthropologists immerse themselves in the society and culture of "others"; while at their writing desk, they view it all from afar. First they write fieldnotes; then only do they write up ethnographies. These efforts coincide neither in focus nor in time. If fieldwork and writing necessarily take place in that order, the respective engagements each entails remain relatively separate. The field situation is mostly an intercultural experience (between ethnographers and the people with whom they interact in the field), while the writing situation is mostly an intracultural undertaking (concerning mainly the ethnographers and the readers who constitute their audiences, even though every day more and more "natives" have access to, thus read and engage, when they do not write, the ethnographers' texts).

Ethnographies transform persons into characters in focusing on circumscribed social objects made up of human subjects marshaled into traditional, thus preconceived and reified, if not poorly reflected, categories. Following the vagaries of its literary genre, an ethnography rounds up and traps between its front and back covers an all-too-well-bounded and defined group of people made to fit the cleavages of anthropological knowledge according to the still pervasive Western nineteenth-century categories of knowledge. Not only have people been willy-nilly molded into groups, but everything happens as if they were all walking in step and looking in the same direction, as if on the verge of some absolute transparency.

The worst possible put-down of an ethnographer's repute is the accusation of self-contradiction, considered less as an accurate reflection of the complexity of social life than as a logical mistake with frequent overtones of fault. Noncontradiction is perceived a virtue, and any conceivable contradiction is viewed suspiciously as if tainted by lies.

And yet, it is exactly the reverse that worries me, not only because one should always be careful with and suspicious of any totalizing model of explanation or interpretation when it comes to social and cultural beings. Social life in and of itself is full of opposing tensions, confused tendencies, cultural oxymorons, unresolved inconsistencies, stirring interferences, murky events, and haphazardous happenstances. In any cultural setting, anything always appears capable not only of "being itself, its opposite or sex," as I remember from my student days (without being able to remember from whom I heard it or read it), but of being anything else as well. For the world as we understand it today is fragmented, and not every contradiction can be dialectically transcended. Consequently our discourses, which quiver in the same trappings, are necessarily plural. An all-too-often hidden propensity to contradict oneself is thus perhaps inherent in how ethnographers apprehend those with whom they engage in their studies, their informants as well as their readers.

In ethnographies, the characters cohere on paper much better than the people ever did in actuality. In short, coherence may not be inherent in the very essence of any social and cultural process but attributed to it ex post facto, deliberately or not, forcefully or not, by the ethnographer. The result of such a *parti pris* is the theatricality, the exaggerated features, the very rationalities that have been grafted onto "natives," thus converting (a dubious term) concrete persons into personages. No wonder, then, that those among them who read our works become upset by our published accounts in which, to their horror and to ours, they fail to recognize themselves and their ways of life.

What has been lost in the writing process is the living texture of social life. Ethnographies end up being reifications in which all the "others" have been gathered together in the similitude of their respective otherness. All the "others" have become grey, undifferentiated in the uniformity of their barbarisms. Not only do they all look and sound alike, but they, absent/present in our monographs, all "read" alike.

If writing ethnography seemingly always does violence to the people under study, if anthropologists impose in their monographs an unwelcome and unwarranted rationality upon the sayings and actions witnessed in their fieldwork, if the ethnographic discourse is indeed at once reifying and politically offensive, is there a way out of this impasse, short of silence?

Although several solutions (critical theory, dialogism, hermeneutics, political economy, rhetorics, post-everything) come to mind, none carries total conviction. Ethnographers remain trapped in the conditions of production of their texts, as they are constrained on the one hand by their fieldwork experiences, by their rapport with the people they studied, and the records they have kept of such encounters, and on the other hand by the climate of opinion, by the prevalent intellectual discourse, as well as by publishing strategies and academic politics. But all those determinants are not equally constraining; at the writing stage especially, even though the memory contained in fieldnotes cannot be extended any further, choices can still be made in interpreting past events and in selecting a style of presentation.

In other words, at the writing stage, ethnographers have little leeway concerning the substance of whatever and whomever they represent, since that substance has been almost entirely fixed in the already completed phase of fieldwork. But they still can avail themselves of a large margin of maneuverability in the presentation itself, that is to say, in the use of rhetorical devices.

Perhaps a way of breaking the Western discourse on otherness—a discourse that seems to persist in marking and masking the differences between a "we" and a "they" as well as in blocking the recognition of the multiplicity of all different othernesses—would be to produce for the reader an analog to the fieldwork experience, instead of just relating it. Rather than aiming at a re-presentation of the otherness of the Other—a task doomed from the start—the emphasis could be placed on the representation of the "othering" of the Other, that is, on how that "otherness" is constructed. This takes place on at least two different levels, that of fieldworking and that of writing. Since the anthropologist has encoded the *substance* of this othering process during the course of fieldwork, this substance itself can be a topic of discussion. Were the work of the anthropologist just that, little progress would be made in the end: as the *form* has been unaffected, the process itself would be reified once more in the rhetorics of a rationalized ethnographic text, and we would be back to square one.

In the writing process, however, where ethnographers are presumably in command of their style, their composition, and all other rhetorical devices, nothing prevents them from destabilizing the discourse, from precluding the text's closure on itself (its tautological aspect) by fragmenting it in ways that "represent" in turn the fragmented realities the ethnographer experienced in the field. The reader would thus be forced into experiencing the intellectual discomfort, the emotional disquiet, the unsettling challenge of shattered certitudes that appear as obbligati in anthropological fieldwork.

If the fieldworking experience can be envisioned as a sort of prolonged hermeneutic and maieutic trauma caused by a social and cultural environment where hardly anything makes sense, where little (rather than nothing) can be assumed, where the obvious seems odd, where almost all that has been taken thus far for granted (including previous fieldwork experiences) can be instantly scrapped, where meaning is essentially elusive, and where sometimes the most minute differences become meaningful, its most radical aspect resides in its persistent hints of incoherence.

Although it is both impossible and undesirable to trace the textually inconsistent figure of a lived inconsistency (all solipsisms are private), it is hardly any better to (re)present the finished product of an interpretive process neatly packaged according to long-established monographic tradition. Furthermore, every text, this one included, is bound by reading conventions which guide the readers in their sets of expectations. If the readers of an ethnography are to apprehend the relevant differences—the differences that make a difference—if they are to grasp the texture, the thickness of ethnographic experience, if they are to feel the coarseness of grain that roughens the surface of anthropological encounters, instead of having them planed away in the logical and progressive cohesion of a traditional monograph, the ethnographic genre needs some refurbishing, even though no rhetorical action can ever be ethically and politically sufficient.

Such a rhetorical focus, however, often encounters a prejudicial objection. The most generous formulation would be in terms of aesthetism or, with decreasing tolerance, in terms of mannerism or even preciosity. But this objection aims at the political content of my argument, or rather at its absence. Since I recognize that every totalization is totalitarian, should I not produce a text that states so explicitly? The contents of my text should be addressed to the political issue that I claim to be of concern to me, instead of "playing" with the formal aspects of my prose. But this is to misunderstand fundamentally the previous failures of ethnographic realism in which the anthropologist's message, no matter how generous, was never really "heard." Otherwise, for example, all the previous and repeated anthropological texts "proving" that racism is unfounded would have had a greater impact on Western societies. In short, this misunderstanding consists in failing to appreciate that the form of a text is itself constitutive of its content and thus in itself a political tool.

It should go without saying that all this is easier said than done. It is one thing to think of oneself as an apostle of ruptured interpretations and another to resist even partially the temptation of neat packaging. Be that as it may, the present work is, after two false starts that I would indeed find difficult to repudiate (Dumont 1985a, 1985b), an all too modest effort in that direction. Tentative as it may be, it is meant as an instance, not as a model. Whether it succeeds in displacing the responsibility for interpretive closure, in opening up the ethnographic discourse to fuller resonances, in disengaging the ethnographers' authority from their awesome monopoly, thus forcing

Western readers to more active involvements and ultimately sensitizing them to the nuances of *différance,* can only be judged by the readers themselves.

THE THEORETICAL STATEMENTS above stand as an almost regrettable sort of authorial admission of intent. So to dot the programmatic "i's" and cross the epistemic "t's" is troublesome indeed for one who cherishes the explanatory value of descriptions and the very embeddedness of anthropological theory in mere ethnographic prose. Relief is at hand, however, for it is now time to abandon such theoretical speculations, which run so strongly against the general intent of this text; time to reach at last the island of Siquijor and to meet the first character in my narrative.

2

Auntie Diding

FROM THE VANTAGE POINT of her sixty years, "Auntie" Diding, born Quilicot, was a personage if ever there was one, a character escaped from, or more accurately as it turns out, ready-made to enter a book. "High blood" had made her a widow. Excessive blood pressure may in truth have caused her husband Pedro Dagatan's death, but several in her entourage doubted that. In passing and with half-hushed voices, some villagers, less poised than the august widow, had reached a different conclusion. They invoked no biomedical reason for Pedro's demise but spoke with conviction of the witchcraft to which he had fallen victim. Indeed, some people did not hesitate to name, albeit in whispers, the alleged manipulator of such supernatural and deadly forces. *Unsa gani* ("anyway"), as Auntie Diding would say of her marriage, she still had five living children and more than twice as many grandchildren (see fig. 1).

Her life spent raising a family, tending her cow, her pig(s), her small field, and her coconuts, as well as making her strong presence felt in her neighborhood, had clearly not exhausted her. If anything, she liked being active—helping here, rushing there, visiting or gossiping with people she had known since her marriage had brought her to the hamlet (*sitio*) of Camingawan in the village (*barangay*) of Lapyahan from a neighboring municipality.

Svelte, agile, and without major ailments, she radiated a youthful energy that her assured ways, her purposeful walking, and her cheerful manners underlined. Age was only written in the callouses on her hands and in the wrinkles of her face. All-too-often moistened by sea mists and exposed day after day to the drying sun despite her efforts to shelter herself under a battered straw hat, her skin had in time assumed a leathery aspect that the light brown of her complexion

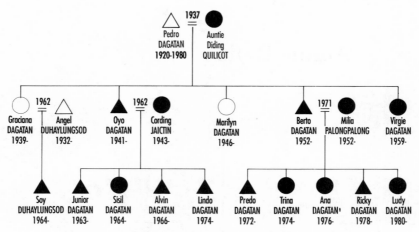

FIG. 1. Auntie Diding's descendants (and in-marrying
spouses) living in Camingawan

accentuated. The twinkling in her eyes, however, seemed to open
a window to the vivacity of her mind. A touch of gaiety emanated
from her, enhanced by her propensity to smile and often burst into
laughter.

Quick at figuring out the still undeclared purpose of a visit and
at perceiving the latent humor in a social situation, she would take
unusual initiatives, especially for a woman who lived in a society
where unassertiveness—the militant disengagement that being *ulaw*
("bashful") entailed[2]—was better regarded than its opposite.

With faint innocence, I inquired about her social future. Would
she not remarry? The mere thought of it provoked explosive hilarity.
I must have been out of my mind, I, such a distinguished note-taker,
asking so silly a question. And yet it was obviously hard work for her,
a widow, to maintain her household. So she was not shocked, just
amused.

She would describe the routine of her daily activities in terms
which at first struck me with the simplicity of the bucolic life they
seemed to reveal. Undoubtedly sensitive to the poetry of the initial
alliteration, as well as to the prosody of the phrase, she expressed
herself and thus presented her daily work through a sort of Three
B's rule: *bunlay ug sagbot, balhin ug baka, bahug ug baboy.* To translate
this brief text as "to weed the field, to change (the pasture of) the cow,
to feed (leftovers or peels to) the pigs" accurately renders the letter

2. In local English, *ulaw* is rendered at times as "shy" and more frequently as
"ashamed." Depending on the context, the word carries a positive or negative charge.
The semantic extension of *ulaw* is therefore huge, from "reserve" to "embarrassment."

of what she said but leaves out the essential irony of the tone that she used, as well as the lyrical mood she manifestly intended to convey.

That there was indeed a rhetorical intent is undeniable. Otherwise the very rhythm of the sentence would make little sense. People, even in the Philippines, do not generally speak in verse, and if they go to the trouble of doing so, it is because they intend to produce a special effect that transcends the literal meaning of their utterance.

In focusing on these three specific activities, Auntie Diding not only presented an incomplete account of her daily life, but she deliberately truncated it, for obviously it was irreducible to and more involved than that. Clearly, she had omitted all the other activities, such as taking care of her grandchildren, tending her chickens, cooking, washing, cleaning, all of which were as characteristic of her working days as the three activities she chose and could have served as synecdoches of her daily tasks. Instead, she chose to present an image, an icon of her activities which was also an emblem, a symbol.

Auntie Diding's presentation of herself focused on the outside, on agricultural activities: it represented an orientation allowing her to escape from her domestic activities and her confinement as a widow within her own house. Since she was, as much as we were, the addressee(s) of that triple statement, she was not just describing activities that took place outside of her abode; it was also a casual presentation of herself.

And indeed, although at first it had sounded to me like a series of particularly monotonous chores to which any and every adult islander was condemned, she had not produced that short list as a complaint. To the contrary, this program described alluring possibilities. Full of energy, she could throw herself into the implementation of such productive activities.

By the same token she devalued, or at least de-emphasized, her domestic activities. It could be said that she turned her back on them and the narrow confinement they imposed upon her, while placing a lyrical accent on the *travaux des champs* that she embraced with determination, and even—or so it seemed at times—with enthusiasm. What she had lost in terms of social insertion through her widowhood, she was determined to regain in productive effervescence. In short, her thrice-proclaimed commitment to agriculture was self-centering.

And yet, something else, something quite different, was also implied, for otherwise Auntie Diding would not have had any need to have my wife and me participate in her work program. Myself a self-proclaimed *manunulat,* "scribe of things Visayan," able to lead neither a cow nor a plow and certainly not both together through a straight furrow, and my wife, always a book in hand and wary of being flea-bitten when feeding a pig—we both had it easy in her eyes. Were we not rich and leisurely? Did we not scoot into town at will on our motorcycle? Were we not beautiful with our long noses and untanned skin, our hands impeccably smooth and stained neither by earthly dirt (a fate reserved for the rural proletariat) nor by mechanical grease (a prerogative of the petty bourgeoisie) but only by an occasional ink blot (the privilege of a literate aristocracy)?

And so there was irony in her statement, a mocking denunciation, however indirect and almost muted, of our privileges over her station in life. Powerful we were, for sure, like all *Amerikano* who passed by. We did not have to weed fields, move the cow, nor feed the pig. In fact, we were not even allowed to do so, for when we acquired a pig and began to feed him, she was prompt to urge us to buy the feed and leave feeding to Virgie, her daughter, who—and how could we miss it?—could do that much better than we ever would.

Even though her statement had been a glorification of sorts, it was also not so much a complaint as an accusation: this is what *our* privileges brought to *her*. She was left with the work that we who belonged to an upper class did not, could not, would not do, out of idleness or out of ignorance. In the end, although the phrase exhibited some manifest pride in her agricultural duties, it claimed mastery over us, who were so ignorant that everything in the local tradition had to be spelled out, mainly at my insistence, so that I could consign as much as possible to the squiggles in my notebooks.

This was by no means the only way Auntie Diding had of exerting power over us. Indeed, we who were so dependent upon her for our food and lodgings, for locating people, keeping connected with the other inhabitants of the neighborhood, and getting in on the gossip du jour, were more than happy to recognize her real expertise in all things native.

In exchange for the respect and reverence (*tahud*) that we paid her, she was an exceptionally accommodating hostess, always attentive to our well-being, not only to our physical comfort but to smooth interpersonal integration into the neighborhood.

This is not to say that capriciousness did not frequently spring from her playful personality. But it was as if Auntie Diding had to reassure herself once in a while that, although progressing in our knowledge of the Cebuano language, the village who's who, and the intricate relations that people conducted with the supernatural, we were still properly and hopelessly ignorant, gullible for sure, and cautious to an extreme—one going in hand with the other, since I always checked and rechecked my (mis-)understandings and thus was led to ask the same or similar questions time and time again.

ONE DAY, shortly after our arrival, my wife and I were working inside "our" hut. I cannot remember now what had kept us so busy. Was it some grammatical difficulty, some contradiction in my kinship charts, or the simple yet time-consuming task of transcribing fieldnotes? At any rate, we were suddenly disturbed by a bizarre sound that made us jump.

We were more puzzled than alarmed. It was not the noise of a child, nor was it the sound of an animal. It was not even the wind playing through the slats and thatch of our hut. What was it, then? We searched a moment for an explanation.

Outside, the softly whistling sonorescence sounded once more, and an artificially guttural, cavernous, theatrical voice slowly uttered: "*balbal.*" Recognizing Auntie Diding's voice and seeing her face at our window, we felt immediately reassured, especially since she could no longer repress her laughter at the effect her supernatural impersonation had caused. Were we to believe—or to believe that she believed—that she was what she pretended to be, a *balbal,* that is, someone possessed by supernatural powers and thus driven to seek fresh but sick human liver and human blood?

Perhaps not, since it had been meant as a joke, and it had been especially successful at disrupting our routine. Returning from moving her cow to a new pasture, she had approached the side of our house and popped up at our window unexpectedly enough to startle us. And indeed, Auntie Diding, who was always reliable in her promises and her information, although she could speak tongue-in-cheek with great ease, was also always ready to tease. At least in the immediacy of the experience, her jokes sometimes made greater sense to her than to us. Partly because of her natural joviality, partly because we provided her with a distraction from her routine, partly because we were so childish in our cultural ignorance, we were all too easy prey for a good prank.

She also liked to be a bit testy with us. Clearly she herself had ambiguous feelings about the supernatural in general and the *balbal* in particular. Of course they existed, even though she had never met any. And of course they were creatures of superstition, but she prayed to the Roman Catholic God not to place any on her path. She did, and at the same time did not, believe in those supernatural beings whose intervention on earth complicated the lives of human beings. She knew the priest's official line against these devilish creatures, but she also trusted her peasant faith.

In effect, in couching her joke in supernatural terms, she displayed her own metaphysical hesitancy. In addition to startling us, she was also reassuring herself on several accounts. First, she successfully made fun of us. Second, she also poked fun at the spirit world as well as at her faith, albeit vacillating, in the world of superstition, and so revealed her own sense of ambiguity. Finally, the addressee of her prank was perhaps neither us, nor herself, nor even the supernatural, but all of these together, as well as the entire neighborhood—among whom the news of our discomfiture traveled fast.

More importantly, her prank was a way of turning the tables on our power relation. She remained ultimately in control of all things native and in particular of our acceptability in her neighborhood. Whatever real and imaginary power we had in her eyes, she knew—and she had just asserted it in no uncertain terms—that ultimately we depended upon her as repository of the Siquijorian tradition(s) whose study justified my temporary existence in her village. My ethnographic dependence upon her was so great that I could only defer, if not surrender, to her and her people—something that my wife and I, disquieted and fooled by her impersonation of the supernatural, had just done with moving perfection.

The joke did not exhaust itself in its execution. On the contrary, it acquired a momentum of its own. It begged for repetition. In truth, there was no need for Auntie Diding to startle us any more; no need for us even to pretend to be startled when she reiterated her interjection: *Balbal!* But we laughed at its utterance, for the phrase had acquired a private meaning, a knowledge she and I shared. Ever since, each time she threw such a *balbal!* at me—which she often did—we laughed together. The word *balbal* in that context had lost its ordinary connotation. Becoming disengaged from its religious reference, the word appeared instead more and more frequently in my conversations with Auntie Diding as a marker of our intimacy.

It was also a permanent reminder of my necessary deference to her as an informant, a reminder of the bond which linked us. To diffuse any possible tension, I could throw the expression back at her whenever she appeared reticent about one of my questions. It would always make her laugh. She would take a leaf of tobacco, roll it, and place it in her *hunsoy* (more a cigarette holder than a pipe), and light it. She was ready to talk.

The interjected substantive had become a verbal wink.

3

Imagine an Island

E

VEN BEFORE I met Auntie Diding, I had
to imagine an island, an ideal island, not too large, though large
enough for an ethnographer to feel at ease, if not at home, with a
handful of people whose story I would one day tell. This situation
appeared to me both the servitude and the grandeur of the profession. Whose story would it be ultimately—mine? theirs? a dialogue,
perhaps? At the time this did not seem to be, or at least was not yet,
the problem that it has since become.

In my still unrealized quest, I was hoping for an "island" that
could offer me the comfortable illusion the word itself evoked, with
its double guarantee of relative "insularity" and "isolation." If I had
not opened an old atlas, if my attention had not been drawn to what
looked at first like a defect or a blot on the page, if I had not recognized that what appeared at first a purely typographical disorder was
an intentional printing mark meant to designate a small yet sizeable
island—if, in short, I had not noticed the intentional trace on the
surface of the map, I would never have met Auntie Diding nor any
of her friends and relatives.

I had often contemplated that map but never noticed the island
that, years before, a cartographer had marked. Where I thought
there had been nothing, there was a trace, marking the coagulated
intentions of the now dead cartographer who, in all likelihood, had
never set foot on the island he had brought to my attention. It was
also, at that moment, the present trace of my future experience.

Thus preunderstood and thus preconceived, this very pretext of
the island was meant to determine, to generate, to manipulate, to
transform continuously my perception of the island as I experienced
it. In other words, the understanding of the island that I would "end

up" having would necessarily be determined by the preconception that I had had and that I continued having, even though it was never exactly the same.

Understanding is always momentary, caught as it is in the dialectic of duration. The ever-changing preconception informs an ever-changing interpretation. Such indeed is the paradox of prejudices that are at once static as providers of idées fixes and dynamic as products of an interpretive effort—minimal as it may be—that experience disturbs and that disturbs experience.

And yet there are, as we all know, mishaps in interpretation. There are times when I may look intensely and see but a vision. These moments linger when a preconception congeals and disintegrates in truth. After the question, the dogma; after the image, the cliché; after a hermeneutic, a scholastic. Forget to pay attention, and suddenly the imagined island lies there lifeless. It is time to go there.

The notion of space, of expanse, that I have emphasized here was not the only trait defining the idea of an island that I carried with me on my way to the island itself—a concrete island with too many rocks and too poor soil for its flesh-and-blood inhabitants. To be sure, it is difficult now to grasp again my preunderstanding. There was also a musical resonance which to my ears was the very mark of the island, its signature, as it were. I am referring to its name its proper name, precisely that which had made me notice it on the map: Siquijor.

"Siquijor" had a musicality that bewitched me. How could I remain deaf to the whistling call of the initial consonant, indifferent to the acute seduction of the first vowels, unmoved by the enigmatic and mellifluous explosion of the last syllable that troubled my hesitant ear? Several possible pronunciations added to the alluring charm of the as yet unknown. And in fact, in the euphony I imputed to such an anapest, the three syllables of Siquijor hid and augured charms all the more ineffable compared with the unforgivably flat spondees in the rather uninspiring names of the neighboring islands: Negros, Cebu, Bohol.

No matter how lyrical my vision, because of its exclusive reliance on preliminary appearances, such an interpretation will appear so highly personal that the reader may object. Such a complacent fantasy, a private reverie, betrays self-indulgence and distracts from the more serious business of anthropology. And yet, my initial awareness of the island had been through the drifting of my imagination, through an individual prejudgment and thus through a personal prejudice I could not deny.

In fact, I should not deny it. Before individual works are consumed, they are first produced. Inasmuch as my perception was a construct, it was not taking place on a tabula rasa of conceptual noth-ingness. Undoubtedly, others (other individuals, since this is who we are in the West) would have been struck by something else and would have expressed the process of attraction and seduction in entirely dif-ferent ways. The rhythm of the word, the appeal of this sonority, the pleasure derived from the minimalism of the sign, all revealed less the objective properties of the island of Siquijor than the historical and sociocultural milieu whence came the anthropologist who noticed them.

In my anticipation, I imagined an enchanting Siquijor because my own culture—French by birth and education, American by mar-riage and orientation; at any rate Western—exploited with ease, greed, and carelessness an aestheticism hastily spliced to a most un-reflected-upon orientalism. At once seedy and luxurious, opulent and outlandish, tropical and squalid, the imaginary Orient that I con-structed resembled all too much the one that Said (1978) had im-pugned when he assumed a strongly militant tone in a discourse that others (e.g., Condominas 1965) had entered into earlier.

Prudent, I mitigated my own, albeit shared, exotic vision of palm trees, pink sunsets, and other Club-Med paraphernalia. To this im-aginary landscape I added more miserabilist expectations: a plethora of malnourished children among the many other attributes of under-development. But that was because, once more, my own culture, full of fin-de-siècle compromises, tolerated all too easily the double re-sponse of seduction and repulsion through which it adopted a strained—at once romantic and realistic—vision of the Third World.

Thus I approached Siquijor, arrived in the field with a bulky yet necessary piece of mental luggage I had acquired in the process of my own enculturation; it was not even the private fantasy of a partic-ular individual. (In evoking my preunderstanding, in pushing to the fore my rhetorical devices, I strive neither to fall victim to introspec-tive subjectivism nor cavalierly to prefer self-indulgence to the ques-tion of otherness. I am only making explicit what most texts hide.)

Incisive yet prudent as he can be, Lévi-Strauss noted that indeed:

All individual works are potential myths, but only if they are adopted
by the collectivity as a whole do they achieve 'mythic' status. ([1971]
1981:627)[3]

In my own case, both things occurred. My prejudice was infor-mative of the kind of perception that I would (be able to) acquire by

3. What Lévi-Strauss actually wrote was: "Les oeuvres individuelles sont toutes des mythes en puissance, mais c'est leur adoption sur le mode collectif qui actualise, le cas échéant, leur 'mythisme'" (1971:560).

having gone there. To a large extent, it was constitutive of the data to be gathered on the island; yet it was also, already, entirely constituted. It was less a private concern between me and myself than a phenomenon that was the product of a specific—social, historical, cultural—context, such that I carried around with me a fragment of it and a version of it. In other words, my prejudice was necessarily the variant of a Western myth, perhaps even of *the* Western myth of Otherness.

But of course, I was not the only carrier of a mythical perception of Siquijor.

THERE ARE, I understand, 7,109 islands in the Philippine archipelago. Luzon in the north is impressive in size, as is Mindanao in the south. The Visayan islands in between are more fragmented. Many of these islands are nothing more than tiny islets altogether inhospitable or unable to sustain any prolonged occupation by human beings (see map 1).

As a Southeast-Asian nation-state, the Philippines were under the Marcos regime divided into administrative regions made up of provinces where the authority of a civil governor competed all too often with that of an army or police commander. Big islands were divided into several provinces, while small islands were regrouped into single provinces. But some islands were just right. Fit for bureaucratic perfection, they were province-islands where physical geography and political destiny coincided.

Such has been the case, since 1972, of Siquijor, in the Bohol Sea, the southernmost island of Region VII, Central Visayas, located between the islands of Negros, Cebu, Bohol, and Mindanao. Small without being tiny, its 343.5 square kilometers (about the combined area of the boroughs of Queens and Manhattan) comprised only 0.11 percent of the total land mass of the country. Its seventy thousand residents, the Siquihodnon, were but 0.2 percent of the total population of the nation (see Philippines, N.C.S.O. 1975, 1982a, 1982b).

Even to a casual visitor, Siquijor offered the very image of homogeneity: a cultural, linguistic, economic, and religious togetherness of which many of its inhabitants were conscious and prompt to emphasize for the benefit of any stranger. Perhaps because of its boundedness as an island, its "gentle beauty" struck the Siquihodnon with the force of evidence, and in their eyes, the harmony of their way of life came close to perfection. Neighborly coziness and familiar intimacy combined to present the unique attraction of a paradisial lure.

Some numeric data even conspire, it seems, to corroborate this viewpoint. For instance, in the census of 1975 (see Philippines, N.C.S.O. 1975:25) 99.56 percent of the islanders declared Cebuano as their mother tongue, while only 0.11 percent were native speakers of Tagalog. Such uniformity is strikingly reflected in the pool of last names revealing a Siquijorian identity immediately to the outsider. The majority of last names (for instance Baguio, Paglinawan, Gabas, Aso, Duhaylungsod) are putative or actual lexical derivations (respectively "typhoon," "peacefulness," "to saw," "smoke," "two towns") from the Cebuano language.

Among the individuals who reported gainful occupation, over 77 percent were involved in fishing, agriculture, or both (see Philippines, N.C.S.O. 1975:26–61). However, I never met an adult male on Siquijor who did not have some kind of active involvement with fishing. Whereas all who farmed also fished (even people from the hilly interior who reached the sea only on occasion), the reverse was not true.

And although the census did not collect data on religious affiliation, the overwhelming predominance not only of Christianity but of Roman Catholicism was immediately apparent. My own data suggest that over eighty percent of the Siquihodnon were at least nominally Roman Catholics, the rest being unequally distributed between Aglipayan and several Protestant denominations.[4]

From a political standpoint, the island was firmly in the grip of the KBL, Marcos's political party.[5] Numerical data on this topic are more than difficult to obtain, of course. The opposition parties of the time, however, did maintain a very low profile—but they had to.

Administratively, the island was divided into six municipalities (see map 2)—roughly equivalent to U.S. counties—and seven parishes. The civil and religious entities had coincided until the establishment of the seventh parish, carved out of the territory of three different municipalities. Whether this indicated that a seventh municipality was in the offing, I could not say. The governor denied it, and so did

4. Established in August 1902, the Philippine Independent Church under the leadership of Isabelo de los Reyes and Bishop Gregorio Aglipay reacted against the then-overwhelming domination of the Roman Catholic clergy by Spaniards. In essence a nationalist church, its followers do not recognize the authority of Rome but do consider themselves Catholics.

About a year after my initial fieldwork during the rest of the 1980s, the concept of liberation theology and of basic Christian communities flourished in Lazi as in the rest of the Philippines. The competition between an established though perhaps stale Roman Catholicism and a charismatic version of Protestantism appealing to the most disaffected town residents picked up in intensity. On my last visit in 1986, the Seventh-Day Adventists could boast a permanent foothold in town and palliated the paucity of recruits with the intensity of their religious ardor. Not truly threatened, the Roman Catholics were nonetheless shaken and had reacted by organizing their own Bible-reading groups.

5. KBL is the acronym for *Kilusang Bagong Lipunan*, rendered in English as New Society Movement. A "new society" was what martial law was to have brought about.

the Philippine constabulary commander. The interested priests denied it too, and so did the concerned mayors, who were not at all
eager to see parts of their jurisdictional territory amputated. But traditionally, with the Church always a step ahead of the state, the establishment of a parish was forewarning of the imminent constitution of
a new municipality.

The mayor of Lazi[6] oversaw about one-fifth of the island and between a fifth and a fourth of its inhabitants, who were themselves
scattered among eighteen villages or *barangay,* defined in official
terms as "the smallest political subdivision[s] in the country" (Philippines, N.C.S.O. 1975:xii). Each one had at its head a *barangay* captain—Victor Saplot in Lapyahan to which *sitio* Camingawan belonged. Unlike a *barangay,* a *sitio* does not have any official existence.

TWO MODEST TOWNS on the island of Siquijor, Larena on the north
coast and Lazi on the south coast, were visited more or less regularly
twice a week by small and aging coasting-vessels that assured the
transportation of goods and passengers to and from Cebu City and
the northern coast of Mindanao, occasionally touching the port of
Tagbilaran on Bohol or Dumaguete on Negros. At the time of my
arrival in Dumaguete, no ship was scheduled in the foreseeable future; and I had to rely upon a smaller category of boat for a preliminary tour of the island of Siquijor. Everyday, weather permitting,
"pumpboats" (*pumbuts*) completed the round-trip between the town
or surroundings of Siquijor proper and Dumaguete, a voyage that
ranged from wearisome but stable to swift but fearsome.

Pumpboats are "double-outrigger canoes with inboard engines
. . . in use in every coastal and island community in the central and
western Visayas" (Spoehr 1980:43). They came into existence as a
technological innovation after World War II, when jeep motors could
be recycled. As a means of passenger transportation, pumpboats were
introduced in Siquijor as late as 1962 under circumstances described
in a newspaper article of the time:

> During the rainy season when [the] interisland ships reduced trips or
> failed to show up altogether, business in Siquijor was at standstill. . . .
> But today, Siquijor inhabitants are rejoicing. There is transportation
> whenever they want it, thanks to the pump-boat, which was introduced only
> last year.

6. "Lazi" refers either to the entire municipality or to the "town proper" (*lungsod*)
where lay the administrative center (*munisipyu*) of the municipality. Further confusion
arises with "Siquijor" that refers (1) to the island or the province of Siquijor; (2) to the
municipality of Siquijor in the island of Siquijor; or (3) to the town of Siquijor in the
municipality of Siquijor.

A Boholano fisherman created this pump-boat era. He had come to Siquijor to try its fishing grounds, but noted this lack of transportation. He returned to Bohol, then came back with a boat powered by a 9-horsepower water pump engine. His boat made a trial run with 25 passengers that was successful, and Siquijor people patronized his service immediately . . .

Each motor boat makes the Siquijor–Dumaguete run in one hour and 30 minutes, against the interisland ship's time of two hours. . . . (Espedido 1963:24)

This last sentence showed a fundamentally optimistic evaluation of the swiftness of the voyage. In 1980 three or four such boats provided transportation to Siquijor. As the pumpboat did not dock but stayed at sea, passengers—their shoes and socks in hand as they were carried on the shoulders of young men waist-deep in water—were boarded from a beach in the surroundings of Dumaguete, unceremoniously delivered on board together with about twice as many other passengers as elementary safety rules would warrant and a heterogeneous if colorful cargo of already pungent jackfruit, fighting cocks, groaning pigs, hands of banana, sacks of root crops, and baskets of fresh comestible seaweed. Crammed under the roof, either on the window side where fresh air could be breathed at the risk of being soaked by slapping waves or at the center where disconcerting odors of engine fumes and vomit melded into an unhappy mixture, the passengers, ready to do anything to escape the consciousness of their precarious position, engaged readily in conversation.

"Yes, I am visiting the island for the first time." "No, I am not a business man." "No, I am not in the Peace Corps." "Yes, my wife will come with me next time." "No, my name is not 'Joe'; yes, just like the Pope." "Yes, I am a teacher; maybe, I shall write a book."

As we approached the other shore, the wind picked up strength and rain threatened. The keel had already rattled several times against coral reefs, as agitated crew members gave apparently contradictory instructions to the helmsman. Some women fingered their rosaries, but their mumbling pleas for divine mercy competed poorly with the polyphony of the elements.

Had I been able to concentrate more on the landscape than on our means of transportation, I would have seen the rugged and hilly character of the island, except for the flat, almost level cape extending west of the town of Siquijor proper. Eventually I had plenty of time to catch up on this, too, because our boat became stuck on a reef and the crewmen dove in to try to dislodge her from this unfortunate spot.

The town of Siquijor itself was now visible, with its tired-looking stone constructions, its zinc-roofed presbytery, and its decaying belfry, once used as a watch tower against Moslem raids in centuries past. Along the coast on the right, a seaside cemetery reflected the sunlight. Stilted bamboo huts were dispersed along the beach front, scattered among an abundance of coconut trees. The deforestation and subsequent effects of erosion were strikingly reminiscent of what could be observed on the island of Cebu. At the end of such travel it was a relief indeed to be able to distinguish on the small jetty the gathering of jeepneys and pedicabs waiting to load up for their appointed rounds throughout the island.

A first impression of Siquijor could be gained quickly by riding on the only road that deserved the word. No more than the fifteen kilometers that separated Siquijor from Larena were asphalted, but its seventy-two kilometers could be traveled without difficulty all year around. As it circled the island, following the narrow coastal plains whenever feasible, it revealed the ruggedness of an interior that was almost entirely hilly rather than truly mountainous. The conformity of the island with the rest of the central Visayas was striking, and what Wernstedt and Spencer wrote about them held true for Siquijor:

> Virtually everywhere . . . sedimentary materials are much in evidence. Calcareous-derived deposits clothe both the uplands and low areas with thick mantles of limestones and marls. . . . Relief in the uplands has been generally subdued to rolling hills. . . . Evidences of accelerated erosion are extremely widespread. . . . The entire region . . . has undergone periods of profound, relatively simultaneous inundations, allowing thick accumulations of marine sediments. Relatively arable land is confined to narrow coastal strips usually at, or near, to the mouths of the many short, swift, and often ephemeral rivers (Wernstedt and Spencer [1967] 1978:468).

A more specific focus on Siquijor corroborated the previous characterization of the general area:

> The soils of the island consist of . . . clay, underlain by coralline limestone rock. The whole island consists of coralline limestone and the soils have developed from this parent rock material. . . . On steep slopes the coralline rock and gravel are exposed and can be seen at a distance of a mile away. An erosion pavement of lime rock and gravel is now the characteristic feature of the soil of the island. (Rosell 1938:418)

There is little doubt that population pressure on the island was responsible for such an alarming situation, dating back to the nineteenth century when Siquijor received, mainly from Bohol and occasionally from Cebu, an influx of refugees who attempted to escape the grip of Spanish authorities one way or the other. The contrast between a before and an after was depicted in vivid terms, even though at times one wonders whether Rosell did not overplay the golden aspect of a bygone age:

At one time [presumably the first half of the nineteenth century], Siqui-jor island was very prosperous. It was rich in forest products, abaca and other crops grew everywhere, and the luscious lanzone[7] was abundant. The best horses used in Cebu, Bohol, and Oriente Negros came from Siquijor, and Cebu and Bohol also got most of their carabaos [water buffaloes] and cows from the island. Corn grew there three meters high and rice yielded as much as 100 cavans[8] a hectare. Bananas of all kinds flourished and tobacco grew very well. Fish were plentiful. The people were contented and happy. (Rosell 1938:418)

Maybe so; but perhaps this last statement slightly exaggerates the relation of causality between the bounty of the land and the felicity of its cultivators. What is certain, however, is that all this was already a thing of the past by 1938, since the same author continues without transition:

But as time went on, the population increased. Forest trees were cut down for building homes and the extra lumber was sold. The mountain slopes were bared, and continuous erosion brought the poor and rocky up-land soil down over the fertile lowland soils and made them equally poor. Today [and nothing has changed since 1938 in this respect] the uplands can-not even support a grass vegetation for animals to graze on, and the low-lands can hardly grow a fair yield of corn, rice, or tobacco. . . . The coconut has of late years been the mainstay of the island. (Rosell 1938:418)

The circling road that I was now following had been built, like the wharf of Larena, in the first decade of this century, at the behest of an American administrator, James Fugate, the only American who not only affected directly the islanders' lives but whose fame in their memory approaches that of General MacArthur:

During the early part of the American occupation of the Philippines, to be precise in 1908, James R. Fugate, a sergeant of the California volunteers, U.S. Army, was appointed by Governor Smith as the Lieutenant-Governor of Siquijor, which was then under semi-military government. (Maypa 1960:25)

Undoubtedly, the main reason the road roughly paralleled the coast was that construction there entailed lesser technical difficulties. The road could remain basically level and relatively unwinding as long as a few minor bridges were constructed. Without underestimat-ing the influence of the terrain, there was another reason for avoid-

7. In his dictionary, Wolff describes this fruit as "whitish-yellow, up to 6 cm. long, growing in bunches from stalks which come out of the larger branches and trunk (of a tall, slender tree), and has juicy translucent pulp encasing one or two irregularly shaped seeds: *Lansium domesticum*" (Wolff 1972:II, 579, art. *lansúnis*).
8. One cavan equals twenty-five gantas; one ganta equals three liters.

ing the mountainous interior, namely the settlement pattern of the island.

In the interior, arable lands were scarce and soils were poor, which was only accentuated by the effects of erosion. By contrast, the coastal areas were relatively richer, with more arable lands less damaged by erosion. And in a precious few cases, the southeast in particular, a few hectares of rice paddies could even be cultivated at the mouth of small rivers flowing into the respective bays of Lazi and Maria. Furthermore, the nearby, irregular coastline provided access to fishing grounds, available all around the island but nowhere better than on the western coast, west of the towns of San Juan and Siquijor. Although inhabited, the interior could support many fewer people than the coast, where the bulk of the population indeed could be found.

AMONG THE EIGHTEEN *barangay* ("villages") of Lazi, Lapyahan, a few kilometers down the road from the town proper, was a strictly rural area on the seaside. In 1975, it had 1,356 people scattered in 259 households (Philippines, N.C.S.O. 1975:2). Five years later, it had, according to my own census, 1,404 residents—717 males and 687 females—living in 291 households, clustered in turn into various named *sitio* or "hamlets," the juxtaposition of which made up a *barangay* or "village." In *barangay* Lapyahan, adjacent to the sea, was a *sitio* named Camingawan. And there in *sitio* Camingawan lived Auntie Diding.

4

A Touristic Attraction

W ITHOUT BEING BREATHTAKING, the charms of Siquijor are genuine enough for anyone who might succumb to the rustic lures of a South Seas island: the sensuous undulation of coconut palms, the eeriness of calm moonscapes, the iridescence of dawning suns, the luxurious exuberance of forming coral reefs, the nearly perfect transparency of the ocean—all of that and more.[9]

Among the moderately successful entrepreneurs in town, some nurtured and proclaimed grandiosely unrealistic plans for the development of tourism in the municipality of Lazi, plans sustained by the old dream of "making it big." This fantasy, charming in the freshness of its naïveté and depressing in the actuality of its economic details, had sprung from the brief visits of a high official of the Philippine government. Enjoying the privileges due his rank, he would on occasion fly from Manila on the only plane to land on the Siquijor airstrip during our sojourn and would relish scuba diving off the Lazi shores, thereby creating among the local elite a minifad of underwater activities.

What hampered the dreamed development of tourism on Siquijor was linked not just to problems of "infrastructure." The housing facilities on the island were as elemental as the transportation, if not more so. Only in Larena could a modest "guest house" be found; on the rest of the island, the passing stranger had to rely exclusively on native hospitality. And to be sure, the main function of the Larena hostel was not to accommodate the elusive tourist but to house a steady flow of various functionaries on inspection tours. The building had even served temporarily as a rather comfortable jail when the

9. Most of the material that constitutes the rest of this chapter has been published under a slightly different form in Dumont 1984.

number of arrested suspects in a case of government embezzlement exceeded the capacity of the island's correctional facility.

Given what could only be perceived by outsiders as its aleatory transportation system and its rudimentary housing facilities, it is hardly surprising that Siquijor appealed only to a very narrow category of tourists: a few Western Europeans in their twenties ready to rough it for the sheer pleasure of having reached, maybe "experienced," an authentically unspoiled island. A dozen of these adventuring youths registered at the Larena guesthouse during our stay, but no more than half of them "did" the side of the island where my wife and I had settled.

Apart from these sporadic visitors, few other outsiders—four, to be precise—disturbed the ethnic homogeneity of the island. There was a "Japanese businessman" in Lazi whose presence was at first a mystery to me, since local anti-Japanese feelings left over from the 1940s were still strong. But this mild-mannered entrepreneur, although of Japanese descent, was a Filipino national married to a Cebuana, trying to organize the production of shark-liver oil by local fishermen for the lucrative Japanese market. As he became moderately successful in his commercial venture, he began to fade into the social landscape. Such was also the fate, though to a lesser extent, of an American Peace Corps volunteer, assigned for two years to the small rural bank in Larena, whose Cebuano was exceptionally fluent.

My wife's and my social integration took a different course. We were the most recent foreigners to settle on the island. We were the denizens of Auntie Diding's *payag,* a hut constructed quite recently for a Peace Corps volunteer who had left after six months. Although everyone in the *sitio* and most people in town knew that I was a "teacher writing a book about the farmers and fishermen of Siquijor," even by the end of our stay I was still occasionally referred to and addressed by the name of my predecessor in that hut. Despite my efforts I had not completely dispelled the belief that I belonged to the Peace Corps. Apart from the nuisance of being deprived of my own identity, it carried no nefarious sanction and was thus rather inconsequential.

The issue was further muddled in the *barangay* by my being French-born but living in the United States. I pointed East toward the States, West toward France; I even displayed a world map with the Philippines at the center. But there were still individuals who asked me in which state was France. Most people's geographical horizons were functionally limited to Japan as villain and the United States as liberator, still with nuances of a never-never land. Since Spain had long lost its local relevance, the rest of the international scene remained blurred.

Neither in the eyes of the town bourgeoisie nor in those of the *barangay* fishermen and farmers were we ever confused with tourists. We were much too visible in the community, as well as too familiar with it; and we spoke too fluently (a hopelessly ungrammatical) Cebuano for such confusion to have arisen. There was no ambiguity at all—at least none of that sort—for the townspeople with whom we had regular relations, because their intellectual and geographical horizons were generally wider. Constituting an elite, they had either received a much better education or enjoyed greater wealth, if not both. Since being an anthropologist was to them an unproblematic if not transparent raison d'être that concerned them little because "the true traditions of the island [were] to be found in the *barangay* and not in town," my wife and I were their peers. And yet we were Americans, we remained outsiders, and we were consequently lumped together with any other strangers. This was indicated by the fact that every single tourist or official visitor who appeared in Lazi was brought from town to our hut, as if this commonality of status was supposed to entail an empathic mutuality of compatible interests as well.

At the same time, this commonality marked our proximity to and our distance from the townspeople: our proximity, since we were made to share in their obligation of hospitality and forced to approve of their openness to what and to who came from beyond the island; our distance, since we were also a diversion from their daily routine, and what was solicited from us was nothing more than a mock approval of their feigned cosmopolitan interests. In short, we were definitely worth a detour. Not considered tourists, we were partly transformed into a touristic attraction, as indicated by the interminable flow of people who appeared at the threshold of our home and with whom we had to reverse temporarily but repeatedly the relationship of host and guest.

Our status as strangers also determined, in part, our position vis-à-vis the people of *barangay* Lapyahan, for whom anthropology, respectable as it may have been, was certainly infinitely more mysterious an activity, not necessarily problematical but at least opaque. They too came and visited us frequently but chose to stay at the periphery of our hut even when we invited them to come in, baffled by the free spectacle that we undoubtedly offered. They were curious about us and amused by us, but they were also seeking, timidly at first, our patronage in the same way they did from their town patrons. Although we had no inclination to relate to them as patron to client, they had no other model for social interaction with people like us who were not previously acquainted with or related to them. Our being neither one "of them" nor even "of the *barangay*" was what obviously constituted our appeal. But their curiosity was not a purely and im-

mediately intellectual one. Quite the contrary, we were Americans
and from their viewpoint this was fine indeed, especially since it was
vague enough in their minds. To them we were rich, and the rich they
knew were their patrons, the townspeople.

We were therefore almost like the townspeople. As a matter of
fact, since our work was not a productive activity, since we were not
involved in agriculture or fishing, since we were involved "but in paper" as they would say of us and of bureaucrats, our research activities would reinforce in their eyes our association—I should probably
even say our merging identification—with the townspeople, whom
they rarely saw working. And there was a good reason why they
rarely saw them working, for they rarely worked, and never with the
energy with which the *barangay* people tilled the soil and cast their
nets. What they saw were the townspeople involved in their favorite
afternoon activity, playing mah-jongg. The townspeople, being patrons, let their capital fructify and their clients work for them, both
in their stead and for their profit.

For the people in the *barangay*, we were equal to but different
from the town elite. The main difference was that we could be more
readily manipulated, since intercourse with us, even if it followed an
established pattern, had not yet been solidified by practice. We therefore could be observed much more openly than any townspeople; we
could even be drawn into social relationships that the town elite would
have resisted. And yet this very difference, immediately obvious in
our physical features and no less subtly in our behavior, was too disturbing to be recognized as such in their experience. There was a
difference that could be manipulated, but it was not deemed a true
difference and accordingly was immediately reduced to a stylistic variation. In other words, we displayed a difference that did not make
any difference. Their experience of us could not and did not register
with them since, by being reduced to our similarities with the dominant social class, we were really not experienced by them at all. At a
conceptual level as well as a practical one, the *barangay* people knew
how to cope with the dominance of their patrons, which was the only
otherness that their culture let them truly experience. Anyone else
was bound to be dissolved into irrelevance or, like us, to be considered
as an extreme variant in the stylistic range available to them in their
relationship with their patrons.

That which appeared to us as a blatant misapprehension of our
social reality, and which on another plane was a culturally acceptable
way—if not the only one—of constructing our social reality, received
a corresponding confirmation from the ways in which the townspeople coped with our presence. For the town elite, too, we were

equal to but different from them. Since that was the case, it is understandable that they would have wanted to and did associate with us, yet not with the insistence with which they did. Our equality made us socially acceptable; our difference provided the incentive for the visits.

Since they felt little concern for our work, which they continued to perceive as focused on their clients rather than on themselves, they were not eager—at least never on a sustained basis; in fact, they were quite uninterested—to cope with me on a professional basis, that is, as informants relating to an anthropologist. "Forget about your book and enjoy yourself," was the advice they would most sincerely give me. Along the same lines someone would ask me, "Not finished yet?" half seriously and half humorously, with a slight tinge of irony that needed to be tempered immediately by a cascade of giggling laughter. Any effort on my part at systematic interviews with them was less than successful. At the same time they were more than eager to interact with us on a social basis. Clearly, we were supposed to be entertaining and entertained without stint. Any possible notion of work or even effort, no matter how minimal, had to be dismissed unless disguised by some jocularity, a style of interaction that at times I found burdensome. Once understood, however, the flow of information kept on, uninterrupted though formidably disorganized. The counterproductivity of frowned-upon interviews was indeed largely compensated for by the amount of information that my wife and I could retrieve from purely social small talk.

I must hasten to say, lest I give the impression of having been perfectly attuned at all times to what was going on, that at the same time we must have irretrievably lost a wealth of information that was displayed right there. Despite our presence, we were not properly part of the multiple dialogues that were being simultaneously engaged in. Although we could and certainly did take advantage of the situation to ask questions, which then were not perceived as inquiries but simply as points of information allowing the dialogues to continue, these dialogues were taking place between the townspeople themselves, who were in their own eyes not disclosing anything substantial to us but relating bits of news and gossip to themselves and only incidentally to us. Inasmuch as these stories could not make sense to us who knew neither the characters, the cultural implications, nor the context, we had to interrupt them constantly, not only to find out what was going on but more importantly in the hope of reconstructing the cultural significance of these related incidents. We were eavesdropping, as it were, on conversations not directed at us. They were willing to repeat and to rephrase—not at all for our an-

thropological benefit, since in their eyes those stories were more performative than informative, but for our social benefit, since we were
de facto their hosts.

If they were rather apathetic toward my anthropological endeav-
ors, the fact that we came from the United States was decidedly a plus
and piqued their interest. Given the history of the Philippines since
the Spanish-American War of 1898, this could not possibly have been
a neutral, objective "interestedness" but one which was informed by
a historical concatenation of memories and experiences concerning
the United States of America. There were among the oldest residents
of the town, a handful of *balikbayan*[10] who had retired to their native
island after having spent their entire life in the States, as well as a
number of still middle-aged men receiving a dollar pension as World
War II veterans of the USAFFE.[11] In addition, every one of the townspeople had, if not a close kinsperson or friend, at least a more distant
relative or acquaintance presently residing in the States. Furthermore, the members of that social class, even the most marginal members of that bourgeoisie, had confronted at some point in their life,
openly or secretly, the moral dilemma of migrating or not migrating
to America. Although relatively few individuals ended up making
such a radical move, many had applied for an entrance visa. When
this is compounded with the manifest aspects of an American cultural
superstratum to which softball, Coca-Cola, graduation rings, as well
as the English language itself belonged, it becomes strikingly obvious
that the absence-presence of America had been engrained in the native bourgeois *mentalité*. No wonder we were visited frequently and
with great familiarity.

As individuals we were unseen: their looks at us did not penetrate
at all but slipped off us to lose themselves in a different, preestab-
lished, and faraway horizon. One indication was the altogether stu-
pendous lack of curiosity the townspeople exhibited toward our particulars. Any questioning of our enterprise, any scrutiny of our past,
any insistent examination of our mores was at best superficial. Rather,
they did not relate to us as individuals but as Americans, according
to a technically prejudicial and extraordinarily rigid preunderstanding of what the States was all about. Inasmuch as such an attitude left
little or no room for our individual behaviors to contradict the model

10. A *balikbayan* is literally a "returnee to the country." This term is a borrowing
from Tagalog. *Balik* means "to come back" in both Tagalog and Cebuano. *Bayan* means
"country," "homeland" in Tagalog; its Cebuano equivalent would be *nasud*.

11. The United States Armed Forces in the Far East, made up of Americans and
Filipinos, were in 1941 under the command of General Douglas MacArthur. The acronym USAFFE is in common usage throughout the Philippines.

of America that they carried around with them, not only were we objectified but we were preconceived as well. We were, from their viewpoint, the United States they had always "known," at once experienced and imagined. Since, in a sense, they had invented us, any intercourse with us had to remain absolutely unchallenging and ultimately was only a form of association among themselves.

There was even more than that. For any strangeness, any radical otherness that we might have displayed by our mere presence was immediately diffused by the authentically native framework in which we lived. Our hut had become a stage on which we exhibited ourselves as puppets in their objectivated fantasy, and they did not—but could they?—tire of the excursion to—or was it an incursion into?—our abode, which had become a sort of tourist bubble, a "pseudo-place" (Fussell 1980:43)[12] where they could experiment on and display the consciousness of their sociocultural identity.

The very liminality of our hut—at once a modest Visayan traditional bamboo construction in a Lazi *barangay* and the residence of *the* two Americans—commanded a rather formidable contradiction. If they saw us as an expansion and an extension of themselves, if they looked up at us as an orientation for themselves, and if all this allowed them to reverse comfortably our mutual host-guest relationship, then in coming to us for social interaction they were undertaking the most undisturbing miniature journey to the United States of which our hut was the minuscule synecdoche.

Those who had actually stayed at any length in the United States, having seen it all, as it were, were noticeably unconcerned by us and appeared rarely on our premises unless there was a quite definite practical reason for their visit, such as bringing, borrowing, or returning something. But for those who only knew the States secondhand from hearsay and, at best, from a handful of haphazardly encountered Americans, we were the real thing, no matter how fabricated by their cultural imagination. If our authenticity was staged, it was most certainly not by us but by the *Lazihadnon* who could erase so easily and immediately the real discontinuities that separated us.

Although we had not constructed the stage itself, we nevertheless had provided it. Catalysts of their own interaction, we were not completely innocent of, or in, what was happening, nor did we discourage the townspeople from coming to visit us. Consciously or unconsciously, in subtle and not so subtle ways, we invited them to interact in front of us, since it was clearly such a splendid and serendipitous source of data and a rather obvious way of learning what they were

12. Fussell's felicitous expression is modeled on Boorstin's "pseudo-events" (Boorstin 1961).

up to. This said, we certainly offered enough latitude for their fantasies to develop fully. Our hut had, indeed, acquired all the characteristics of a pseudo-place. The fact that it was our residence had become immaterial; it had become for some townspeople a meeting place away from their conventional meeting places, such as the cockfighting ring, the billiard parlor, the market, or the church. At the same time, our presence also had acquired the characteristics of a pseudo-event, and although it had provided the occasion, socializing could proceed with or without our active participation.

The extraterritoriality with which our hut had thus been invested was further reinforced by the type of interaction that could take place there and that contrasted with the normal flow of social interaction in town. In these circumstances, a number of cultural constraints normally de rigueur in town were bound to erode so that a certain license began to prevail. All barriers did not instantly collapse, yet as time passed unusual conversations emerged between persons who were not likely to have interacted with such ease in the town context. Persons who belonged to different factions were careful to maintain their avoidance relationship and abstained from visiting us simultaneously. But persons who would have remained very formal with each other in town, on entering a different setting as they came to our premises, could become almost familiar with each other. For instance, the traditional terms of address which so strongly marked respect toward relatively older individuals tended to disappear and be replaced by a more egalitarian use of first names or nicknames. This abnormality in and of itself signaled a significant behavior modification.

There were more restraints yet to fall in such a context. Among our regular visitors, a number of women would not hesitate to accept a shot of rum from us, while ordinarily they would have rather been caught dead than been seen drinking in public. Furthermore, the generally valued reserve that prevailed in town was replaced by a seemingly liberated flow of unending stories and narrated incidents, perfectly trivial in themselves but eagerly produced and avidly consumed. Even in selecting themes of conservation, locutors could glide easily from the expected bashfulness that constrained them in town to an obviously freer style. Not only could gossip here become quite nasty and acquire detailed vividness, but even women who in town maintained a façade of repressed respectability would dare to manipulate in public the double entendre of some risqué stores amid explosions of embarrassed laughter. The crux of the matter is that in "touring" us, as it were, the townspeople relaxed some of their cultural inhibitions, as if they were actors on a theatrical stage where social and cultural experimentation was given free rein. It is not so much that every cultural aspect of their life broke down, for in fact most of them did not, but that "our" stage offered them the pretext and the possibility of daring, albeit momentarily, to behave in nonconformity with their expected standards.

For individuals who have been encultured to feel acutely *ka-ulaw* (that is, embarrassment or shame at what other people think[13] to the point of not answering a simple question for fear of giving the wrong answer), our stage provided a domain of improvisation, a place to test oneself as well as one's peers. There, one could *ulaw-ulaw* someone else (that is, could tease someone else by saying embarrassing things) while at the same time commenting on the reaction thus provoked. As we (over)heard once after some of our visitors had departed (although I cannot remember what had generated this little exchange), *gihatagan niyag ka-ulawan ang lalake* ("he gave great shame to that man"). Then somebody else replied, still in Cebuano, *piro nagpaka-ulaw na siya* ("but he had already put himself to shame").

That the experimentation was not always successful is not the point here. What seems so striking to me is not only that these cultural experimentations were occurring but that they also so strongly resembled the situation in which tourists everywhere find themselves. What and whom they tour are largely inconsequential since ultimately their real, if not only, concern is an experiment on themselves as individual, social, and cultural entities. If this is exactly what prevents tourists from seeing "reality as it is," from perceiving the otherness of others, it is also what prevented the townspeople from seeing us either as individuals or as persons. Looking at us, they were really looking at a certain image of themselves with which they could play. In a way we had quickly lost our identity and were reduced to our use function as catalysts of their own self-reflection. Literally, we had become for them indifferent.

Such an indifference to us, such nonengagement did not prevent either the *barangay* inhabitants or the townspeople from undertaking their trips. Indeed, it was the frequency and the regularity of such round trips to our hut that made the indifference noticeable. And thus, for the duration of our stay, people from the town and to a lesser extent from the *barangay* kept looking at us as an attraction. Their blindness to us as "us" was a construction on their part by which we were almost immediately eliminated as persons, as we had been the pretext of their self-experimentation. As persons we had been dissolved into a generic nothingness. Not only were they in a hurry

13. The Cebuano concept of *ulaw* is equivalent to the Tagalog concept of *hiya*. For a historical analysis of the latter, the reader may wish to consult Rafael's masterful *Contracting Colonialism* (1988).

to find a conceptual niche for us, they were also very little disposed to suspend even for a moment their disbelief. In other words, we could only fit into a preconception that, no matter what we did or said, no matter who we were, informed *ne varietur* the sensible and intelligible aspects of our presence on their island. In fitting us into a prefabricated mold of their own, they prevented themselves from relating to us but forced us into playing the role of Americans on display. Finally, as Americans, we had been reduced to something previously apprehended, to an already known, within their fantasy of themselves. In short, there was no escape from our transformation into pure cliché.

As an anthropologist, I would be a fool if I failed to perceive and emphasize that the Siquijorians' conceptual approach to our sociocultural reality was both mimetic and parodic of my own ethnographic curiosity. That recognition acted as a constant reminder to me of the humility with which anthropologists must hold the all too fugitive totalizations that they call their interpretations.

And, of course, I shall have to bear this in mind in my attempt to describe Auntie Diding, interpret my interaction with her family and with her neighbors, and thereby transform concrete Siquijorians into ethnographic characters.

5

Full Provincial Status

T HROUGHOUT ITS HISTORY the island of Siquijor has had a tortuous administrative destiny. Too small in area and population to be governed on its own, it was always subordinated to some other neighboring island in the Visayas, its identity trampled at the periphery of larger entities, the concerns of which were rarely consonant with its own needs. The repeated changes of status imposed on Siquijor during the nineteenth and twentieth centuries express the unease with which Siquijorians seem to have experienced such varied tutelage and inconsequent governance.

In the first half of the nineteenth century, the island was administered as part of the Province of Cebu, one of the thirty-five provinces that constituted the Philippine archipelago and that Buzeta and Bravo described in their contemporary compendium:

> A First Class Mayor with the title of military commander is in charge of the administration of justice and the collection of head taxes in this province made up of a multitude of islands, most of them insignificant due to their scant importance. The main islands are Cebu, Bohol or Bojol, Siquijor or of Fire, Camotes, Mactan, Bantayan, Mino, Davis, and Panglao. (Buzeta and Bravo 1850:I, 546; my trans.)[14]

The neighboring island of Negros, which had been a "corregimiento" from the beginning of the seventeenth century, became in 1839 a province in its own right as "alcaldía mayor de ascenso" (Buzeta and

---

14. The original Spanish text reads as follows: "Fórmase esta prov., mandada por un alc. m. de término, encargado de la adm. de justicia y de la cobranza de los trib. con el título de capitan á guerra, de multitud de islas, la mayor parte insignificantes por su escasa importancia. Las principales son Cebú, Bohol, ó Bojol, Siquijor ó del Fuego, Camotes, Mactan, Bantayan, Mino, Davis, ó Dauis, y Panglao."

Bravo 1850:II, 357), which in turn became in 1855 a "gobierno político-militar" (see Martínez Cuesta 1974:141–42).

By the middle of the nineteenth century, an important administrative shake-up occurred in the Philippines, with the creation of the politico-military provinces. The fate of Siquijor changed when

> Bohol became a separate province on July 22, 1854, when by a royal decree it was constituted into a politico-military province, together with the island of Siquijor. (Putong 1965:24)

Simple geographical proximity should have dictated that Siquijor be made a part of the province of Negros rather than of the province of Bohol; but the seat of the mayoralty, rather than the nearby town of Dumaguete, was Bacolod, on the west coast of Negros, far away from Siquijor. Tagbilaran on the west coast of Bohol was decidedly easier to reach.

A few years later, however, circumstances were quite different. From Bacolod, it turned out to be almost impossible to administer the east coast of Negros, and as early as 1864, the governor of the Visayas in Cebu proposed the creation of a new "politico-military government" (*gobierno político-militar*) to control the eastern part of the island (Martínez Cuesta 1980:289). The proposal suggested:

> that Dumaguete should be the capital of the Oriental coast and that the Island of Siquijor which was made up of four towns should be added to the Oriental coast because it is nearer (7 miles of distance) to this place while it is some 20 miles distant from Bohol where it belongs at present. (Manila: National Archives of the Philippines, *Erección de Pueblo, Isla de Negros*, leg.109, no.32, quoted in Hernaez Romero 1974:42)

It would be thirteen years before the island of Negros would be administratively cut in half. A royal decree of October 25, 1889, which was implemented the following year, brought the politico-military government of Negros Oriental into being. Siquijor, however, had not been included in the new province.

The Governor-General of the Philippines in his memoranda to Madrid could only repeat previous arguments, namely, that it was more convenient for Siquijor to be part of Negros Oriental than part of Bohol. He further represented that, in addition, the Siquijorians longed for this new affiliation (see Madrid, Archivo Histórico Nacional, *Ultramar* 5282, no. 71, in Martínez Cuesta 1980:324–25). Drawing from the *Libro de Cosas Notables* for Dumaguete, Martínez Cuesta summarizes the successful conclusion of these efforts:

> The decree of union [joining the island of Siquijor to the new province of Negros Oriental], signed by Gen[eral Valeriano] Weyler [Governor-

General of the Philippines] on Jan[uary] 19, 1892, was ratified by a Real Order dated Dec[ember] 3 of the same year, [published] in Gaceta [sic], February 7, 1893. Manuel de la Reguera, Commander of Escalante and Tanjay, was appointed temporary Governor of the Province until May, 1890 when its first proprietary Governor, commander of the Cavalry Joaquin Tavira took possession of it. (Martínez Cuesta 1980:357)

But new arrangement or not, Siquijor still remained under the hegemony of a larger and more powerful neighbor. In many respects, it was with Negros Oriental as it had been with Bohol: Siquijor was remarkably remote. In reality, it was almost out of reach for administrators who did not reside there, who rarely visited it, and whose interests and concerns clearly lay with the larger of the two islands. Perhaps an advantage of this relative geographical and consequent political isolation was that little of the turmoil that rocked the entire island of Negros and much of the Philippines during the nationalist revolution of 1896 and the Spanish-American war of 1898, as well as the ensuing takeover of the archipelago by the Americans, ever affected it.

By May 1, 1901, the province of Negros Oriental was reaffirmed in its limits and returned to the rule of a civilian government headed by Demetrio Larena, who thus became the first Filipino provincial governor of Negros Oriental. Soon after, Siquijor became a "subprovince" administered by a lieutenant governor. James Fugate, a scout with the California Volunteers of the U.S. Infantry, was appointed and served in that capacity from 1901 to 1913. Curiously perhaps, his presence and his engineering deeds—the construction of roads, bridges, schools, and a wharf, among others—were still vividly remembered in 1980, at least in the towns, if not in the *barangay* of Siquijor.

In a way, it is certainly ironic that the actual residence on Siquijor of that American—often mentioned as "an adoptive son of Siquijor"—seemed to have represented the achievement of aspirations manifested by the island elite throughout the nineteenth century. While the Spanish administration had been incapable of treating the Siquijorians with the seriousness they longed for, the Americans made a coup by sending an actual lieutenant governor to reside among them. In Siquijor, the fact that Fugate was American rather than Filipino, let alone Siquijorian, was irrelevant. It was his very presence that was taken to represent the seriousness with which finally the capital of the province had taken their small island.

The events that jolted the Philippines at the turn of the century had bypassed Siquijor, which remained slightly out of synchronization with the rest of the nation. The elite seemed satisfied with the attention Siquijor had received from Dumaguete. As I was told by an informant in town, "Siquijor was already a subprovince but not yet a province." This would occur only years later.

In contemporary (1980) memories, twentieth-century landmarks were few and far between. Pablo Bueno was the first lieutenant governor of Siquijor to have been elected. A native of Dumaguete, he served for two years after a vote in 1914 by the councillors of the six municipalities of Siquijor; but the significance of this had been forgotten. His immediate successor, Tomas Padayhag, a native of Larena who served from 1916 to 1918, was the first Siquijorian to occupy this position. But this too had been forgotten.

However, what was vividly remembered—mainly in the Siquijor towns—in terms of the political and administrative fate of the island were events which took place after World War II. This period marked the advent of what some people called emphatically, if not theatrically, the "independence" of Siquijor. Without having been at the center of military action, the Siquijorians had not been entirely bypassed by World War II. A Japanese detachment had occupied the island, guerillas had engaged in sabotage, and the interaction had wreaked havoc. General MacArthur, in being true to his word, was perceived as a sort of James Fugate on a grand scale. After the political independence of the Philippines from American control was "granted" on July 4, 1946, the Siquijorians were less disposed than ever to forego their own identity, as if, in addition to cementing a national consciousness, the war had planted the seed for their renewed "islandism."

Even with the presence of an elected Siquijorian as lieutenant governor, being administered from the outside from Dumaguete did not necessarily create smooth interaction and prefect harmony within the province. Siquijor was a secondary and distant dependency for Negros Oriental, and Siquijorians, at least the town elite, began to feel increasingly neglected, if not frankly abandoned.

In a sometimes vitriolic style, Apol B. de la Peña, a journalist and a Siquijorian, makes in a short article (1968) a powerful argument for what he calls the "provinciation" of Siquijor. First, he complains about the congressman representing the second legislative district of Negros Oriental (four municipalities in Negros and the six municipalities of Siquijor):

> Rep. Lamberto L. Macias . . . seldom visits the Island . . . not only because he comes from Dumaguete City, where he has his mansion, although he hails—legally—from the municipality of Siaton on the southernmost fringes of the mainland of Negros Oriental, but because he stays most of the time in Manila, where he has acquired a costly residential house and lot, and from here he, like his fellow millionaire-colleagues, manages by remote control the affairs of his district. (de la Peña 1968:12 and 16)

In other words, the representative of Siquijor seemed incapable of representing Siquijorians, and thus his competence was called into question. In the same article, under a photograph of the politician Eulogio Omictin, Jr., the caption reads:

His title of Lieutenant-Governor (of the subprovince) was changed by Congressman Macias to 'Governor' through legislative fiat—an act of which only the congressman himself knows the why and wherefore? (de la Peña 1968:12)

It is easy to infer that de la Peña condemned the futility of the congressman's actions in having thought he had taken care of Siquijor with this symbolic act instead of introducing legislation "for the provinciation of Siquijor in accordance with the longstanding desire and aspiration of its masses" (de la Peña 1968:16). De la Peña further argued that a precedent had been set by the creation of other provinces "no better than Siquijor in area, population, income, as well as in other aspects of qualification for provincehood" (de la Peña 1968:16). Rather than placing his faith in the integrity and efficiency of "a native congressman of Siquijor," de la Peña painted a bleak picture of the Siquijorian reality:

As it is, the Island, after many long years of political vassalage to powerful gods from the mainland, has never had even a smell of economic progress, although it has heard countless promises of a better future. School buildings are lacking, roads are not paved (except portions of national roads in the poblaciones), municipal buildings remain unfinished or are still the old structures that they have been since Spanish times, the hills and small mountains have remained bald and unproductive, streams have dried up as a result of defoliation, unscientific farming, and apathy on the part of the authorities, the supply of fish around the Island has dwindled largely due to tolerance of illegal fishing with explosives, and the general conditions on the Island are agonizing for attention and care on the part of the authorities. No real progress in the economy of the Island is in sight. (de la Peña 1968:16–17)

In such a realistico-romantic presentation, it is interesting to note the quasi-personification vested in "the Island," which is always written with a capital "I." De la Peña's appeal left the congressman unmoved, although a newly created "Siquijor Island Elected Municipal Officials League" or SIEMOL in Resolution No. 1 of December 28, 1968, urged him to propose a bill making Siquijor a separate province. On February 21, 1970, a newly created "National Association of Siquijorians" published a manifesto on page two of the daily *Manila Bulletin,* which put pressure on the congressman:

Congressman Macias, who, luckily enough, has gotten reelected for a fifth consecutive term in the House of Representatives with overwhelming

votes by *Siquijorian* electors last November 11 [1969], has remained unmoved and he continues to ignore the legitimate aspiration of the people of
the sub-province, and all other moves toward the same direction are likewise
not availing and have produced no sign of any foreseeable favorable result.
(Reproduced in de la Peña 1970:13)

In addition to forcing Macias to budge and introduce the desired
legislation, the manifesto revealed two other aspects of the issue. On
the one hand, the bill for the "provinciation" of Siquijor meant the
dismantling of Macias's own district, then straddling two islands. On
the other hand, he was drawing enough votes to be elected from the
barangay peasants of Siquijor, even though he had become unpopular
with the Siquijorian elite.

For the rural masses, it did not make a great difference whether
or not Siquijor acquired the status of a province, any more than they
cared if they were part of the province of Bohol or the province of
Negros Oriental. For the local bourgeoisie, being a province was indeed as significant in the twentieth century as it had been in the nineteenth century for the *ilustrados*. It was they who in the past had business interests and had to consider the distance to the administrative
center. And it was their heirs who now had, in addition to the proclaimed ideology of "islandism," something to gain in being independent politically from the control of Dumaguete and economically
from the more highly capitalized concerns on the "mainland" which
prevented, or at least threatened, their own growth.

Republic Act No.6398 "separating the subprovince of Siquijor
from the province of Oriental Negros and establishing it as an independent province" was passed by the Seventh Congress of the Republic of the Philippines. It was approved on September 17, 1971, by
President Ferdinand E. Marcos and ratified by the electors of Siquijor
in a plebiscite at local elections on November 8, 1971. Finally, the
Province of Siquijor was inaugurated on January 8, 1972.

On that occasion a 186-page *Inauguration Souvenir Program* was
published. An impressive 27.3 cm. by 21.2 cm. in-folio, it contained
portraits and congratulatory messages from Philippine officials, bio-
graphical sketches of the new Siquijor administrators, a roster of civil
servants and elected officials in the new province and its municipalities, as well as a calendar of activities complete with a picture of the
mutya sa lalawigan—"Pearl of the Province"—of course the winner of
the beauty pageant. The rich iconicity of its cover (see frontispiece)
deserves further comment.

At the bottom, just above the phrases "Siquijor, Siquijor" on the
left and "Jan. 8, 1972" on the right, the picture of a heavy, dark chain
has been painted. Two of its links are broken: one is still in position

as if it had just snapped, and the other one hangs. Above the chain a map of the new province with its municipalities is superimposed on a profile of the island. On the side, the figure of a young, dark-haired, brown-skinned Filipina in a full-length skirt and a loose short-sleeved blouse, stands in a posture obviously inspired by the Statue of Liberty. In her left hand, she holds a scroll with an inscription, of which only "RA 6398" is legible. Her right hand is raised as she holds a torch, the flame of which shines—as the sun would—in all directions but particularly over herself, presumably the metonym of the Siquijorians, and over the entire island, which is thus assured of a "bright future."

This description would remain incomplete if I did not mention, appearing under the title "Inauguration Souvenir Program" (each word in different lettering on a new line), the "official seal" of the "Province of Siquijor." In addition to those five words, the white periphery of the round seal contains six yellow stars, each representing a municipality of the province. The seal itself is divided in pie-like fashion into three equal portions, respectively blue, white, and red, like the Philippine flag.

Each portion also contains some black superimposed drawings, the meaning of which were less than clear to me. Such impressions over the basic elements of the Philippine flag allowed Siquijor to stand out, that is to manifest its identity. In short, it was the signature of the islands as the Siquijorian elite had wanted it to appear publicly. When I inquired of the townspeople, who visited us in our hut in Camingawan, I obtained interpretations that may not have coincided with the symbolism originally intended, but which revealed their sense of self-representation and the ways in which they constructed their island.

In the blue section were two stylized coconut trees, although this black overprint is difficult to see because of the dark blue background.

> This is for our farmers in the *barangay* who drawn their livelihood everyday from the coconut and drink *tuba,* because this is mostly a rural province.

In the red section, a miner's hat, a pick, a shovel, and a lamp are clearly delineated and are easily identifiable. While this suggests the presence of an industrial activity, in fact it is only the recollection of a past activity and the suggestion of one desired in the future:

> This is for old-time sake. It is already finished. There were mines [actually one mine of manganese] in Larena but it stopped already.

As I learned later, it had been hoped that Siquijor, as a province, would be able to resume the extraction of manganese ore, an activity that had flourished during the American regime but had ceased in the fifties. Either the ore was not rich enough or the deposit had been exhausted, for the extraction was never renewed. The island seemed to be lacking exploitable natural resources.

In the white section was the sea with a sailboat on its surface, a profile of the island in the background and a (presumably rising) sun. In the Philippine flag the sun is indeed at the center of the white section, and I was anticipating what then seemed obvious to me, namely an allegory of fishing on the island. But my question elicited a different answer:

> This is for the bright future of the island. The sea, the beach [none appeared in the drawing], this is for the future, for the development of the island, for attracting tourists on our beautiful beaches.

A common theme in 1980, it was often repeated, as if tourism was the universal panacea that would lift the rather depressed economy of the island and make Siquijorians wealthy once and for all. In the *barangay*, however, getting rich was of less concern than knowing whether there would be enough fresh fish for the next meal. Despite their shared past, it was as if the town bourgeoisie and the *barangay* peasantry had lived and constructed quite different histories.

6

Auntie Diding's Household

O N LOSING HER HUSBAND about a year before our arrival, Auntie Diding could not have been said to be thoroughly devastated. She properly mourned him. But in many conversations I could judge from her way of referring, directly or indirectly, to her relationship with Pedro that they had not been very close to each other for a long time. Had there ever been any romance, any *gugma*, in that marriage, contracted long ago in an era when people were betrothed and wed by the will of their respective families rather than by their own? It would be difficult to say. Rather than loving each other, which would have been expressed by *gugma*, it might be more appropriate to state, as she did, that they *tahuray*, that they "respected each other," a more reserved, austere, and public demonstration of their involvement.

In many respects, it was obvious that the old man had been a burden to her. Widowhood suited her well. She could even be said to have acquired a new appetite for life. Hence her laughs. No, she was definitely not interested in remarrying. As she put it jokingly—but not gratuitously—now she was only interested in *kaun ug inuminum*, in "eating and (social) drinking."

Her late husband had left her enough to satisfy those needs. She owned some three acres of arable land. Not particularly fertile, it was so stony that it was always a challenge to cut straight furrows; at almost every other step, she had to lift the plowshare to avoid the rocks. The red lateritic soil was so poor that a good deal of her corn and peanuts—her two staple crops—failed lamentably, and occasional sea mist (by all accounts not the best of fertilizers) all too generously moistened her land, which lay adjacent to the beach.

Her coconuts, some fifty trees, however, fared better and in fact were thriving—no small irony, for the price of copra (the dried coconut meat, a volatile commodity) had drastically collapsed in the past year or two. Nonetheless, being a coconut producer offered the advantage of a life insurance policy underwritten by the administration of Cocofed, one of the bureaucratic concoctions of the Marcos administration. She had received but a fraction—less than a thousand pesos, at the equivalent rate of seven Philippine pesos to the U.S. dollar—of what she understood to be her due.

Her chattel was limited, especially since, as is customary, she had had to sacrifice most of it the year before to feed the mourning party. Nonetheless she had a pregnant cow to pull the plow, a sow complete with a fresh litter of piglets, and another pig which, fastened to the stilts of our nearby hut, graced our dawns with its grunts and our nights with its fleas.

Not least of all, she had retained from her late husband the quite large and solid dwelling where, following the traditional pattern whereby women move to their husband's residence, she and Pedro had lived all their married life. Built on stilts like all traditional Visayan buildings, the house stood on the beach amidst the undulating coconut trees, at the very center of an informal cluster of loosely related households known as *sitio* Camingawan.

In close proximity to that house, she also owned a small *payag*, a bamboo-built, thatched-roofed hut erected the year before to shelter an American Peace Corps volunteer for a few months. After his departure, the hut had been converted to a storehouse for fishing gear. For the modest rent of one hundred pesos a month, it became ours for the duration of our stay. Since the floor was made not of wooden boards but of split bamboo through which air could circulate, it was pleasantly "air-con," as one of our neighbors put it. From it, we had a magnificent, panoptic view of Mindanao across the sea, the town of Lazi on the other side of the bay, the cluster of households in our vicinity, the surrounding fields, and the beach from which fishermen came and went day and night.

Through her marriage, Auntie Diding had also achieved the enviable status in the community of a mature woman surrounded by her married sons, the venerability of a matron of local influence whose words were respected, especially since she had a sharp tongue that matched her determination.

Auntie Diding, in her widowhood, was thus far from being destitute, even though she was not well off. For her, to be *datu*, to be "rich," would have required a reserve of cash and a source of income incompatible with the rural life of a peasant. She may have pretended to be *pinobre pareho sa tanan*, "poor like everyone else," but she always had enough to treat herself to a drink of *tuba* (the fermented coconut sap) or to some tobacco leaf for her small pipe.

Her poverty, real though it was in comparison to us or to the bourgeoisie of the nearby town, was not striking when compared to that of her neighbors. When she complained, it always seemed part of the proper way to conduct a cross-class conversation. Her complaints were, as with any of her neighbors, a discreet and entirely indirect solicitation, always presented and never answered. In a more relaxed moment of candor, for instance over the cup of hot chocolate to which we had invited her, she would tell us that in fact she considered herself to be *husto pa*, which can be rendered by "still OK" or "just fine, still."

There was nonetheless something of which the loss of her husband had deprived her. Death had truncated her household; there was no man in the house. And a manless household was a fishless one. Although women are involved in beachcombing from which they gather some shellfish and edible seaweed, fishing by any technique (angling, netting, or spearing) is a strictly male activity. Women can ride any boat, from the smallest *baroto* (the most common small dugout canoe with double outrigger) up to the biggest ships, but women are prevented from joining fishing parties lest they jinx the whole effort.

As a consequence, Auntie Diding's household was deprived of the steady supply of fresh fish that in his lifetime Pedro had secured. For animal protein, she now had to rely upon the culturally prescribed generosity of her fishing sons. For her to maintain, keep, or perhaps recover, her independence, required an adjustment to her new circumstances, an additional change in the composition of her now manless household.

WHEN AUNTIE DIDING lost her husband, her five children were all alive. She had had no miscarriage, and death had not snatched away any of her offspring.

"*Wa pa*," she would say, "not yet."

She would pause a moment, then add with a large smile: "*Gasa sa Dyus*," "God's gift."

I was not sure I had perfectly understood.

"*Unsang gasa*, Auntie Diding?"—"which gift, Auntie Diding?"

"*Nga buhi pa ang akong lima ka bata*," "that my five children are still alive."

She would draw a puff on her pipe, spit, look back at me, and interject, thoroughly happy with her wit:

"*Lagi,* JP," which meant "of course, JP" but really meant "How dumb can you be, JP?"

To which, exerting my fieldworker's privilege and eager to avoid too much embarrassment, I found my most professional and neutral tone to repeat sheepishly:

"*Lagi,* Auntie Diding."

As the reader might appreciate, the number of children was fairly small, especially in Camingawan, where until recently no effort at family planning had ever been made and where those exposed to the concept were loath to practice it, preferring to laugh it away.

ALL THE WIDOW'S CHILDREN, three daughters and two sons, were grown. Her sons Oyo and Berto Dagatan were not only married but each one had already given Auntie Diding four grandchildren; Berto's fifth child was born during our stay in Camingawan. They thus had their own families and each his own *balay,* "house." Though the very modest accommodation resembled less a house than a hut, it was nonetheless their *panimalay,* their home. In addition, the *balay* was where their immediate family, their own *banay,* lived in proximity with their own *kabanayan,* the group of their blood relatives, who were concentrated mainly in the same *sitio.* Following tradition, they had settled in a different house from that of their parents but very close to their childhood house, so that they inhabited the same settlement as their mother and were her closest neighbors.

Auntie Diding was fortunate that both her sons had followed the traditional pattern of postmarital residence, which keeps sons from dispersing while sending daughters away to join their husband's household. What kept this from being a completely happy story was that in following the traditional residence pattern, Oyo and Berto had accepted—or had been forced by tradition and circumstance to accept—their fate as poor fishermen, thus depriving themselves of the greater economic opportunities that the northern coast of Mindanao might have provided.

For those neither particularly adventurous, blessed with any capital, nor properly educated, Mindanao offered more the lure than the reality of a last frontier to the south. For people, however, with nothing but their own labor, classic proletarians, there was not much to lose in attempting to better their conditions on a less depressed island. No wonder that so many young people outmigrated from the overpopulated and quite resourceless Siquijor to Mindanao, in an attempt to escape their poverty. They were not unaware of the eco-

nomic as well as physical risks incurred in this collective encroach-
ment into Moslem territories by lowland Christians. But the risks
there were often easier to chance than assuming the despair at home.
Sometimes, just the attraction of a change of pace in one's life or an
enticement from a friend or relative already settled on the southern
island provided sufficient motivation. But neither Oyo nor Berto had
been reduced to economic despair or sufficiently seduced by anyone
else's tale of pioneering triumph. Their entrepreneurial abilities were
modest, and their lack of education made them unlikely candidates
to break away from their native island. In many respects the two
brothers were traditionalists, conservative in life style, and attached
to Lapyahan, the *barangay* of their birth.

Auntie Diding's eldest child, a daughter, Graciana, had obviously
married a different sort of man. Angel Duhaylungsod, whom I never
met as he never appeared in Camingawan during our stay, had taken
her to reside on the northern shore of Mindanao, in the vicinity of
Iligan. There he apparently fished with no greater success than he
had on the island of Siquijor, but he was able to supplement his income with diverse odd jobs. In following her husband to Mindanao,
Graciana had behaved as she was expected to. But without friends or
relatives, away from everything she knew and cherished, without a
kauban ("companion"; literally "someone to go with") or a *barkada* ("a
group of coeval friends"), she would have found herself isolated and
trapped in a situation almost unbearable in a culture in which the
greatest value is attached to sociability. For that reason she convinced
one of her younger sisters, Marilyn, to accompany her to Mindanao.

It took little convincing; for Marilyn, who was not yet married
and languished at home longing for a Prince Charming known only
vicariously through the daily romances carried over the radio waves,
it was an attractive opportunity to move from the island of Siquijor
and explore what the world outside had to offer by way of a potential
spouse and possible income. When I met her on her annual visit
home, she was still looking for both. For the time being, she had
found some domestic security in a position as "helper." Employers
and employees alike used this English word—more frequently than
its Cebuano equivalent *alagad*—as a standard euphemism to refer to
servants or live-in maids. Sheltered and fed, people in her position
often managed to save enough money to send home and to come
home on occasion, out of salaries generally closer to one hundred
than to two hundred pesos a month (at an exchange rate of about
seven pesos to the U.S. dollar). To the best of my knowledge, Marilyn
did not send money home, at least not to Auntie Diding, but she came
back once or twice a year for brief visits to Lapyahan.

All this, however, left Auntie Diding by herself. Or rather, she would have been alone had there not been Virgie.

VIRGIE DAGATAN was the youngest of the widow's children. Like her sister Marilyn, she was a *dalaga*. This term designates females (*babaye*) who cannot be considered children (*bata*) anymore, as they have reached puberty (*kahingkuran*). One remains a *dalaga* until marriage (*kaminyuun*). Although Cebuano speakers must express time through the frequent use of particles such as "*na*" meaning "already" and "*pa*" meaning "still," at eighteen, Virgie could not be said to be either *dalaga na* or *dalaga pa*, but *dalaga ra*, that is "*dalaga* only"—neither too young nor too old, perfectly marriageable.

Attractive and outgoing, always energetic and involved in all sorts of civic or church-related projects—a dance, a basket ball game, a prayer meeting—she was certainly gregarious and by the same token popular among the available men (*ulitawo*) of her age. But there was nothing pressing so far as marriage was concerned. If anything, her celibacy had been, for the time being, a blessing for her mother, since under normal circumstances the rule of postmarital residence would have compelled Virgie to move out of her mother's house and live with her in-laws.

She might have been tempted to imitate her sisters by looking for a different future in Mindanao, but her father died just at the time when she might have been ready to make such a move. Even without a direct word from Auntie Diding or any of her older siblings, her culture surely placed tremendous pressure upon her not to leave. Indeed, it would have been unacceptable for her to leave her mother alone in a society where being *inusaranhun* ("all by oneself," derived from the verb *inusara*, "to be alone," itself based upon the root *usa*, "one," combined with the particle *ra*, "only," and preceded by the adjectivizing infix *in*) is considered almost a social disgrace. In addition, a strict principle of seniority demands that juniors show *tahud* ("respect") to their seniors, so that Virgie could not have moved to Mindanao, just on an impulse, unless she wanted to rebel and act against the grain of her culture.

Prior to any intended departure, she would have had to ask and receive the express consent not only of her mother but of her elder siblings as well. Thus, for a number of reasons—partly perceived duty on her part, partly knowledge that a request to leave was unlikely to be granted by her elders at the time, partly attachment to her mother, partly enjoyment of her popularity in the *barangay*—she said that she had no desire to leave. And so, for the time being, she continued living at home. Not only did she thus provide an excellent adult *kauban* ("companion") for her mother, but she was also able to perform or share strenuous tasks such as ploughing, fetching water, or collecting edible shellfish at low tide, an activity which tired Auntie Diding quickly.

Virgie's presence was well and good, but there was still no man living at the home of Auntie Diding.

WHEN MY WIFE and I, as yet innocent of all this, arrived in Camingawan, Virgie, under her mother's fussy supervision, gave the finishing touches to the cleaning of the hut. When we proposed to pay her "helper" wages for domestic chores—mainly cooking and cleaning— she accepted in broken English but with enthusiasm. To us, her help was invaluable, as she knew how to light a fire inside our hut without setting it on fire, how to cook, and where to find fuel. She was not a particularly good informant and did not care to be trained as such, but she knew very well the social life of the entire *barangay*. From her viewpoint, however, for an hour or so at most of daily work, she did not have to go to Mindanao, in fact did not have to change anything in her routine. As she lived with Auntie Diding, who housed and fed her and who did not need her money, she could save all her wages.

We were still missing one thing however: *tubig*, fresh water, available at a *pusu*, a well operated with a pump, about half a kilometer inland. Water was carried in plastic jerricans, most of the time by hand and on occasion in a rudimentary wheelbarrow, a *karetilya*. The traditional way of carrying water in big bamboo tubes had almost disappeared, because bamboo groves were no longer plentiful and plastic containers were sturdy and relatively cheap. Virgie volunteered her nephew, a young teenager, to guarantee us a permanent supply of fresh water, and he arrived every morning before going to high school, emptied his jerricans of water in our tank, and collected his daily peso.

Soy Duhaylungsod, for that was the name of our water-carrier, was a shy teenager. As Auntie Diding expressed it, he was *ulitawo na*, "already a bachelor," a phrase which made him blush immediately. At fifteen or so, with juvenile more than masculine traits, he observed to a fault the code of etiquette demanding that he be *ulaw*, or "reserved, unassertive" with us. In local English, this can be translated as "shy," but it was clear that there was more than mere institutional shyness in Soy. At any rate, he was, as we were to learn, the man—if a "little" one—in Auntie Diding's house.

It was Soy and only Soy, through the fishing in which he engaged after school with boys of his age, who provided her household directly with a fresh supply of fish. He already excelled at diving with a harpoon, which he enjoyed more than just angling; and he rarely came back to shore empty handed, even if the catch of the day was not always sufficient to feed everyone in the widow's house. As a fisherman, he had already acquired most of the skills needed for a lifetime.

Soy was Auntie Diding's grandson, the son of Graciana and Angel Duhaylungsod. Because his parents wanted him to finish high school, it was easier for him to go to school in Lazi and return each evening to Auntie Diding's. But the main reason for his residing in Auntie Diding's household had been Pedro's death. Having left home, Graciana felt obligated to send her eldest son back to her mother, and although not quite an adult, he almost was. The obvious intent of the arrangement was that he would settle more or less permanently in Camingawan and that, having been fostered by Auntie Diding in his *ulitao* days, he would later take care of her forever.

But there was someone else who was being raised in Auntie Diding's household. Trina was a little girl of six to whom I had great difficulty relating because as soon as I tried to talk to her she would retreat and hide inside the house. Even as time passed and she got used to my presence, it was still proper behavior for a little girl to display how *ulaw* she was and thus to refuse to engage in any relationship whatsoever with an older male not a member of her immediate family. I found this avoidance a nuisance, but of course the child had been socialized in that way. In my presence, both Virgie and Auntie Diding politely and overtly instructed Trina not to be afraid (*hadlok*) of me. Yet they approved as well as encouraged Trina's manifestations of her *kaulaw*, that is, the maintenance of distance, the denial of any engagement—an etiquette of utter restraint.

Trina was Auntie Diding's granddaughter, the second child of her son Berto, and therefore another of Virgie's *pagumangkon*, a term which refers to both "nieces" and "nephews." It is gender-blind like the kinship terms of reference for "children," *anak;* for "grandchildren," *apo;* for "grandparents," *apohan;* for "siblings," *igsoon;* for "siblings-in-law," *bayaw;* for "parents-in-law," *ugangan;* and for "cousins," *igagaw.*

At first, I misunderstood Trina's relationship with Auntie Diding. Since the *balay* of her parents was so close, perhaps less than a hundred meters away, I thought she was just visiting. When I realized that she stayed overnight at Auntie Diding's house, I wondered why. Auntie Diding tried to explain to me that, *dili sinagup siya piro sinakup diri*, "she had not been adopted but belonged right here." Auntie Diding was happy with herself, visibly amused at her own pun. She repeated the phrase until I wrote it down in my notebook. That there was a pun was manifest, but its meaning was way above my command of the language at the time. Even when I realized there was a play on words between the root *sakup*, "to belong," and *sagup*, "to adopt," I was not sure what it meant. Trina belonged in Auntie Diding's home but was not adopted. Fortunately, Virgie helped me out of my puzzlement, explaining, *binuhi ba* to mean, literally "she is raised," "she is fostered." Like Soy, Trina was also being raised by Auntie Diding and thus was also considered to be her foster child.

Parents quite commonly sent a child to live with, to be raised by, or to serve as a companion to, either aging kin or childless couples. These fosterage arrangements between households with a surplus of young children and those without offspring or threatened with severe disruption by a recent death were considered to be mutually advantageous. The exchange of a child between two households had the structural effect of maintaining one of the households that was deficient or in threat of collapse. In addition, it had an emotional effect, that of asserting, reaffirming, or strengthening the links between the members of the exchanging households, even though the exchanged person—a child or an adolescent—had little say in the deal, either because of age or because a decision taken by older kin was incontrovertible.

In the case of Trina, for whom Virgie played a motherly role teaching her the bulk of what she would have to know to function properly in her culture, real affection had also developed between her and the other members of the foster household. Besides, she was an active link between her present household and that of her parents. Not only did she convey messages, but she was often sent on errands from one to the other to borrow domestic items—a fishing line, a piece of soap, some preserved fish (*ginamus*), a cupful of *bugas* (husked corn or rice)—or carrying small gifts of food—a fish, a couple of plantain bananas, some peanuts.

Perhaps the most important role that Trina had in this minidrama was her apprenticeship to womanhood under the direction of her two female elders. Of course, she played with children of her age, including her own siblings; but she prayed with Virgie and Auntie Diding, and her most intense games were at cooking and ironing and washing, and cleaning with Virgie. And so, it was clear to all that she was being groomed as an able replacement for Virgie, for the day when the latter would move away from Lapyahan, away from Lazi, perhaps even away from Siquijor, as far as across the sea to somewhere in Mindanao—a prospect that Auntie Diding could only dread, be it silently.

7

Views from Afar

$\boxed{W}$ HEN SIQUIJOR ACQUIRED administrative autonomy in 1972, it was the smallest province-island in the Philippines. Probably because of the geographical and demographic irrelevance of Siquijor, many a Filipino[15] failed to notice that Siquijor was no longer a subprovince of Negros Oriental, choosing instead to remember only its reputation for witchcraft (see Lieban [1967] 1977; Maghanoy 1977) or just unaware of its mere existence. Today, from the outside, Siquijor still tends to be perceived either as insignificant or quaint.

Even close by, as in Dumaguete, the provincial capital of Negros Oriental—from which, barring bad weather, the sight of Siquijor could not be missed—or in any of the neighboring islands and in fact throughout the Visayas, the island of Siquijor or mere mention of its name carried strongly negative overtones. It was as if people took a perverse pleasure in sounding for us only discordances, refuting the visible charm we saw, and creating pictures other than those that the island offered to anyone's eyes.

Being close by did not help. In the Central Visayas, where people are native speakers of Cebuano, linguistic particularities were still strong. "Accents" provided sufficient excuses to draw lines, in other words, for people to be provincial in the linguistic process of "othering." While the city of Cebu, and to a lesser extent Dumaguete, embodied urbane refinement, the islands of Bohol and Siquijor presented enough particularities to stand apart as out-of-the-way, iso-

15. Various authors indiscriminately write "Filipino" or "Pilipino." Since there is no dento-labial fricative in either Cebuano or Tagalog, there is no contrast between an "f" sound and a "p" sound. I use the word "Filipino" to refer to people from the Philippines and "Pilipino" to refer to the national language.

lated islands. Their inhabitants could at best be considered slightly backwards, if not thick-witted.

Concrete examples to the contrary did not alter the situation. Any possible counterproof to this partisan judgment was simply discounted, for the prejudice did not concern any concrete person—neither some distant relative nor some vague acquaintance. Hearsay was enough, and imagination did the rest. What was left was an abstraction, a stereotype as well as a caricature, where several negativities converged. Whereas Bohol inspired the equivalent of "Polish jokes," Siquijor, which was smaller, more aloof, and thus almost negligible, stood as the "Podunk" of the Visayas.

Consigned to the domain of trivia, Siquijor could have been easily forgotten had there not been something preventing that from happening: the Siquijorians were known to meddle dangerously with the supernatural. What made them unforgettable was their reputation for sorcery.

And indeed, outside of Siquijor, once my wife or I had named our destination, we could expect to prompt—midway between jest and heartfelt worry—some sympathy. Raised eyebrows among those who heard us indicated their surprise and slight disbelief, which they adorned with exclamations such as "*uy!*" (more mysterious for its etymology than for its iconicity) or "*sus!*"—an abbreviated and thus milder blasphemy of Jesus's name. The exclamation would often be followed by a cryptic expression tossed out in English: "Witchcraft." When I remained silent, hoping for a less laconic pronouncement, some people, otherwise quite uninterested in my answer, would prod further with: "You're not afraid?"

I could not have been warned any better. Someone sketched in Cebuano the verbal image of the difficulties I would meet on the island just across the water. There was *abat,* which denoted all kinds of more or less frightening apparitions; *barang,* which referred to a type of sorcery in which insects are inserted in the body of an enemy so as to eat from within; *aswang,* which announced the possession of a person who had become the instrument of a sorcerer; and *paktol,* perhaps the most frightening of all, which invoked the magic torture inflicted on a person, using as a medium a skull or a human figurine pierced with needles.

Siquijor may have had other witchcraft techniques; but the ones I have just listed, the potential threats mentioned to us haphazardly in conversations, constituted the paradigm of supernatural afflictions that Siquijorians had in store on their island. Such was the rather unappealing way in which Siquijor had been constructed from without.

Seduction myth as mine had been, or repulsion myth as neighboring islanders imagined—both prejudices shared similar fantasies. Although both constructed Siquijor from without, the island, entirely deprived of ontology, was confined to an instrumental role. It was but the pretext—at once occasion and foreword—of a self-oriented commentary, even though the discursiveness of such a discourse was almost absent here. Such image-texts of Siquijor expressed truths *pour soi*, albeit different in each case, thus partial—and therefore stories that could never sound right.

Rather than the myth of Siquijor, it might be preferable to evoke a mythical theme or motif that is surely identifiable but remains without content as long as it is not set in its network of contextual relations. Taken from the outside, Siquijor constituted either "the-other-for-me," the metonym of a shoddy, stage-set Orient, or "the-other-in-me," which discharged all too easily on a close neighbor the dark side of a troubling identity.

Conceived either as the model of an engaging otherness or of a disgusting identity, perceived from afar or from close by, Siquijor as a reality had disappeared behind its mythical virtualities, even though my pretext was just that—a pre-text meant to change—while the prejudice of the neighbors appeared a concluded affair, a prejudice that events could no longer affect. From that (or those) standpoint(s), Siquijor, or rather its "mythicality," existed *ab origine*. The island had always been there, it seemed, destined from all eternity to enshroud in its timelessness fantasies without history, without genesis, without future. Fixed once and for all, the case of Siquijor was closed.

Tracing the history of the myth—the history of "just-so stories" that present themselves (they all do so) as outside history—might be of interest, but it would frustrate too long my desire—implicit in my way of imagining the island and hereby made explicit—to penetrate the island. The indifference to genesis, common outside of the island, did not hold as soon as the Siquijorians entered the present text. They too of course had constructed their own island, though differently.

FROM THE OUTSIDE, an island has an aspect that is quite illusory, though immensely seductive, particularly as its dimensions are relatively small. It can be embraced at once, in one single glance. Seen from afar, it stands in front of me, neither complex nor complicated, as an almost graspable entity. It is bounded, limited in the immediacy of the view it presents. No need thus to search for the extension of its inhabitants' territory, since the islanders are enveloped, maybe trapped, in the closure of their "natural" habitat. The sea is there at my feet, and I would have only to extend a hand to touch the reality of the island.

And yet, at the very same time, in this still distant approach, everything remains entirely out of focus. Through the haze of the tropical heat, the island's indistinct profile appears only as a blurred image in an uncertain remoteness. With but the sea between me and it, there are only hues to distinguish the island, the sea and the sky, within a mass of blue-green pastels. Some clouds may hang over it. A vague mountain may emerge and slope gently toward the water where the edges of the island hesitate to vanish. No other feature can be seen at this point, just the geographical materiality of the island in its most general appearance; no village, no field, no fishing boat, nothing human yet. All these can quickly be supplied by a minimum of anticipatory imagination. The island is a tropical water lily: its glints of light and refractions undoubtedly belong to Monet; beyond perhaps, still unreachable, Gauguin is at work, brushing onto his canvases social scenes and human landscapes.

For the moment, however, I contemplate an island I embrace as a whole. It has a name, the sheer musicality of which is alluring: it is called Siquijor. For almost a year it is going to be "my" island, even though I am aware of the dubious connotations of this possessive.

At this point in my reverie, I am insistently reminded that my promenade along the beach front of Dumaguete City, on the island of Negros, is not exactly solitary. Children, a whole flock of them, have clustered around me and keep calling me "Joe," as anonymous Westerners have been addressed since World War II, when every American G.I. was known in the Philippines by the all-encompassing name of "Chocolate Joe." Most smile or conspicuously smother giggles, or even burst into half-embarrassed laughter when they have managed to make me look at them—the evident object of their game. As I stroll on the wharf, they invite me to throw a few coins into the water for which they will dive. On this mid-July afternoon, heavy clouds brought by a powerful and persistent *habagat*, the moist southwestern wind, burst overhead and force me to take prudent shelter. Siquijor has now all but disappeared behind the screen of rain. Tomorrow I will have a closer look, but for now I prefer to keep my distance and examine instead the map of the area, taking momentary refuge in its abstraction.

Almost lost in the immensity of insular Southeast Asia, Siquijor will appear, if at all, as a mere speck of dust on large scale maps; even on smaller scale maps of the Philippines, it will take an unfamiliar eye some time to locate it. Its bearings are 9° north latitude and 123°5′ east longitude.

Washed by the Mindanao Sea, it is the southernmost island of the Central Visayas, to which belong the provinces of Negros Oriental, Cebu, and Bohol, spread in a sort of arc north of it. Its southern neighbor, Mindanao, is the second largest island of the archipelago. Well-exposed on the southwest to the Sulu Sea and consequently to the *habagat*, the dominant winds of the rainy season from June to October, Siquijor is more sheltered from the *amihan*, the northeast winds that blow from October to March, bringing moisture until December, when the dry northeast monsoon comes into effect.

Which winds the first Westerners to sight the island of Siquijor sailed with in May 1521 is unknown today. Even though their expedition marked the passage of the Philippines from protohistory to history,[16] their "discovery" of Siquijor was in recorded history a nonevent. This is made clear by Antonio Pigafetta (*ms. ca.* 1525 in Nowell 1962:180), the Italian chronicler whose observational appetite may have lost some of its edge after Magellan's death on Mactan Island and the Spaniards' precipitous withdrawal from Cebu:

> In the midst of the archipelago, at a distance of eighteen leguas[17] from that island of Zubu [Cebu], at the head of the other island called Bohol, we burned the ship 'Conceptione,' for too few men of us were left [to work it]. We stowed the best of its content in the other two ships, and then laid our course toward the south-southwest, coasting along the island called Panilongon [Panglao], where Black men like those in Etiopia [*sic*] live. Then we arrived to a large island.

Pigafetta's last sentence contains indeed an eloquent ellipsis. As the context indicates, the remaining two ships arrived at Quipit on the northwest coast of Mindanao. But from Panglao to Quipit, they had to pass either south or north of the island of Siquijor and, one

16. According to Scott (1984 [1968]:63), "Chinese records contain sufficient reference to the Philippines to indicate regular trade relations during what H. Otley Beyer has not inappropriately called the 'protohistoric period,' i.e., the tenth to fifteenth centuries when imported trade porcelains make rough dating possible even without written records."

17. The value of the Spanish *legua* or league is more difficult to asses than one could anticipate. It was a measure of length equivalent to 5,572.7 meters, or so states the *Enciclopedia Universal Ilustrada Europeo-Americana* (art. "Legua") in its first definition. But to complicate matters, the Spaniards had also, according to the same source, a *legua común* of 5,556 meters, a *legua de camino* of 6,620 meters, a *legua jurídica* of 4,175 meters and a *legua legal* of 6,958 meters. We are concerned here however with yet another measure, the *legua marina* or "sea league."

Blair and Robertson assert twice (1903–1909:I, 320 and III, 201) that the Spanish league (presumably the marine one, since they are commenting on early navigators' reports; but they do not say precisely) amounts to 4.2151 statute miles, although I have no idea how they arrived at that figure. Since a statute mile is equivalent to 1,609.31 meters, a *legua* would equal 6,783.4 meters.

way or the other, they had to sail along its coast. Any mention of Siquijor, however, remains consigned to the unrecorded.

Often more precise than his companion and fastidiously keen on assigning a name to whatever piece of land he can lay his eyes on, Francisco Albo (Blair and Robertson 1903–09:XXXIII, 349),[18] the Greek pilot, was still laconic on that part of his travel: "We left Bohol and sailed southwest toward Quipit and anchored at that settlement on the right hand of a river"—without mentioning having even seen Siquijor.

In fact, the invisibility of that island was to be surprisingly persistent. Clearly, the Portuguese raiders who "as late as 1563 . . . prowled the Visayan waters, plundered Bohol, and killed and enslaved about 1,000 inhabitants" (Zaide 1979:I, 234) were hardly concerned with keeping records of their daring ventures. But not even the *Adelantado*, Miguel López de Legaspi, on his way from Bohol to Cebu, where he arrived on April 27, 1565, seemed to have bothered to note the existence of Siquijor. It is clear, however, that Esteban Rodríguez could not have failed to notice it. Legaspi had dispatched him earlier on a reconnaissance mission, but the pilot "had not anchored at Cebu, because of the violence of the tides" (BR 2:119) but pursued his route further south and circumnavigated the island of Negros.

What is made abundantly clear by all this conspicuous disinclination even to mention a physical encounter with Siquijor is the narrow universe of discourse within which all those early travelers confined themselves. "Plentiful food" for subsistence, "good anchorage" for navigational security, and "gold and ginger" for economic opportunity were key elements in their limited vocabulary. These phrases reflect only too well the commonality of their interests. Hastily bypassed by all for the promises of richer lands and more secure moor-

---

But all the encyclopedias I have consulted, including the Spanish one I mentioned above, agree in stating that a sea league is equal to exactly 3 nautical miles. Hence since a nautical mile is equivalent to 1,851.851 meters, a sea league equals 5,553.553 meters. This however assumes the exact knowledge of the circumference of the earth and the accurate recognition of 20 leagues (or 60 nautical miles) for one degree of the equator (one nautical mile is equal to one minute of angle at the equator). As shown by Spate (1979:xxi), such an assumption is unwarranted: "Following the erroneous Ptolemaic estimate of the circumference of the globe, the Spanish reckoned 16⅔ leagues to a degree instead of the better Portuguese value of 17½: a factor of great importance in the Luso-Castilian debates over the partition of the globe" (Spate 1979:xxi). Consequently the actual value of the Spanish league was 6,666.53 meters and that of the Portuguese was 6,349.20 meters.

With all these figures at hand, readers will have to decide for themselves how to interpret the sixteenth-century text.

18. Blair and Robertson will be cited hereafter as BR followed by the volume number, hence here BR 33:349.

ages, Siquijor, superfluous beacon in an infinite sea of potentiality, remained for the time being altogether unworthy of the merest mention.

Its entrance into colonial history—a modest entrance at that—was not to occur for several more years. It lost its irrelevance only when Legaspi became firmly in control of the situation and began to distribute *encomiendas,* "those tax farms of early years" (Larkin in Echaúz 1978:xiv) that Martínez Cuesta ([1974] 1980:32) defines so well as

a contract between the king, the *encomendero* and the natives, to which only the king and the *encomendero* freely consented. . . . The king ceded to the *encomendero* his right to the annual tribute [a head tax]. In return, the *encomendero* agreed to protect the natives from any danger and to procure for them religious instruction.

Such an arrangement developed after the arrival of Juan de la Isla on Panay with Spanish reinforcements. A few weeks later, Legaspi was able to return to Cebu; and on January 25, 1571,

Negros was distributed among seventeen *encomenderos,* eleven of whom were given two thousand natives each and the remaining six were given one thousand five hundred each so that it would appear that Negros had thirty-one thousand inhabitants. (Martínez Cuesta [1974] 1980:310)

It is on that same date that Siquijor, now exploitable, became the object of a document that indeed consecrated its entrance into written history:

In the city of the Holy Name of Jesus on the 25th of January of 1571, the King's representative [*el Señor Adelantado*] Miguel Lopéz de Legaspi commended [*pusó en encomienda*] to Pedro de Figueroa of the First [*de los Primeros*] the natives [*naturales*] of the island of Camiguin [*Camiguinin*] and of Siquijor [*Isla de Fuegos*].[19]

The Holy Name of Jesus was the name designating Cebu City after Legaspi had officially founded it as the first Spanish city in the Philippines in the same month of January 1571. Pedro de Figueroa had been among the first arrived; he had been part of Legaspi's original party and did not arrive with later reinforcements. The fact that this single person received two islands emphasizes their diminutive size. Without overlooking the religious obligation of each *encomendero,* it is nevertheless obvious that the main object of such distribution was to allow the Spaniards to make a profitable living—in fact, to flourish, thanks to the head taxes (*tributos*) that they could levy on the natives

19. Archivo General de Indias (A.G.I.), Seville, *Patronato,* Legajo 24, Ramo 19, Estados de las Encomiendas, 1571–75.

in the king's name. The number of natives assigned to Pedro de Figueroa's jurisdiction is not mentioned, but it can be assumed that it was in line with the arrangement on Negros. It would thus appear that Camiguin *and* Siquijor together at the time had between fifteen hundred and two thousand inhabitants. Furthermore, since the islands are of comparable size,[20] it would be reasonable to expect that the respective populations supported by each island would have been in a ratio comparable to what they have today.[21] In this speculative vein, to say that Siquijor might then have had between seven hundred fifty and one thousand inhabitants would not be too far off the mark.

Whatever the case, Pedro de Figueroa was not destined to enjoy his privileges on either island for very long,[22] since his *encomienda* was divided less than three years after its creation:

> In the said city [of Cebu], on the 5th of January of 1574, Guido de Levazaris [sic for Lavezaris] commended anew [*reencomendó*] the island of Camiguin [*Camiguinin*] to Domingo de Cuaco and Siquijor [*Isla de Fuegos*] to Agustín Duerto.[23]

Legaspi, at his death on August 20, 1572, in Manila, was succeeded by his Royal Treasurer, Guido de Lavezaris (or Labezares), who thus became interim governor of the Philippines until the arrival on August 25, 1575, of Francisco de Sande. Siquijor's new ruler, Agustín Duerto, was also a member of the original expedition; he had already received as *encomienda* from Legaspi part of the island of Samar on January 25, 1571, and Marepit (on the island of Cebu) on April 11 of the same year (see n.23 above; also BR 34:306, 310).

Some seventeen years later, Siquijor was still part of a larger *encomienda*, as manifested in an account dated May 31, 1591 (BR 8:96–141), prepared as an enclosure to a letter of June 20, 1591, from Governor Gómez Pérez Dasmariñas to the king:

> Francisco de Molina collects in Sámar, Ybabao, Siquión [*sic*] and Maripit, four hundred and seventy-seven tributes, which represent one thousand

20. Respectively, 248.63 square kilometers for Camiguin and 291.81 square kilometers for Siquijor.

21. Respectively 57,126 people in Camiguin and 70,360 in Siquijor in 1980 (Philippines, N.C.S.O. 1982a:3–4).

22. The reason for the redistribution is likely to have been Pedro de Figueroa's death. But I have been unable to verify whether "he died," as indicated by a marginal notation on the archival document, within three years of having received his *encomienda*, or lived long enough to be the same man who accompanied Governor Luis Pérez Dasmariñas in the 1596 expedition to Cambodia, as suggested by Blair and Robertson in their index (BR 54:362; see also BR 16:268).

23. A.G.I., *Patronato*, Legajo 24, Ramo 19, Estado de las Encomiendas, 1571–75.

nine hundred and eight persons. It has no instruction, but has justice. It
needs one minister. (BR 8:130)

The tantalizing brevity of this minitext deserves some commentary. Although I know nothing else concerning this Francisco de Molina, he seems to have acquired, perhaps inherited, the entire *encomienda* that Agustín Duerto once controlled. "Sámar" and "Ybabao"
are actually synonyms, despite the fact that they seem here to refer to
two different places. "Maripit" or Marepit or Malepit or Marepipi are
also synonyms designating a portion of the island of Cebu. Finally
"Siquión"—which is what draws our attention here—is likely to be an
early reference to Siquijor by that name rather than by the old designation of Isla de Fuegos.

The number of collected tributes is likely to be correct; after all,
the Spaniards should have been able to know how much they were
making. But the population figure for this fragmented *encomienda*
should be taken with the greatest circumspection. The figure did not
come from an actual census but rather from the mechanical applica-
tion of a ratio, that is one tribute per four inhabitants. I would suspect
that twenty years later the population of Siquijor was still within the
750–1,000 range estimated for 1571.

Even if Francisco de Molina visited regularly each component of
his *encomienda* (and we do not know that he did), he would have been
more likely to reside in Cebu City or perhaps in its immediate vicinity
at Maripit than on Samar or Siquijor. There was no priest, hence no
instruction, and the justice that it "has" means hardly more than that
the tributes were collected relatively smoothly through native local
administration.

Siquijor, then, was still caught in a haze. Even when the lure of
exploitation gave compelling reasons for the Spaniards to notice it,
Siquijor's entry into history is nothing if not modest. This apparent
historical fuzziness surrounding Siquijor has in fact persisted
through time. Even well into the seventeenth century, not much progress seems to have been made, as attested by a "relation of the Filipinas by a religious who lived there for eighteen years" (BR 29:277–
311), attributed to Diego de Bobadilla,[24] listing "the island of Fuegos"
and "Siquior" as two separate islands among "those subject to the king
of España" (BR 29:281).

SIQUIJOR IS NOT just hard to see; it is also small. I could embrace
it in one single glance from the Dumaguete beachfront. Indeed, its

24. The Jesuit Diego de Bobadilla (1590–1648) came to the Philippines in 1615
and spent fifteen years as an instructor in the Jesuit college at Manila and five years as
its rector (*see* BR 25:232; see also de la Costa 1967:622). His "relation" was thus written
circa 1632.

293 square kilometers[25] represent slightly less than 0.10 percent of the Philippines' total land area. Despite the highly dense population—241 inhabitants per square kilometer (which characterizes the whole of the Central Visayas)—Siquijor's 70,360 inhabitants (in 1980) amounted to less than 0.15 percent of the nation's total population (48,098,460).

In modern literature, descriptions of Siquijor are few and far between, and provide little detail. Geographers such as Wernstedt and Spencer, despite their generally thorough observations, offer no more than this:

> Siquijor, another small island situated approximately 10 miles east of the southeastern Negros island city of Dumaguete, is entirely fringed by coral reefs. The island contains a high and much dissected interior, and

25. One would think that the land area of Siquijor is an easily established fact, impeccable in its objectivity and impervious to doubt. But this would belittle any human ability at erring creatively. Confining myself to a selection of twentieth-century data, I find an incredible range of variation in the area of Siquijor, as reflected by the following table, where values are arranged in ascending order. Since one statute mile equals 1,609.31 meters, one square statute mile is equal to 2.589877 square kilometers; I have used this figure for conversions, but rounded off the results to the second decimal point.

Area in km2	Sources
123.00	U.S., *Census of 1918:*I, 224
274.53	U.S., *Census of 1903:*I, 68
278.87	Maypa 1960:24
278.88	Amor 1977:28
291.81	S.P.D.S. 1983:22–33
292.61	Tumapon [1972]:[37]
293.00	S.P.D.S. 1983:i
332.70	S.M.D.S. 1976:8
335.91	Wernstedt and Spencer [1967] 1978:600
335.96	Espedido 1972:43 Quilicot 1968:11
343.50	N.C.S.O. 1975:xix N.C.S.O. 1983:xxi S.M.D.S. 1976:30

The discrepancies thus displayed not only between different sources but at times within the same publication are not trivial; and the issue is no mere quibble, since it affects directly a number of other data, the density of population, in particular. Not being a cartographer, I make no pretense of reaching the truth in this convoluted matter. I choose to believe the S.P.D.S. figures, whose members were careful in their use of a polar planimeter as well as prudent in their measurements and calculations. The S.P.D.S. nonetheless gives two different figures. The larger is rounded off, but the smaller corresponds exactly to the cumulative area of the municipalities which compose the island, and it is this figure that I most tend to trust.

At the current time, however, the largest figure of 343.5 square kilometers has been repeated in census after census, and for that reason is the most widely used.

near the center reaches an elevation of 2,060 feet [628 meters] on Mount
Malabohoc. Deep limestone deposits cover all of the island's surface. Level
land is limited to narrow flood plains and deltas, particularly along the
southern and northern coasts. ([1967] 1978:28)

The same authors, despite or perhaps because of their modernity,
demonstrate concerns similar to those of the earliest colonists, when
they mention the island once more:

Production of manganese began on Siquijor in 1937, and during pre-
war years the island was a leading producer. The Siquijor deposits were exhausted, however, and are no longer the basis of any significant production.
([1967] 1978:477)

In addition to brevity, early descriptions share the peripheral
view of the island still found today: Siquijor is most often reduced to
its position in relation to other islands considered more important
because the describer is more familiar with them. This was indeed
the case in the writings of Fray[26] Juan Francisco de San Antonio:

The island of Siquijor, called the Island of Fire, is at a distance of two
or three leagues to the south of the point of Panglao at the southwestern
end of the island [of Bohol]. It extends from north to south for some five
leagues and it is two and a half leagues wide. Its southern side is at a distance of twelve or thirteen leagues from the coast of Mindanao, eight or
nine leagues from the coast of this island of Negros to the West, some nine
leagues from the point of the island of Zebu to the northwest and to the
northeast some eight leagues from Baclayon on the island of Bohol. ([1738]
1977:91)

It is hard to visualize such a narrative map without aid of some
commentary (see map 2). Whatever the value chosen for the league
(see n. 16 above), the Franciscan has "moved" the island slightly closer
to Bohol and much further away from Negros and Mindanao than it
actually is. Given the time at which he wrote, such imprecision is not
in itself surprising. More striking, however, is the perspective taken.
Although the text gives the impression that Fray Juan Francisco is
describing Siquijor from "this island of Negros," the map that can be
inferred from his geographical narrative actually indicates that Siquijor has been drawn into the orbit of Bohol, as seen from its southwest
corner. Distortion of perspective pushes Mindanao, Negros, and the
southern tip of Cebu way beyond their actual locations, a distortion
somewhat reminiscent of the popular *New Yorker* cover-map of the

26. Spanish *Fray* (pl. *Frailes*), equivalent to English "Brother" in the religious sense,
always designates a member of the regular clergy. Following common usage, however,
I have not translated this title.

world seen from a Manhattanite's viewpoint. This impression is reinforced in the Franciscan's description, as his only precise points of reference are two southwestern Bohol landmarks, two of the earliest Jesuit missions (see de la Costa 1967:163–66). Baclayon had been founded as early as 1594; the adjacent small (less than one hundred square kilometers) island of Panglao could only be known to the Fray for the even earlier establishment of the mission of Dauis (now Dawis) in 1593.

What is certain is that Fray Juan Francisco de San Antonio's "objective" description of Siquijor is singularly informed, not to say twisted, by the horizon he has chosen. Not only is Siquijor within the administrative domain of the Bohol Jesuits, but it is—most likely unconsciously—at the same time made to fit this religious territoriality. Strikingly, the island remains pure potentiality, an empty locale still to be evangelized. If there are any people there, they are obscured in their projected Christian future, fluttering souls on abstract coordinates.

People—or is it bodies?—appear, at last, some twenty years later, in a description attributed to Sir William Draper, whose focus is understandably of an altogether different nature, since it is part of a "plan of an expedition for the conquest of the Southern Philippines":

> Seguiyod which is a small Island to the Southward of Zebu is inhabited by a valiant people but is remarkable for little else except the number of Fire-Flies from which is said the Name Isla de Fuegos was given it. ([Draper? ca. 1759?] BR 49:37)

There are good reasons to believe that Sir William, or whoever actually wrote this, never set foot on the island. The subtle humor encapsulated in the mention of the abundant fireflies reflects the military hauteur with which the author evaluates from afar the islands he has never seen. The population's valor is evidently thought no match for the projected conquest since, in a remarkable Swiftian move, the people and the fireflies have been implicitly equated. Once their valor has been subdued, both people and insects can be confined to their shared territory, and the conqueror-to-be can move on to more serious sources of potential resistance.

Fray Joaquín Martínez de Zuñiga, who resided in the Philippines from 1768 to 1818, described the area encompassed by the "Province of Cebu" around 1800. Siquijor, Bohol, some towns of Negros and northern Mindanao, together with the island of Cebu, were part of the province of Cebu:

> The island of Siquihol lies southwest of Bohol, between the Island of Negros and the islets of Panglao and Balicasag, which are adjacent to Bohol

and belong to this *alcaldía* [i.e., the province of Cebu]; it is 5 leagues long and 2½ wide; this island is rich because of the abundance of cacao that the natives have planted on it; it had been administered by the secular clergy, and in 1793 the bishop [of Cebu] ceded it to the Recollect Fathers who gave him in exchange two towns in the province of Capis or Panay. (1893:II, 61)

Still brief, the Augustinian's description is slightly more detailed. The geographical position and dimensions of the island are compulsory opening statements, but no mention whatsoever is made of its concrete aspect, of its physical nature; the describer's only true concern seems to have been bureaucratic. The island remains an abstract entity, which can be the object of administrative transactions. Martinez de Zuñiga being a Fray, religion falls within his sphere of interest, but what he sets forth is less the religious than the political fate of the island. Whichever branch of the Church controls the island seems infinitely more important than the flock.

True, the "natives" are mentioned but immediately reduced to their economic instrumentality. If the island is rich, it is a trait of political economy; and the precedence of the economic concern over the religious only reflects with clarity that the evangelization of the island is not exclusively a spiritual affair but also subject to material constraints. And yet, at the same time, the island begins here to emerge from its imputed insignificance; by now, Siquijor is in focus. Even though the Augustinian has probably never been there, and even though he says preciously little in this digest of secondhand knowledge, he is certainly better informed than those previously quoted.

The interpretation of these older texts points to the fact that descriptions are often more revealing about their authors than about the reality that they purport to apprehend. Each text is already a fully constituted interpretation; and although there is truly no way out of this hall of mirrors, the best solution still consists in landing on and taking a closer look at Siquijor itself.

WHEN I LEFT Dumaguete for the first time, my preunderstanding of the geography of the island did not go much further than these printed descriptions and the vision of Siquijor I had had the day before from the wharf. Efforts at talking with Siquijorians who were now residents of Dumaguete had introduced some skepticism, as they displayed what appeared to me the excessive enthusiasm and apparent bias of "expatriates" who choose to emphasize that everything was much better back home. The picture of an enchanting island peopled with hospitable islanders had its charms. But, apart from demonstrating their attachment for their homeland, their comments did little to give more precise contours to my perception. If anything, exactly the opposite was taking place. A flurry of names, of people I should see, of relatives I could count on, of *barangay* I should visit, of *sitio* where I should settle, all of which I could only feverishly jot down without the hope of remembering them, added to my confusion. On the positive side, it was arranged for me to borrow a motorcycle for a brief survey of the island. But even the way of getting there was the object of some conflicting opinion.

For all the qualities that entirely rural island boasts, Siquijor remains remarkably out of the way. For a few years after the island reached provincehood, regularly scheduled flights had linked Siquijor to Dumaguete. The airplane often flew with a single, pampered passenger, and weary of losing so much money, the airline soon abandoned the route. Siquijor became once more entirely dependent on the sea for any link with the outside world.

8

Two Brothers, a Field, and Fifty Coconut Palms

O N AUNTIE DIDING'S well-sheltered and pleasantly ventilated porch, many a resident of Camingawan used to congregate during the day, as if it were a semipublic place. Because of its location so close to the beach where the fishermen landed their catch, because of its owner's sociability, and because of the centrality of her social position in the neighborhood, Auntie Diding's porch had become a focal point where relatives and friends gathered, gossiping and loitering, dozing or relaxing, listening to the radio, or even drinking a bowl or two of palm toddy on Sunday afternoons.

On occasion when Auntie Diding felt less sociable than usual, to take refuge from the games and cries of children or from the noises that teenagers and adults generated in their animated interaction, she climbed the five or six high steps of an inner staircase that led her to the most private section of her house, to one of the two rooms *sa taas* ("upstairs") where only her closest relatives were ever admitted. Sitting by the window sill, she disengaged herself entirely from what happened downstairs, although nothing—and no one—could really escape her attention. From upstairs, she discovered which fisherman was at sea, whose *baroto* ("canoe") was on its way back, and her trained eyes could even identify who appeared to have luck that day and who seemed to have none.

Closer by, she had also a perfect view of the narrow expanse of land in front of her house. No more than thirty yards separated it from the beach itself. It was that space that Virgie struggled to keep under control by sweeping it with a palm frond meticulously every day. Infertile as it looked, the sea-sprayed parcel of land was Auntie Diding's. Grass grew sparsely in its sandy soil, but coconut trees (*lubi*) thrived, and she owned some fifty or so fruit-bearing trees in the narrow stretch of land which extended for about a hundred meters parallel to the beach from just beyond our hut to just beyond Zosing Yano's.

She designated this part of her property *sa ubus* (literally, "beneath," i.e., "downhill"). From the central and maximal elevation of Mt. Bandilaan (a.k.a. Malabahog), the terrain of the island slopes more or less gently toward the sea. Anything located between a Siquijorian and the shore is always considered to be "below," even if, as was indeed the case here, there was no perceptible difference in the level at which Auntie Diding's house and her palm trees stood, no visible slope in the terrain.

But when Auntie Diding referred to the bulk of her property, the land lying in back of her house—that is to say, something farther away from the sea—she talked about it as being *sa ibabaw* (literally, "above," i.e., "uphill") even though the slope here was quite insignificant. Right in back of her house, just far enough from the beach to escape the damaging salt mists, away from the shadow of palm trees, lay over a hectare (1 hectare equals approximately 2.47 acres) of flat, arable if not rich, land. This was the field (*yuta*) that she and her late husband had once cultivated together and upon which three households now relied—Auntie Diding's and that of her two sons.

Across the field from Auntie Diding's house and still adjacent to that piece of land but further "uphill," amidst rocks that would have rendered cultivation impossible, stood two houses. More modest both in size and solidity than Auntie Diding's own, both were built on stilts. The widow's two sons lived there, Oyo and his family in one, Berto and his in the other.

In her marriage to Pedro Dagatan in 1937, Auntie Diding, as the reader may recall, had borne five children. Only the youngest, Virgie, still lived "at home," while her sisters had settled in Mindanao. The two brothers had stayed very close to their birthplace, settling just on the other side of their family land. The presence of the land itself was reason enough for them to have stayed.

Eleven years separated the two brothers, who had both inherited the jolly disposition of their mother. Judging from the only picture of Pedro Dagatan I ever saw, the elder, Oyo, small and sturdy, had acquired his stockiness from his father. This did not make him look any younger, and his general appearance was further impaired by particularly bad dentition that spoiled the grace of his generous laughs and smiles. His charm, however, lay in his personality. Warm and personable, he gave the impression of living harmoniously with his wife, Cording. Two years younger than he, she was also originally from the *barangay* of Lapyahan and thus did not have to move far to follow him when they married in the early sixties. They had produced three children in rapid succession—Junior, born in 1963, Sisil in 1964, and Alvin in 1966, all now teenagers in school—and waited another eight years before having a fourth and last child, Lindo, an intrepid six-year-old who, encouraged by his father and his elders, could, when the occasion arose, sing traditional songs and recite native poetry.

In contrast to Oyo, Berto was so handsome and youthful that he bore hardly any physical resemblance to his brother. Svelte without being frail, attractive without being in the least effeminate, playful without being exasperating, he seemed to have acquired whatever physical qualities he had from his mother.

While he was still a teenager, Berto had met a woman, his elder by one year, when she came from a distant *barangay* in the interior of the island to visit relatives in Lapyahan. They met and, not long after, wed—she, already pregnant; and every two years, with obstinate regularity, they produced a new baby: Predo in 1972, Trina in 1974, Ana in 1976, Ricky in 1978, Ludy in 1980, in an apparently unending series. They lost little time after the weaning of their newest child—which generally occurs a year after its birth—in starting a new pregnancy.

When I ventured to mention family planning to Berto, he dismissed the idea with hilarity. His favorite way of putting such an idea to rest was to use a pun that I heard in English over and over again: "Family planning, family planting," although at other moments he recognized that "*lima, igo ra*," "five (children) were enough." And yet, this phrase itself belied its manifest meaning, for it echoed the governmental poster and slogan that attempted to curb the national population growth. Urging the masses to join in family planning projects, it depicted a couple and their three children and declared: *Tulo, igo ra*, "three are enough."

In this sense, I should not have taken Berto's words literally. Without lying, he certainly had not committed himself one way or the other. Depending on his mood, his fifth child was to be the last one. But nothing prevented him from making an about-face, entering into a more realistic mood and, reversing himself, claiming that he was on his way to a score of children, on his way to setting a record. His wife, Milia, who, more than he, was stuck with this reproductive reality, was less inclined than he to joke about it but did not feel free to explore the issue of family planning all by herself and probably against his will.

At that point in their life, however, neither of them had felt yet any external pressure to put an end to their reproductive enthusiasm—quite the contrary. Their eldest child, a boy, Predo, who attended primary school with less than optimal frequency, was beginning despite his young age to give his parents a hand in different domestic tasks. And their second child, Trina, was no burden at all since she was not raised at home but at Auntie Diding's under her grandmother's and aunt's harmonious supervision.

As far as Virgie was concerned, Oyo, eighteen years her elder, belonged to another generation; he was more fatherly than brotherly to her. She always addressed him properly and respectfully as *manong,* and this formality itself seemed to prevent the expression of any real intimacy between them. Since Virgie was the youngest of that set of siblings, she was still Berto's junior by seven years. As such, she owed him as much *tahud,* as much "respect," as she did her other brother, and she should have addressed both in the same way. But she did not. Berto looked younger than he really was, and Virgie somehow felt too relaxed and comfortable with him, too close to him to call him *manong.* They laughed at the same jokes and teased each other and altogether entertained a mutual state of pleasant intimacy that met with Auntie Diding's approval.

Auntie Diding herself had a markedly different attitude toward her sons. Vis-à-vis Oyo, she manifested a hesitancy that betrayed ambivalence toward her eldest son. It appeared to me that, unintentionally perhaps, she was inconsistent with him, as if pushed and pulled between contradictory feelings. At times, she appeared more reserved with him than she usually was with anyone else, barely paying any attention to his mere presence, only to follow this detachment with bursts of relaxed and solicitous interaction that thus looked a bit forced and theatrical.

Even though his earnestness was counterbalanced by a certain lack of luster, for matters of import Auntie Diding turned to Oyo. Somehow he, with an insistent solemnity that sometimes blurred his usual joviality, seemed to remind her too much of her late husband. And yet, she recognized easily his trustworthy solidity. For matters of judgment, she turned readily to him, for birth order had bestowed responsibilities on Oyo that he took seriously. Consequently, she could count on him.

Reliability may not have been his younger brother's main quality, but Auntie Diding clearly expressed her preference for Berto's frivolity, which her indulgence almost encouraged. Manifestly partial to her younger son, she could see nothing wrong in anything he did, whether he had gambled away money at a cockfight or imbibed too many shots of rum and chased them in turn with too many bowls of palm toddy. She made no mystery of her inclination toward Berto, who tended to be almost as fun-loving as Oyo was serious.

"*DIS-A MAN ka, manang?*"

Manang was the polite and respectful way of addressing a woman who was my elder. Uncertain of my ability to communicate properly in Cebuano, I repeated my question to her in English, as she was returning home:

"Auntie Diding, where have you been?"

There is no ethnography without the nosiness of the anthropologist and the tolerance of the informants, but Auntie Diding was more than amused at my childish efforts at understanding what was going on in Camingawan, at my funny mistakes and my silly questions. As if it should have been perfectly evident to me (as, actually, it was to everyone else) she answered:

"*Ang sagad nako ra, nagbalhin ug baka*"; "just as usual, I moved the cow."

What she meant was that she had gone, as she did every evening, to move her cow to a new grazing spot. This one cow, the sow with her litter of piglets, another pig, and a few chickens were all the domesticated animals left to Auntie Diding after her husband's funeral, for which she had unhappily slaughtered her calf as well as a couple of mature pigs and a half-dozen chickens. The funeral meats may have attested to the deceased's popularity, but to cover the expenses of the funeral, Auntie Diding needed cash, and she had mortgaged (*prenda*) her cow. In exchange for receiving several hundred pesos, she was to repay the sum borrowed in forty-eight months; if she defaulted, she would lose her cow. As interest, every other calf to be born to said cow, starting with the first one, were to be property of the mortgagor.

When we arrived, Auntie Diding had already given away the first calf, and—she could hardly contain her glee—her cow was pregnant again. Her cow was of the utmost importance, since it was the only draft animal she owned. Without a cow there was no possibility of ploughing her field, unless she hired someone to do it, and she saw this as the beginning of a downfall. As she explained to me, this was the dreaded way of passing from owning one's own land to mortgaging it, which is only the first step toward sharecropping. This prospect was understandably most unattractive because tenant farmers (*saup*) must divide their crop into three shares (*bahin*). In this tripartition (*tinulo*), they may keep two thirds of the harvest but must forego one third of it to the landlord.[27]

For Auntie Diding, the fear may have been unrealistic. *Saup* cultivation represented as little as 13.26 percent of all farms on the is-

27. Further discussion of "shares" and "tripartition" will appear in chapter 12 below.

land of Siquijor in 1971, and agrarian reform notwithstanding, it had increased to 15.50 percent in 1980 (see Philippines, N.C.S.O. 1974, 1985). Auntie Diding had chosen to emphasize this worst possible scenario, even though her pregnant cow, her fertile sow, her other pig, and two or three rather scrawny chickens seemed to attest that she was well on her way toward economic recovery from her husband's demise.[28]

IN SHARP CONTRAST with their neighbor Zosing, who defined himself exclusively in terms of fishing, Auntie Diding's two sons considered themselves to be as much *magdadaro* ("farmers") as they were *mananagat* ("fishermen"). They understood that they depended as much upon the bounties of the earth as upon the fortunes of the sea. And although they shared, like Zosing, in what at times was the predatory excitement of fishing, in contrast to him, they had land (small as their parcel was) to rely upon and thus did not loathe involvement with farming activities. Of course, they, too, preferred fishing—altogether a noble, exciting, all-male activity—even though in its actual wet practice, with its scarcity of catch and its endless repetitiveness, it also conveyed a sense of *kalaay*, that is, "great frustration mixed with sheer boredom," since actuality rarely conformed to the fishermen's idealized expectation.

To be sure, farming activities, such as plowing (*daru*), planting (*tanum*), weeding (*bunlay*), or even harvesting (*ani*) rarely offered high excitement, as the tasks to be performed were more often than not tedious as well as strenuous. Instead of the competitive ambiance that prevailed among fishermen at sea and which, not so surprisingly, reinforced mainly among adults a certain male camaraderie on shore, farming activities pulled together other forces. For the cultivation of

28. In reading the following inventory of domesticated animals, the reader should bear in mind first that in the same year the province of Siquijor had a human population of 70,360 (see Philippines, N.C.S.O. 1982b, as well as the table of population below).

ANIMAL INVENTORY FOR THE PROVINCE OF SIQUIJOR IN 1980

Type of Animal	Head Count
Chickens	149,395
Pigs	24,616
Cattle	14,355
Goats	10,195
Water buffalo	801
Horses	92

a field, males and females, children and adults, every member of a family were drawn together to join their efforts, to "co(l)-laborate," as the very word indicates. In Auntie Diding's case, three households, hers and her two sons,' teamed together. Agricultural activities involved her and all her descendants with their in-marrying spouses and their offspring residing at Camingawan, as one single unit of production.

This type of cooperation among people working together in partnership, sharing expenses, labor, and the fruits thereof, was described by the verb *tambayayung*, derived from another verb *yayung*, "to carry together," which connotes the idea of common burden. Customarily, close relatives who lived in proximity or people who were just neighbors cooperated in the cultivation of their respective fields, undertaking some teamwork (*alayun*) and performing chores in each other's field, mainly weeding, on a reciprocal basis (*hunglus*).

Nonetheless—and this is why, at first, I was surprised by this particular arrangement—the explicit norm was for each landed household to cultivate its own land, to grow its own corn (*mais*) and root crops, so that I did not expect two, nor a fortiori three, different households to point to the same patch of land and tell me that just there grew their taro (*gabi*, L. *Colocasia esculenta*), their cassava (*kamuti nga kahuy*, L. *Manihot esculenta*), their sweet potatoes (*kamuti*, L. *Ipomoea batatas*), their yams (*ubi*, L. *Dioscorea alata*), or whatever plant they were cultivating. There were also, of course, households such as Zosing's, which were completely landless.

For any particular household, however, reasons not to conform to the norm were certainly as compelling as reasons to conform. Importance was given to the strong sense of propriety and privacy that one expressed when one mentioned one's *kaugalingun*, that is literally "what is one's own," but this consideration only aggravated the extreme fragmentation of land that other forces such as high birth rate, low mortality, and bilateral inheritance without age or sex bias had helped create. For practical as well as symbolic reasons, a strong pull in the opposite direction prevented individual households from conforming to the norm. And such motivations kept land holdings undivided, as exemplified in the case of Auntie Diding and her two sons.

Actually, whenever Auntie Diding talked to me about the land behind her house, she did not usually speak of it as "hers" but as "theirs." What the exclusive possessive in her expression, *among yuta* ("our land"), covered exactly was vague enough to be ambiguous. Did her "our" refer to her husband and herself, to the couple that death had separated? Did it refer to both of them and their children, as if to underline the unity of the family before the father's demise? Or, was it meant to designate only the survivors, herself and her children? I hesitated in choosing among this array of possible interpretations, but . . . the field rarely seemed to be just "hers."

For all practical purposes, what Pedro Dagatan and his wife had once owned and the household they had established appeared now to be exclusively in his widow's hands: the *balay* ("house") where she resided, as well as the coconut trees and the field that she exploited. Oyo's and Berto's only possessions were their respective *payag*, modest abodes on the fringe of their parents' estate. Before their father's demise, they had already taken up residence there with their own wives and children. Since Auntie Diding could not perform the farming operations all by herself, even with the conjugated help of Virgie and Soy, her two sons only "helped" her to cultivate it.

The verb *tabang*, "to help," and its derivative *tinabangay*, "to help each other," that Auntie Diding as well as Berto and Oyo often used in this context (more readily than the verb "to cooperate," *tambayayung*, even though this was precisely what they were doing), tended to emphasize once more the dominant ideology of family solidarity supposed to permeate the social texture of the entire island. But that native viewpoint, an implicit proclamation of gratifying mutualism, presented only a partial understanding of such land arrangement.

"Helping each other" had a supplementary effect for all the parties involved, as will soon become apparent. To start with, Pedro Dagatan's death had changed little in the exploitation of the land. In respect to the agricultural practice of his family, each family member had just added Pedro's share of work to their own, and it looked rather as if he were only away from home for a while. His estate had remained undivided, and one effect of "helping each other" was for the members of his immediate family surviving him to deny at one level the very happening of his death and thus to reject as a nonoccurrence the structural disbalance mentioned above. Not dividing an estate between the heirs is necessarily—in addition to everything else that it can practically accomplish—a denial and a simulacrum, the pretense that death has not struck.

On the practical side, "helping each other" was a means of consolidating the late Pedro Dagatan's holdings as well as promoting the solidarity of his extended family. In other words, it was a way of maintaining, perhaps artificially, the social order in effect during his lifetime. Above all, it preserved the integrity of his land, certainly an important achievement, which a few numbers can help the reader appreciate.

On the island of Siquijor in 1980, there were 9,597 hectares of cultivated land. This represented a substantial increase in acreage from 1971, when only 8,771 hectares were farmed, and left very little land available for future expansion. Evidence from the 1980 census reveals a more startling change: during the same period of time, there was a staggering increase of 50.52 percent in the number of farms (from 6,653 in 1971 to 10,014 in 1980; see Philippines, N.C.S.O. 1974, 1985).

The population of the island of Siquijor has grown steadily throughout the twentieth century, as reflected in table 1 below,[29] but it increased at its highest rate between 1970 and 1975. While the recorded rate of population increase dropped back between 1975 and 1980, and the population of the island almost reached a plateau, this should not be attributed to any success at family planning efforts. The population pressure was instead relieved by a steady outmigration of peasants to the frontier zone of northern Mindanao. For the period from 1971 to 1980, while the area of farmed land increased by 9.42 percent, the population grew by 11.73 percent, and the number of cultivated hectares per person decreased by 2.07 percent.

Table 1.
TWENTIETH-CENTURY POPULATION OF THE ISLAND OF SIQUIJOR

Date of Census	Population	Mean Annual Growth Rate	Population Density
1903	50,156	—	146
1918	56,774	0.88	165
1939	59,507	0.23	173
1948	57,258	− 0.42	167
1960	59,555	0.33	173
1970	62,976	0.57	183
1975	69,077	1.94	201
1980	70,360	0.37	205

For the Siquijorian peasants who did not opt for outmigration to Mindanao, land was becoming scarcer and scarcer, as generation after generation it was further fragmented to accommodate more and more heirs. That the size of farms shrank drastically within that nine-year period is attested by even a scanty perusal of the censuses (see Philippines, N.C.S.O. 1974, 1985) from which I have adapted table 2. Consequently, in having over a hectare of farming land, including the part which could not be tilled but could be planted with

29. Density reflects the number of inhabitants per square kilometer. For the sake of consistency, calculations have been made on the basis of a total area of 343.5 square kilometers (i.e. 34,350 hectares or 132.68 square miles) for the island of Siquijor. Sources for the table are Philippine Commission 1905; Philippines, B.C.S. 1956; Philippines, N.C.S.O. 1975, 1982a, 1982b, 1983.

coconut trees, Pedro Dagatan and even more so Auntie Diding and their sons were not among the most deprived for the time, either on the island as a whole or in their own *barangay*.

Table 2.
SIZE OF FARMS ON THE ISLAND OF SIQUIJOR

Size of Farms in Hectares	1971			1980		
	tNo. of Farms	No. of Hectares	% of Farms	No. of Farms	No. of Hectares	% of Farms
<1.00	2,728	1,295	41.00	6,549	2,746	65.33
1.00–2.99	3,333	5,035	50.10	2,976	5,035	29.69
3.00–4.99	487	1,769	7.32	340	1,233	3.39
5.00–9.99	104	662	1.56	142	662	1.42
10.00–over	1	11	0.02	17	218	0.17
Total	6,653	8,771	100.00	10,024	9,597	100.00

Today, however, with her children grown up, some of whom had outmigrated while others had successfully reproduced, Auntie Diding was living on relatively less and less land. As time passed, the same area had to support an increasing number of mouths. She had lived off the same land throughout her married life. At the beginning of their marriage only the two of them tilled the piece of land they had acquired early on from his side of the family. With young children to raise, the land had fed all of them without too much difficulty. By now, however, things had changed. Even with the outmigration of two daughters and with Pedro's death, with three people less to feed, many more people depended on the exact same piece of land. Now there was not one household but three of them banding together. In addition to Auntie Diding's own household, there were also Berto, his wife and their five children, and Oyo, his wife and their four children: in all it came to sixteen people.

"Helping each other" thus had one negative aspect. It encouraged the members of the three households to stay together and so it tended to increase the population pressure on a fixed, small area of land. But any alternative would have been worse, since it would have fragmented and thus dispersed either the estate or the family or both.

As I understood local legal matters, Auntie Diding owned half of the land. The other half, Pedro's, could have been divided equally among their five offspring. In the worst scenario, it would have led to the creation of new parcels of what seemed to everyone a ridiculously small size (one tenth of a hectare going to each child, about a quarter of an acre each). Although no one can cultivate such small fields, I was told of one succession in a different *barangay* in which thirteen children had insisted upon the fair division of a hectare or two of land they had inherited. Since they could not get along, all thirteen lost: their land remained uncultivated and all thirteen of them, landless, had to emigrate . . . and were never seen again. This exemplary narrative, complete with the Christian aura overtones on the number thirteen, was perhaps nothing but a moral tale; but nonetheless it illustrated perfectly the kind of quagmire that everyone wished to avoid. For that reason, I always suspected the story to have been spread, if not completely invented, by local lawyers, who wished to maximize their profits by encouraging peasants to write wills.

In the reality of Camingawan, things did not need to take such a theatrical turn. The possibilities were scary enough. For instance, in Auntie Diding's case, one of the inheritors—presumably a son, since women were supposed to marry out and reside with their husband's family—could have consolidated his land holdings and buy out the others, but this would have been extremely difficult because it would have required capital (several thousands of pesos) that neither Oyo nor Berto had. Another possibility—and this was by far the most common solution in Lapyahan—would have been for one of the sons to take charge, to cultivate the entire field and pay a small rent to his brother. Instead of dividing the field into tiny and unmanageable plots; instead of forcing Berto, Oyo, or both into a Mindanaoan adventure; instead of letting one of the brothers buy the other one completely out; instead of turning one of them into a miniature absentee landlord and the other one into a tenant farmer—everyone in "helping each other" cooperated and left Pedro Dagatan's estate intact and undivided.

According to the municipal records, the office of the Bureau of Land Management had recorded both Pedro Dagatan and his wife as owners (*tag-iya*, a noun composed of the agentive prefix *tag* and the genetive form of the third person singular personal pronoun *iya*) of a continuous piece of land in Camingawan, delimited by other parcels and extending to the shore. A bar across his name and a marginal notation indicated Pedro's death. Not only had the land not been further divided, but his succession had not really taken place because, as is common among *barangay* peasants whose material possessions are relatively modest, he had neglected to write a will (*tugun sa kabilin*, from *tugun*, "to leave instructions with someone to do something" and *bilin*, "to leave behind"). As long as there was no real friction between the widow and the children nor among the children themselves, there was no pressure whatsoever to divide the land.

COLLECTIVELY, DESPITE death and emigration, the three associated households continued to increase in size. While they accumulated progressively more persons to consume what they produced, they also increased the number of hands to work at tilling the land. In other words, land was scarce, but its cultivation more labor-intensive. Of course, all sixteen members of the three households did not participate, or did not participate equally, in the different aspects and phases of agricultural production.

While children—all of Berto's offspring and Oyo's youngest— were left to play freely, teenagers were occasionally expected to contribute labor. Alvin, his older brother Junior, and their cousin Soy, in tune with all the other teenage boys in the *barangay*, did not display a great deal of enthusiasm for school and preferred even the physical hardship of plowing a field to the intellectual duress of the classroom. Sisil, who saw for herself a different future than the limited horizon of her *barangay* and therefore attended school more assiduously than her brothers, worked in the field after hours and on her days off from school.

As for Oyo and Berto, whom I could often see, sweating and panting, under a sack of fertilizer or behind a plow, they were when necessary unexpectedly vigorous in their efforts, already at work in the cool hours of the early morning and still at it under the suffocating afternoon sun. Between the necessary, relatively secure, slowly maturing investment that, as they understood it, cultivation represented and the risky, nerve-racking immediacy of the economic gamble that fishing was for them, the latter might have been more fun. In a way, they had, if not exactly the choice, at least the possibility of anticipating a pleasant change of rhythm in their activities, of foreseeing relief from the hardship they experienced in the field.

Women did not even have that. Day after day, Auntie Diding and Virgie, Cording and Milia worked in the field. Although there was no formal and specific division of labor, the most back-breaking and boring of all tasks fell to these women who—and this was perhaps the compensation—could maintain uninterrupted conversations working side by side. And indeed the task of *bunlay ug sagbot* was arduous and painful, consisting as it did of weeding the field with the help of a blunted cutlass, bending over the soil for hours at a time. Even plowing, a job that neither Virgie nor Auntie Diding hesitated to perform when the men went fishing, was less of a chore, although perhaps more lonely. The main difficulties of plowing came from a double impossibility: controlling the erratic drafting abilities of Auntie Diding's meager cow and the rather hostile nature of the soil. In order to make a straight furrow, one had to lift the plow constantly to avoid the rocks. Every field in Camingawan that had been brought to cultivation within this century was bordered by stones that year after year the tillers had picked from their furrows and thrown on the outskirts of their fields.

Such labor-intensive occupation took four women and two men with the intermittent participation of four teenagers to cultivate slightly over a hectare of land that, year after year, had insured the survival of the extended family. In addition to less than 0.3 metric tons of peanuts grown as a cash crop, the plot yielded approximately 0.6 metric tons of corn—the staple food on Siquijor—and 0.3 metric tons of root crops, both of which were used exclusively for the subsistence needs of their producers.[30] When I inquired about the price of corn and root crops, it was Virgie who replied:

> I told you, I do not know; Auntie Diding does not know because it is not sold; it is just for eating, just here. I can tell you about peanuts. I sell peanut, dry peanut for eighty to eighty-five pesos each *sako;* peanut that is not dry for sixty-five to seventy pesos each *sako.* You know that there are four 'tin cans' in each *sako,* don't forget to write that in your book, there are nineteen liters in each 'tin can.' Don't forget!

Aside from the products of her plowed field, Auntie Diding had another cash crop at her disposal: coconuts. According to her, year in year out, her fifty trees brought to her between six hundred fifty and eight hundred nuts. The productivity of coconut trees depended largely upon their maturity, so that Auntie Diding, as a prudent

30. In order to help the reader place Auntie Diding's field in its regional context, the table below, adapted from census data for the year 1980 (Philippines, N.C.S.O. 1985), summarizes the agricultural production for the entire island of Siquijor.

Only crops production greater than fifty metric tons has been entered in this table. Note that no sugarcane is grown on Siquijor, and unlike the situation in some *barangay* of the interior, the amount of tobacco grown, delightful though it may have been to local smokers and chewers, was negligible here. Note also the relative scarcity of rice in Siquijor, where the staple food is boiled corn grits. The table omits coconuts because it is almost impossible to convert the yield of 338,878 trees, producing 5,071,200 nuts into tons of copra. Finally, because of the practice of intercropping, the same farm or the same area may have been tabulated under more than one crop category.

AGRICULTURAL PRODUCTION OF THE PROVINCE OF SIQUIJOR IN 1980

Nature of Crop	Number of Farms	Area Harvested in Hectares	Production in Metric Tons
Corn	9,173	7,279	4,438
Tubers, Roots, Bulbs	7,014	3,538	2,112
Rice (Palay)	909	801	589
Bananas	NA	NA	370
Peanuts	1,365	556	308

farmer, had to make sure to plan several years ahead, to replace fallen or otherwise destroyed trees by planting new ones for future harvests. Other circumstances that affected the size and quality of the nuts, droughts for instance, were well beyond her or her children's control. Much beyond their control, too, were the hectic variations in the price of copra that pushed buyers in town to offer less money for the same weight of copra while demanding at the same time a drier and drier pulp. This could push the primary producer like Auntie Diding into playing a complementary game, which consisted in attempting to fool the buyers by selling them less dry, hence more bulky and heavier copra for a greater price. In the ensuing give-and-take between habitual commercial partners, the town buyer, who worked with more capital, was certainly better equipped to win, but both parties perceived the very process of bargaining (*panghangyohangyo*) as a most enjoyable and subtle form of gambling.

Not only did coconuts bring cash—and almost fun cash at that—but in sharp contrast to the labor-intensive activity that corn or peanuts required, coconuts demanded little effort. Working with coconut trees appeared foolproof and trouble-free. Once planted successfully, the trees did not require any specific maintenance and could be harvested year after year. One of the attractions of working as a producer of coconuts was the sort of casual, relaxed labor arrangement that it permitted. Working with and around them could be made to fit any schedule, to be interspersed with other activities, after school, before fishing, after a laundry trip to the spring of Caliguwan, or before going to the well to get a load of fresh water as well as a cooling shower.

Gathering coconuts in front of Auntie Diding's house, husking them out, scattering the pieces of kernel in the sun, turning them regularly to make them dry evenly as copra, all were tedious tasks that could be easily interrupted and restarted almost at will. More often than not, it was also an occasion for Virgie or for Soy to socialize with whoever happened to pass by, renew a conversation, gossip and joke, all at the same time. Above all, with exception of shelling corn, this was the only agricultural task that could be performed without being exposed to the harshness of the afternoon sun.

Judging from the laughs which such gatherings occasioned, Virgie or anyone in her immediate entourage could give the illusion of transforming into an easy pastime the arduous task of separating the coconut husks from the flesh. Coconuts were indeed a product apart, perhaps mostly due to the almost infinite variety of uses to which coconut trees could be put. To mention only a few, the trunks gave wood, the fronds thatching material, and dry coconut husks were ordinarily cooking fuel. Although the fresh gelatinous and refreshing flesh of the young coconut (*butong*) was a sweet delicacy, coconuts were not eaten per se. They provided milk (*gata*) and oil (*lana*), which were essential ingredients in the local cuisine.

But of all the products derived from coconut trees, I have omitted so far the one that everyone in Camingawan thought the most interesting. And certainly it stood out for its social importance. Coconut flower buds (*bulak*) were incised, bled, and tapped for the production of a readily available intoxicating drink called *tuba*, derived from the palm toddy that gave its name to the drink. This is the work of a specialist, a *tuba* gatherer (*mananggot*) who, more often than not, introduced himself as our local "coconut pilot." It was he who climbed the coconut trees at dawn and after dusk to collect the sap that was quite sweet at first but that fermented almost as soon as extracted. It was he, too, who pushed his wheelbarrow filled with four jerricans of *tuba* by Auntie Diding's house on weekends, bringing, at twenty-five cents a large bowl, more than merriment and excitement to the *sitio*. And it was I who had to prove—and prove again every week—that *bisan pag Amerikano, hinginum kag tuba,* "although American, you can drink toddy."

9

Conflict of Interpretation

I N CONTRAST to the general and amused indifference that outsiders and neighbors professed toward the genesis of the island, the Siquihodnon, as one could expect, were at variance. They too had constructed, and mythified, the island upon which they lived.

There is a popular song, perhaps the most popular and famous of Cebuano songs, that everyone on the island knew and knew by heart. Anyone could sing it, at least hum it and recite its words. It is—what else?—a love song in which a lover pleads his or her own cause against the bad reputation in which he or she is generally held. It starts this way:

Matud nila, aku dili angay.

In local English, this is rendered as:

According to them, I am not worthy.

What, in a rather clumsy way, "worthy" (implying "worthy of you") tries to express is the notion conveyed by *angay*, a word which offers some resistance to translation. Despite multiple connotations, it refers to a general notion of propriety, what the English auxiliary "ought to" expresses. It therefore calls upon what is fitting, what is proper, what is suitable, as it evokes the right time, the right situation, an evenness of cuts, of spacings, an appropriate spatial rhythm. *Angay* thus expresses a notion of desirable balance, evenness, and harmony. In underlining what "they" ([s]*ila*), ignorant others, assert on the lover's account, the text establishes the exact opposite, that is, the value of the offered and proffered love. In stating that "according to them, I am not worthy of you," it follows that "in reality"—at least in the reality of the text—"I am worthy of you."

In the song itself and by virtue of this being a song, moral value and aesthetic judgment are merged in the text. As a consequence, what in the end is "worthy of you" is the song itself, rather than the love it evokes. It also follows that the "I" of the text and the concrete performing "I" may merge so as to create a courting ambiguity.

The first line of the song clearly reveals a two-part conformity. First, *matud nila,* "according to them," resounds with the extraordinary weight of public opinion that makes and breaks reputations. Second, *angay* points at the recognized desirability of gentle harmony between people in general and lovers in particular. To be acceptable, not only do they need to conform to the social norms in vogue but they need to fit or match each other.

Some Siquijorians, like our town-dwelling friends Ned Pasco and his wife Minay, were aware of their island's reputation among the neighboring provinces as a hotbed of witchcraft; but they did not immediately appear to be upset by it. Although no one coopted it, they easily could have, for instance, by reappropriating "witchcraft" to their own benefit and extolling with pride whatever cultural heritage it represented. Its presence on the island was not denied either. To the *barangay* peasants like Auntie Diding who cared much about local opinion in Camingawan and little beyond, "witchcraft" under whatever name was either a matter of concern (if directed against her) or a mode of action (whenever other channels of action had failed).

But to the local bourgeoisie, witchcraft was an embarrassment, an annoyance, or a threat, or any combination of these, depending on how strongly they believed (or disbelieved) in its powers. They expressed this concern in subtle ways. Some, like Ned and Minay, merely used a mild sanction and laughed it off; but there were not many of those. Some others, like the physicians (it was incompatible with their rationality) or the Aglipayan and Catholic priests (it clashed with their faith), used a stronger sanction and manifested their annoyance by restating their commitment to eliminate such backwardness in country beliefs. There were not many of those, either. Being just ignored by the denizens of other islands was no solace, either. And so, tirelessly, throughout our stay on the island, the same English catchphrase was repeated to us over and over again.

What Minay would say in English was:

"Siquijor is an island of gentle beauty where we form one whole big happy family."

It sounded strange, as if lifted from a book. This polished and formal statement bore little resemblance to her habitual way of speaking.

And then, a day or two later, with his usual soothing smile, Ned would say:

"Siquijor is an island of gentle beauty where we form one whole big happy family."

Word for word, the same sentence as his wife. And so did others. The sentence had been learned; there was little doubt about that. But more than that, it had obviously stuck in the heads of those who uttered it because it rang true to them. This was the way they chose to perceive and present themselves.

Such a saying conveyed almost exactly the same ideas as did the first line of the song: gentleness, beauty, abundance, happiness, togetherness. Could an island be more homey? Could social life be more cozy? Could harmony be more perfect?

Because at the time I failed to appreciate the performative aspect of the statement, I grew tired of hearing it, as my receptivity to *matud nila* had become dulled by repetition. Yet, just like the song, the phrase concerning Siquijor expressed the general feeling, even though it could only be uttered by those who knew English and who dared to speak it, that is, by the more or less urban and relatively well-off members of an educated bourgeoisie.

"Siquijor is an island of gentle beauty where we form one whole big happy family." In the *barangay*, the rural proletarians could not say it quite that way. But they expressed the same idea when they extolled the exquisite taste of coconut toddy, the abundance—no matter how illusory—of local food, or the affectionate feelings that wove kin and neighbors into a community of islanders, *kaming kaliwat* (literally, "our descent," "our breed"). That was what counted on the island: its people, the islanders. The use of the exclusive *kami* clearly eliminated me, the ethnographer, from their midst, but it also conveyed a subtle ambiguity as far as the town bourgeoisie was concerned, which in a way undermined the boasted and insular togetherness.

The (all-too-)perfect harmony that the islanders claimed as their lot was of course disengaged from time, from any social process—in short, from history. It remained illusory, an ideological statement. And yet, this was indeed the very light that many people chose to shed on themselves, a cultural program. The some seventy-five thousand residents of Siquijor may have shared a rather idyllic understanding of social life on their island, but they maintained a different awareness of their common origin. In other words, despite their proclaimed cultural homogeneity, they had not had a uniform experience with their cultural tradition.

To say that all the islanders did not live on the same island would be perhaps too strong a trope. Greater accuracy might be reached by stating—notwithstanding what has been claimed above and the apparent paradox this constitutes—that on Siquijor a multiplicity of voices could be heard.

And indeed, how could it have been otherwise? In and of itself, Siquijor did not constitute a complex society, but it was part of one— a Philippine island and a Philippine province. In that loose fragment, faults, and cleavages were multiple and multidirectional. The schism between townspeople and villagers was undoubtedly dominant. But there were others, which overlapped each other without ever exactly matching any precisely. Gross correspondences existed. Roughly speaking, schools were better attended for longer years and with greater achievement in town than in the *barangay;* the villagers had almost no competence in English, while townspeople had some. In ethnic terms, people of Chinese descent, often hard-working, successful, and generally resented merchants, inhabited the very center of town. Socially, the center of town sheltered the local elite rather than common people, who dwelled dispersed in the surroundings. Finally and most importantly, in economic terms, the well-off tended to be town residents, while the *barangay* had to contend with the poverty of its rural masses. Strikingly indeed, the Siquijorian society unabashedly sustained a two-tiered social structure, with a merchant bourgeoisie and a rural proletariat.

And yet, I should not push too far the rigor of such a duality, lest my sketch decay into caricature. Other distinctions, other differences, other discrepancies were more blurred and more subtle. For instance, religious affiliation or political allegiance did not seem to follow any other rationale. Furthermore, other slippages provided enough obvious exceptions to undermine the perfection of the model I have just proposed. In addition, kinship networks crisscrossed and permeated everything to such an extent that this fragment of complex society appeared ready to crack under the weight of all sorts of contradictions.

The origin myth of the island did not escape this general confusion. Before proceeding to the *barangay* with questions on such an august topic, I had first to acquire a liberating if minimal proficiency in Cebuano. This is why I had already begun to ask questions in town. There, English, despite its obvious limitations, was an acceptable, if not compulsory, medium for my investigation. Almost anything that could have resembled a myth of origin would have delighted me, but already an entrenched official mythism was there, to which, whatever the procedures I used, every investigation necessarily led. By asking about the origins of the island, I was not, of course, expecting answers from everybody. But I had hoped that in the end at least one talkative informant, perhaps less timid (*ulaw*) or less inhibited than the others, would have led me through the arcane byways of the local tradition. Vain hope.

The answers I received surprised me at first, but the logic they revealed was incontrovertible. They also led me in a direction I had not anticipated. To start with, the townspeople I knew manifested very little if any interest in the past in general and theirs in particular, be it mythical or historical. It was as if they had neither awareness nor remembrance. They could elude—and did—my queries by proclaiming their indifferent ignorance. Sometimes they even turned the tables on me: it was not their concern, but mine.

After all, I was the one who had arrived in their midst with one stock phrase in Cebuano as a way of introducing myself. I had often stated to anyone who asked that I had come to their island *aron mag-sulat ug libro bahin sa mga magdadaro ug mga mananagat sa Siquijor*, "to write a book about the peasants and fishermen of Siquijor." If that was so, who else, if not I, could know the answer to the question of Siquijor origins? And if I who was manifestly "learned," as some people said, if I who was of my own admission a "writer" and even a "professor," if even I did not know, how could I seriously expect them to provide me with any answer?

Sometimes to get rid of me but as often with the sincere desire to be helpful, someone in town would direct me to this or that person who was either supposed to be "very knowledgeable" or who had the reputation of "knowing everything." This often marked the beginning of a wild-goose chase, which I knew to be vain before it even started. The privileged informant was ever evasive, declaring his or her incompetence, and sending me back once more to someone truly more knowledgeable who—a sure bet—in turn would shy away or refer me to someone else, even more competent. Knowledge was always deferred, and I felt trapped in a circle of indifference.

But I also received another type of answer. It denoted a militancy and a self-assurance that I could only admire.

"Everybody knows that this is not a volcanic island. *Bisan aku* [even I]. Just limestone."

Here too, and even more so, I was frustrated in my expectations. Somehow contrite and not to lose face, unwilling both to show and to disguise too strongly my disappointment, I hastened to reply,

"Of course, I know."

And I attempted to reorient the conversation toward the revelation of a less sophomoric answer. I nearly thought I had reached a solution to my problem when I heard the same person, after some reflection, utter:

"God."

Had I heard correctly? Or was it for that informant a way of expressing impatience toward me? I asked her to repeat.

"Like all the islands. Like everything else. Siquijor has been created by the Lord God."

I had made little progress; this verbal icon encapsulated the mythical blocking that was taking place. For there was still no narration, neither scientific nor religious. What was left was only a sort of abstract reference through which the informant was sending me back to someone else (again), a physician or a lawyer who, curious about geology, could have told me "the whole story" or to the parish priest who could have read me Genesis.

In all cases, the preceding tradition, if there had ever been one, had been erased systematically by two successive colonial powers, that of the Spaniards with their Catholic Church and that of the Americans with their positivistic schools. Each had brought with them their respective ideological supplies.

In town therefore, the island was an extremely quiet and unassuming entity, island among islands, be it a raised coral reef or an effect of divine providence. Without style and without trope, its unadorned, coarse, gross mythism sounded empty. Deprived of narrativity, it had become but an isolated element, almost irrelevant, as it was either lost as an object within a haphazard collection of scientific knowledge or dissolved as an indistinct creature within the universal Creation. The only thing which seemed to remain was the trace of a lapsed colonial discourse.

Of a previous or local tradition, nothing was left, nothing so long as I insisted in "discovering" an indigenous tradition coming from the depths of an absolute anteriority, uncontaminated by the quiverings of actual life.

But the townspeople were able to answer my questions in yet another way. Instead of sending me on the track of an identical other, the bourgeois but elusive bearer of an ever-deferred knowledge, they would also direct me beyond the class barrier to a different other. Although indirect, it was their manner of indicating there was still something else beside the mythism left by successive colonial powers. If churches and schools had exerted their influence in forming the individual consciousness of the town inhabitants, the state had also played its role. As I was told:

"Here in town, we know nothing. We are ignorant."

By then, I was convinced of it; perhaps more importantly, I had grown impatient with such indirectness, because at the time I could not understand what it meant nor what caused it. And then, probably satisfied with the suggestion, my informant would add with disarming candor:

"You should rather ask around in the *barangay*."

Before following this judicious advice, I must stop a moment and look closely at this term. Since 1974 (martial law had been declared in 1972), *barangay* referred to "the smallest political division in the country" (Philippines, N.C.S.O. 1975:xii). This definition did not introduce a change of facts, only a change of name, for it served to replace the word *barrio*, which until then had designated the same administrative unit. I focus on this apparently banal change of name for a simple reason. Had it been insignificant, it would not have taken place. More to the point, the civil servants in town, who in general were unconcerned or perhaps amused by my cultural and linguistic blunders, went to great trouble and with admirable persistence to correct me each time that I erred and, following the villagers' usage and their relative indifference to administrative regulations, uttered the officially obsolete word *barrio*.

The political intent of this unusual sensitivity to the imperfections of my speech was sufficient indication that the Philippine state had been able to manipulate, with art but without subtlety, just what it needed of mythical elements to establish its authority comfortably. It was to the advantage of the independent state to base its legitimacy on ancient local traditions. In so doing, not only did it maintain its distance from the colonial powers of the past but it also rejected its neocolonial present status. Thus the *barrio*, the basic territorial and administrative unit that (too reminiscent of its hispanicity) would disappear, was nominally replaced by the *barangay*. And everybody knew—or should have known, for it had been trumpeted enough in the schools— that it was an ancient word which belonged to the same semantic domain as *sa una* ("long ago") and *kaniadtong panahuna* ("once upon a time"), to a distant beginning where myth and history were entangled. History textbooks indeed state that before the (Spanish) conquest:

> The *barangay* was the unit of government and consisted of from thirty to 100 families. . . . Each *barangay* was independent and ruled by a chieftain. There was no king in those days, although some chieftains were more powerful than others and consequently respected by the other chiefs. The multiplicity of *barangays* implies that there was no national or central government. (Agoncillo and Guerrero 1978:45)

But the *barangays* also persist in a way which points at the mythical manipulation:

The word '*barangay*' originally denotes a sailboat used by Asian immigrants in coming to the Philippines. Later it came to mean the village unit politically speaking. Currently [in 1968], it connotes solidarity on the barrio level. (Robles 1969:20)

The change of name was thus a means for the government to unite with its past (be it a mythical one), to reach for the very root of what I must call "Philippinitude." In the beginning there were the *barangay*. Rather frail in the legitimacy of its power, the Marcos state had cleverly anchored itself in the origins it wished it had.[31] But that was enough of a legitimizing move to impress favorably the Siquijorian bourgeois, enough for them to perceive my linguistic mistakes as (ever so slightly) subversive. In that process, the state that pretended to be independent repeated the old feats of the Spanish church and of the American school; namely, it reduced the island to an anonymous generality. For in effect, everything which held true "here" held true anywhere else throughout the Philippine archipelago.

As for the townspeople themselves—at least those (they were the majority) who accepted the legitimacy of the mythical manipulation performed by the government—they deferred to the knowledge, always a bit murky, of the peasant masses. Profiteering from the produced surplus and monopolizing the nationalist ideology sufficed for the greed of the bourgeois class; it did not need in addition to exert its control over the fantasies of a strictly localized tradition.

This said, two contradictory attitudes prevailed in this abandonment of tradition to a lower class. On the one hand, a sort of nostalgic lament could be heard. Townspeople did not know anything any more. The villagers were the last source of a tradition about to vanish, as if there had been a previous Golden Age, whose values had almost but not quite disappeared. The rural memory was thus an archival repository, and the villagers themselves embodied a surviving past rather than a living present. They were pregnant with the myth of origin. In fact, it was all too easy to overstate the town troubles and to "mythify" endlessly the rural virtues. But no one argued for going back to the village(s) where life would have been *makapapiskay* ("en-

31. Under the Marcos regime, the longing for historical (including protohistorical and prehistorical) depth, roots, and thus legitimacy was particularly sharp. In this regard, the reader might wish to consult my reflections on the Tasaday controversy (Dumont 1987, 1988a).

ergetic"), for sure, but too *mabudlay* ("exhausting") for people whom the town's delightful trappings had spoiled.

On the other hand, the deference (which was also a deferment) by some bourgeois to the rural knowledge of the peasant could take the reverse orientation. Undoubtedly, the villagers embodied a surviving past, but it was now a different past, at once disparaged, despised, and rejected. They offered in their very lives the show of History with a capital H, congealed and reified in the gigantic *tableau vivant* that the *barangay* represented. Survivors from a still recent but already bygone era, the villagers were supposed to know a (or the) local tradition especially well considering they did not know anything else. In the hyperrealism thus drawn, such human beings, ignorant because of their poverty and poor because of their ignorance, constituted a dangerous class, even though it had the ill-deserved reputation of not being a very industrious one.

From this standpoint, anything could serve as a pretext to denigrate the "qualities" of that social class. To reinforce the argument, there was always a ready-made person, a denizen of the *barangay* to fit the prejudicial model all too well. Was it not *tinuud* ("true") that Ishong had accumulated debts? He fished without success. He neglected his field. He had incurred debts playing *piyatpiyat* (a sort of poker game played with ten cards) as well as *tigbakay* (this term refers to "illegal cockfighting" and figuratively to "extramarital affairs"). Flanked by a wife and a half-score of kids, he clearly preferred fornication to cultivation and, as the oft-repeated play on words went, was better at "family planting" than at "family planning."

For the townspeople, the difference that the rural others represented was attractive and positive as it guaranteed a common cultural heritage; the peasants exerted the "natural" attraction of continuity and contiguity. Or was it the reverse? The difference induced fear and scorn for a common, but presumably amputated, origin. Thus the bourgeoisie could claim two contradictory attitudes in regard to the *barangay* people, one of identity and one of otherness. In this way, people from the town could be proud of their *barangay* origins or they could loathe them. Still, the proximity in space and time of the peasants was such that ambivalence prevailed.

Such an attraction/repulsion also characterized the relationship that the townspeople entertained with "their" island. Surely, the insularity of Siquijor guaranteed the identity of the Siquihodnon, who claimed it fully in their interaction with the outside world—to that effect, had they not constituted an Association of Siquijorians in Manila? But that same insularity encircled them in its rather inactive

perimeter and forced them to a slow lifestyle. Tired of this confinement, they were constantly on the move, incessantly busy, and, for the
most futile of reasons, escaped to Dumaguete, to Cebu City, to Manila, to the United States, to endlessly renewed elsewheres. In a way
and paradoxically, the ancestral *barangay,* although already here on
the island itself, was one of those elsewheres to which, from time to
time, it was good to pay a visit.

10
Ned and Minay

NED PASCO arrived after dark at our *payag*, our hut, visibly muddied, bruised, and furious. He had run through a cow rope. He had told "them" a hundred times not to put their cow to pasture in the middle of the road. It was too much. He was going to sue them; he was going to complain to Victor Saplot, the *barangay* captain. He would have them jailed, that would teach them. He would go all the way to the governor if necessary.

Since he was angry, his monologue was animated and, for me, hard to follow. He switched back and forth between English and Cebuano, and I had difficulty interrupting him:

"Who do you mean 'them'?"

"Them, *lagi, kuan, Si Kuan, ang putol.*" ("Them, of course, er, what's-his-name, the cut-up guy").

This was cryptic enough, but the reference to *ang putol,* "the cut-up guy," indexed all too well, even for me, the family of Loloy Tundag, a man in his late forties, who lived a few hundred yards behind Auntie Diding's house.

To Auntie Diding, Loloy was a *silingan ra,* "just a neighbor." He was neither a *kabanay,* that is, a person to whom she could trace her relationship, nor was he even a *kaubanan* (derived from *kauban* "companion," itself from the root *uban,* "with"), that is, a relative, but one with whom the step-by-step relation could not be traced. In fact, he had married a Dagatan girl, and his wife Teofista Dagatan was a first cousin of Auntie Diding's husband (see fig. 2). Younger than Auntie Diding, Loloy had to address her with respect as "*manang* Diding," while she could be informal and call him directly by his nickname, Loloy, the short form of his first name used as a term of endearment. He was indeed a habitué of Auntie Diding's porch, where he came

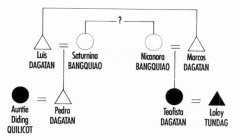

FIG. 2. Affinal links between Loloy Tundag and Auntie Diding

often, as most people from Camingawan did, toward the evening after the return of the fishermen or on Saturday afternoon to drink a pot or two of *tuba,* the coconut palm toddy.

He had no kinship relationship to Ned either, at least none they could mutually acknowledge. Approximately the same age, they should have addressed each other informally. Ned indeed did address Loloy by name, but he in turn called Ned "*manong* Ned." This mark of formality indicated a disparity in social status which overrode the informality generally expected between coevals. Ned, who more than most, had a great sense of practical etiquette apropos a de facto situation (and who knew how to manipulate matters to his advantage), complained, with a touch of calculated bad faith, that he was not receiving from Loloy the respect he was due. But—I anticipate.

Loloy had lost his right arm. The amputation had left him with a well-healed stump above the elbow, so that he could still use what was left of the arm to carry things, to block his harpoon while rearming it with his other hand, and so on. Pushed by necessity, he had so well adapted to his physical impairment that his fishing and farming activities were barely hampered.

The war (World War II) had brought to Siquijor, as to the rest of the Philippines, more than just the grimness of Japanese occupation and the glory of Philippine resistance. Not only did it profoundly disrupt the traditional fishing and farming of the islanders, it also exposed them to entirely new techniques of production. One of these had the irresistible appeal of complete efficiency combined with minimal exertion: fishing with dynamite sticks, an abundant material then and for years to come.

Despite, or more precisely because of, its efficiency, the fishing technique was disastrous for the fish itself, since it killed indiscriminately everything that swam close to the point of impact. More seriously, it damaged permanently the coral reef, the very habitat of the coastal marine fauna upon which the fishermen based their existence.

Dynamiting was not an activity that could be sustained on a large scale for a long time. By 1972 when martial law was declared, the ready supply of dynamite had vanished, dynamite fishing had become illegal, and fishermen complained about the scarcity of available fish. On occasion some individuals were still tempted by such miraculous means of production, even though the fear of being discovered by or denounced to the dreaded Philippine constabulary prevented most from engaging in this detrimental activity. By the time of my fieldwork, it had all but disappeared.

In addition to the fear of punishment and the difficulty and expense of securing dynamite, one of the reasons most people seemed to obey the law prohibiting this fishing technique was the daily contemplation of the likes of Loloy. For, although dynamite fishing demanded little effort, it required a certain amount of skill. Thrown too early, the cartridge got wet and did not explode; thrown too late, it took the fisherman's life or—as was Loloy's luck in 1966—just his arm.

"But," I asked Ned out of concern for our neighbor, "you want to send Loloy to jail for allowing his cow to feed in the middle of the road?"

"No, but it will scare him enough," he replied.

He was still animated, but I could see that his anger was subsiding and that he was beginning to recover his usual bonhomie.

Ned would not have gone to yell directly at Loloy, because this simply was not done. It would have run against the Visayan sense of propriety, according to which indirectness—exemplified by allusions, innuendos, third-party testimonies—was preferable to any immediate confrontation because it preserved a smooth surface for interaction. Conflict, if at all possible, was articulated through a third party.

And so Ned never went beyond complaining to Victor Saplot, the *barangay* captain, about the cows pasturing on the road, about his having been almost killed when he ran into the rope linking the cow to her post on the other side of the road, about the general backwardness of irresponsible *barangay* people who by their neglect precluded any progress in their lives. By the time he reported the incident to Victor, Ned was not sure whose cow it was—it might have been Loloy's—but he had now forgotten and, anyway, had never seen it very well in the dark.

THE TOWN OF LAZI lay at the bottom of the bay. From our neighborhood with Auntie Diding's home at its center, the shortest way to reach town was still by *baroto* (the traditional small double-outrigger canoes), an easy ride along the shoreline. The same distance was

often covered on foot by those who preferred to follow the beach at
low tide, although they had to ford a stream or two on their way.

But Camingawan was also the end of a path that led into Auntie
Diding's palm foliage and then vanished on the beach. Starting at
Auntie Diding's, the path meandered through the entire *barangay*,
crossing different *sitio*, passing the artesian well where Soy refilled his
jerricans, and continuing toward Lapyahan center, where it reached
the *barangay* chapel, the small peanut co-op, a cemented yard (alter-
nately basketball court or dance floor), as well as one or two "convenience" (*sarisari*) stores around which people of both sexes and all
ages drank, gossiped, and dawdled before returning home. From
there the road led to the spring of Caliguwan, a busy place where
people fetched water, washed clothes, bathed, and brought their
cattle to drink. A few hundred meters more down the road was the
junction with what some people occasionally and ceremoniously referred to in English as the "highway," the seventy-two-kilometer long,
still-to-be-asphalted circular road that sequentially connected all the
island municipalities. All sorts of motorized vehicles traveled this seg-
ment between the municipality of Lazi and that of San Juan. Still a
few kilometers down the road, one reached the *municipio* of Lazi, the
town proper at the center of the municipality.

By far the most traveled way of reaching town was yet a longer
route. A murky track behind Auntie Diding's house wandered
through Lapyahan before joining the circular main road. This route
was no less adventurous than that following the beach, because with
any rain the little-traveled way between Camingawan and Lapyahan
center became extremely hazardous. On four or three wheels, it was
a bumpy and slippery ride; on two wheels, it was a challenge to one's
sense of balance.

Since the people of Lapyahan did not own any means of transportation—no motor, no bicycle—the track was not much traveled
except on foot. An occasional tricycle carrying bags of rice, copra,
corn, or peanuts, and once in a while a jeep "for official use only"
passed by. Ned, who came on his motorcycle to visit us several times
a week, and my wife and I on our Yamaha 100 were in fact its most
frequent users.

The *barangay* residents found that grass grew beautifully on the
road and along its sides, and for the people who lived by its side, the
road was the closest available pasture. A cow at the end of a rope
fastened to a stave at the roadside could not damage anyone's crop
field even if it pulled out its rope and grazed across the road.

For about a week following this incident, the villagers, who had
been warned by their *barangay* captain that *usa ka tawo*, "one person,"

had complained about *usa ka baka,* "one cow," rid the road of its animal obstacles. Thereafter, the situation went gradually back to normal, and Loloy's cow, like others in the vicinity, returned to graze in the middle of the road. No name was ever mentioned. Anonymity triumphed. No one could possibly be offended. Yet everybody knew. And so the relationship between Ned and Loloy never warmed up. It never deteriorated very much, either, because the two men almost ceased interacting with each other. And yet, paradoxically, they still maintained a business relationship, as we shall see below.

INTRODUCING NED as a character is a task that I find difficult because, as a middle-aged middleman from the middle class, he embodied so many contradictory traits. His appearance, itself emblematic of his whole person, displayed those characteristics. He was still in good physical shape for a man in his forties, with a cherub's face (despite a receding hairline), the beginning of a paunch, and a laugh revealing several artificial teeth. Altogether, he was good-natured, with an engaging personality whose limits had presumably been reached in the incident with Loloy.

Sometimes a character cannot be described in isolation, and that is the case with Ned. I could not depict him without his motorcycle, a ten-year-old, 175-cc. monster that he and his wife, Minay (he at the commands and she as passenger, most often ignoring mundane perils with superb dignity), rode imperially over at times improbable paths and often over such short distances that walking would have been less trouble than turning the machine, finding the keys, starting the engine, and sitting astride before reaching, perhaps a hundred meters away, their destination.

But it would be even more difficult to introduce Ned without his wife, Minay Dalugdug, a skilled and dedicated nurse, who was looking forward with excited anticipation to a promotion that would eventually bring her further away from Tagaw, her *barangay* of origin. They lived *sa lungsod,* "in town," behind the imposing Roman Catholic Church and beside the Aglipayan Church, close to the municipal building and the *galingan,* the "mill," where people from different *barangay* brought their bags of corn or rice to be processed. Their children were already grown and only their youngest daughter, a teenager, still lived at home; the others were students in Dumaguete, Cebu, and Manila.

Ned and Minay belonged to the local bourgeoisie. They did not own much land. Ned's auto mechanic shop, a few steps away from their house, catered to jeepney and motorcycle owners and at all hours exuded penetrating odors of burnt motor oil. His supervision of vehicle maintenance and repair obliged him to undertake inter-island travels to get spare parts in Cebu and sometimes even in Manila. His business was relatively lucrative, as his clientele extended well beyond the limits of the municipality of Lazi, to neighboring Maria and the easternmost part of San Juan.

Ned saved part of his profits; the children's education could be costly, and he had to think about his old age. Although he certainly did not live extravagantly, he had a house that was comfortable by local standards. Built of cement block walls and covered with a zinc roof, it was equipped with an ingenious plumbing system that allowed him to have running water in the kitchen and in the bath. He also had enough money to indulge in one of his favorite activities, deep-sea diving, with costly equipment.

As a member of the local bourgeoisie, he was always on the lookout for a productive investment. Ned's house not only sheltered his immediate family and a servant; on the premises he raised—giving a penetrating and acrid smell to the surroundings—several hogs he had bought as piglets that would bring him a healthy profit once fattened. This was a risky business, despite the presence of a veterinarian in town. Pigs die easily, I was told, but promise a high return on a minimal investment in a short time—hence the attraction.

Hardly more rewarding as an investment was his attempt to derive some profit from fishing done in the *barangay*. He could thus speak of *akong mga mananagat sa Camingawan,* "my fishermen in Camingawan." He used a small amount of capital, less than a thousand pesos (at the time less than two hundred dollars), to acquire a *baroto* (a small canoe with double outriggers) and a *pokot* (a one hundred-meter-long fishnet).

He was even thinking of investing in a secondhand pedicab (a motorcycle with a sidecar used for hire), but, as he would say, *wa pay siguro,* "it was not yet sure."

What was certain, however, was that he knew how to diversify his financial interests. Almost anything could titillate his entrepreneurial sense. Making money as a businessman was an end in and of itself and did not need to be justified, but he was also a dreamer whom his wife regularly brought back to earth. Did he not dream of unrealistic developmental projects on the island, as if the postponed tarring of the highway and the announced arrival of electricity in town would be the panacea for the island's poverty and the key to his own financial triumph?

The fishing interest that Ned had acquired happily combined finance and pleasure. The operation was potentially profitable, although that had not been the determining factor in his involvement. In the first place, it allowed him to justify his diving hobby to himself and to his entourage. Not only was the initial equipment and its main-tenance expensive, but even the bottles of oxygen had to be refilled outside of Siquijor, either in Dumaguete or in Cebu City. Now it had become part of his production costs, a necessary expense if he was to be successful in the fishing venture. He dived amidst "his" fishermen, whom he could thus coach directly and presumably more efficiently. Like everyone in the *barangay*, they tended to be, at least in the eyes of a town entrepreneur, both *dili kasaligan* ("unreliable," "untrustwor-thy") and *tapulan* ("lazy").

Whether they needed coaching was another matter. There could be little doubt that Ned was there more for the fun of it than out of duty. More importantly and perhaps paradoxically, Ned enjoyed the company of "his" fishermen, the camaraderie of fishing teams on one boat, the after-the-fact exegesis of their efforts, the possible sharing of the catch on the beach, the commensality of *kinilaw* (a dish of any-thing unripe or raw, in this case fish seasoned with *suka*, palm toddy vinegar), *sinugba* (anything broiled, generally on coals of coconut husks), or *tuba* (the palm toddy).

ALTHOUGH HE WAS a town entrepreneur, a bourgeois, Ned had a strong orientation toward the *barangay*. After all, either in his shop or with his fishermen, he derived most of his profits from exploiting its resources. This could have had the reverse effect and have pushed him more toward the town lifestyle than toward *barangay* activities. In fact, he and his wife Minay were both ambiguously bourgeois, he by birth and she by profession.

As a *barangay* nurse who had been born and raised where she now worked, Minay's attachment to the rural area of her ancestors was evident. At the same time, she was educated and had "married up," into one of the best families of the town bourgeoisie. The ambiguity of her social position, thus of her identity, was only reinforced by this marriage.

Ned's position was no less ambiguous, and for reasons that, though related, were not entirely identical. Ned was born to the fam-ily into which she had entered only by marriage. In at least two re-spects, it was a good match. First, they cared for each other. Some twenty-five years of marriage and four children later, they still en-joyed each other's company and, at least publicly, displayed mutual affection. In addition, both had "married up": she had espoused him and the resonance of his name; he had espoused her and the luster of her education. His economic position was respectable, although there were copra dealers, lawyers, store owners, and others who were better off.

However, bearing the family name of Pasco was assuredly, in and of itself, an immeasurable asset, which carried prestige and even power. Consider this: from the beginning of the twentieth century until today (1988), seventeen different mayors—even though the label has varied from *capitán* and *alcalde mayor* to *presidente* and finally "mayor"—have headed the administration of the municipality of Lazi. Ten of these mayors were related as father and son (see fig. 3). In only two cases was I unable to trace actual kinship relationships between the mayor and another.[32] While Ned's maternal grandfather (Jose Veradio) had also served in that capacity, there had been two mayors bearing the Pasco name: first, the late Antonio Pasco (a brother of Ned's only recognized paternal grandparent); second, Antonio's son, Victoriano Pasco, who was still alive and whose own son, Victoriano Pasco, Jr., was himself a town official at the time of my fieldwork.

Thus the political grip that a few elite families undoubtedly exerted over the entire town is clear. And there was indeed a politically active town bourgeoisie, eager to exert its class privileges, to profit and prosper, to dominate the economic life of the municipality, and to do so by absolute control over the decision-making process and, in particular, over the appointment of civil servants. Leadership and exploitation went hand-in-hand, since the elite controlled not only the resources but all the methods of access to them. They had, or more accurately they were, the legitimate power, and they were recognized as such. Unusually mighty under the Marcos regime, the weight of law and order was on their side. Because they could afford generosity toward the Church, they were doubly blessed. Education had endowed them with grace, social and otherwise. Furthermore, their linguistic facility in English as well as Cebuano gave them the rhetorical control necessary to persuade their clients, in particular the proletariat of the *barangay*.

The mere mention in town of the Pasco family name would have been sufficient to conjure up images of this sort. However, Ned himself had some obscure origins. He certainly was a Pasco, but was he the right Pasco? And had Minay married the right man for love but the wrong one to satisfy her social ambitions?

---

32. Even so, one of these two late ex-mayors had begotten a son who at the time of this writing (1988) had become a highly visible political figure. But this is another story.

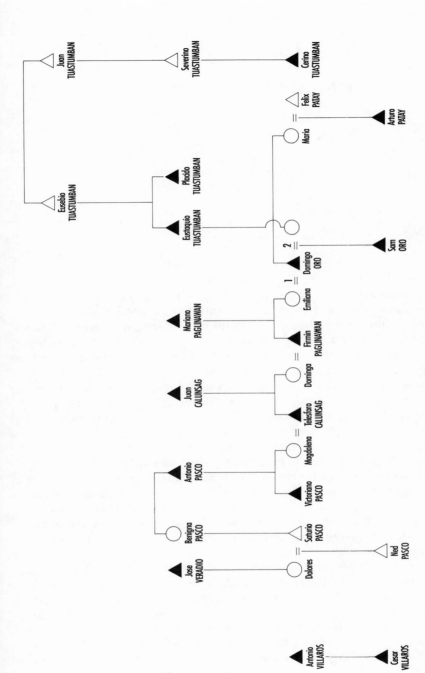

FIG. 3. Interrelatedness of Lazi mayors, ca. 1900 to 1988

11

A Lame Story

I N THE *BARANGAY*, only a few people escaped poverty. Many just scraped along, while others barely survived. For those who lived there permanently on the modest products of their fishing and farming, the island of Siquijor constrained, rather rigorously, their activities. To begin with, it limited their movements. They did go to visit kin and friends in other *barangay*, and it was only a few kilometers' walk to town. On Sundays, people converged there less for the morning dominical Mass than for the serious business of cockfighting. Men gathered en masse in and around the *bulangan* (the "cockpit"), while women shopped along the main street, socializing and gossiping with relatives and friends who had come here for the same reasons. By midafternoon on Sunday the town was almost bustling. Many men were no longer completely sober. Jeepneys and pedicab honked endlessly trying to rally passengers returning to distant *barangay* or to another municipality. Perhaps even a ship on her way to Cebu City or to Mindanao called briefly at the municipal pier. By sunset, if the ship had sailed away, the main street was again deserted, and the town fell back into a seeming torpor until the following weekend.

But most *barangay* residents could not escape the island at will, certainly not with the same ease as the townspeople. Boat fares, already expensive for a member of the bourgeoisie, reached a virtually prohibitive price for ordinary villagers. For them, getting out of Siquijor most often meant going into exile, to Mindanao, toward that southern frontier zone where all hopes could still be fulfilled. I thus could expect villagers' mythism to be different from that of the townspeople. In truth, the two groups did not always seem to live on the same island.

Because of his repeated trips to Camingawan, Ned had lost some of the glamor that being a town resident conferred. With him, Auntie Diding joked rather freely, Virgie felt at ease, Tropio Quilicot and Leon Isoy liked his company. In general, everyone enjoyed his easygoing personality; the people of Camingawan had grown accustomed to his presence. When members of the town bourgeoisie appeared on their beach, the people from the *barangay* normally kept their distance. Speaking to strangers, much less to foreigners, was always a bit daring. It went against the local ethos. All too commonly I would ask a question of someone who felt immediately embarrassed by the situation and who, unsure as to what to do, would walk away without having said a word, even when my question had been understood perfectly.

Of course, time created familiarity and granted us an intimacy sufficient to facilitate the flow of communication with our neighbors. One day, Virgie, who thus far had come and gone on different errands without ever engaging in much conversation, brought us some fish and, her delivery done, lingered a while on our porch. From her viewpoint, as a young woman concerned with her social position in the village, this was more than daring. Although generally *ulaw* ("abashed" as well as "ashamed"; see note 2 on *ulaw*), she seemed this time willing to engage in conversation instead of returning straight to Auntie Diding's home.

Had she been alone, it would have been scandalous, but she had a *kauban*, as little Trina had accompanied her. Also, the presence on our porch at that very moment of several of Dadoy Quilicot's siblings, her cousins, made the situation altogether acceptable.

Peter Quilicot, who was almost as good-looking as his older brother, was in his late teens. Trying to assert himself was appropriate to his age, even though it ran contrary to his own shyness as well as to the reserve that his culture prescribed. He would clown in front of me, amused by the fact that my name was the same as *Juan Pablo, pareho sa Santo Papa* ("John Paul, like the Holy Father"), while his own name brought him close to *San Pedro, ang ika-primerong,* that is "Saint Peter, the first (of the Popes)."

His brother Diego, an even younger teenager and not completely at ease in this setting, contented himself with smiling in silence at his elder brother's witticisms, all the while nervously adjusting and readjusting his diving goggles.

There was also their younger sister Susie, a *dalaga na,* who could not prevent herself from giggling and blushing both from amusement and intrigued embarrassment at witnessing Peter's behavior and observing me. She and Diego would also exchange asides with each other, spoken so quickly and so softly that, although intrigued, I could never catch the words.

At any rate, the three of them were just there, sitting and settled, watching me and my wife, observing us and commenting on our writing with at least as much eagerness as I displayed in observing and commenting on their comments.

Too shy to join them on our porch, although surely as curious, two or three adult women leaned against our hut as they waited for the return of several fishermen. Hands in front of their mouths, they talked to each other. Although they stared at us, they liked to gossip among themselves rather than engage in conversation with us. Only when asked did they reply and then often with only a laconic *oo* ("yes").

Virgie came and stayed only because there were other people around whose presence could mitigate any potential and imagined danger in our own presence and unplanned interaction.

As for me, in the process of writing notes on our porch toward the end of the day, I often asked—since there was often someone to ask—for a scrap of information, or how to pronounce a word, or what was the nickname of such and such a person, and so on. It was very informal, and whoever was around could answer and help me check something about which I was unsure. Often I learned, in that way, something new. I cannot remember with any certainty (having forgotten to write it down in the excitement of the action) how or even why in that context I had asked about the meaning of the word *kihud* that I must have heard, noticed, and noted that very day. With the older women's approval—they marked it with rapid and repeated raising of their eyebrows—and in front of the teenagers' impassive indifference, Virgie proceeded to narrate as follows:

> *Sa una, kuan,* the Spaniards, she come. The name of Siquijor she don't know. There was a man on the beach when the Spaniards are coming. She ask the name. *Sa ato pa,* uh, *kuan,* she ask the name because the Spaniard she don't know. His companion, he makes mistakes. He believes the Spaniard she asks the name of his companion. He says that he tchok, tchok, tchok [the informant and some auditors mimic limps]. *Sa binisaya,* the tchok, tchok, tchok, *kihud, nagkihud siya.* The Spaniards she ask the name, the companion he say the name *Kihud,* because the bad way she walks. The Spaniards she understands wrong, because *Si Kihud* and Siquijor. It's OK *lang* now; *kuan,* OK *ba na lang?* finished in your book? I'll be go home now.

Virgie had spoken *sa ininglis,* even though it was in a hesitating English interspersed with Cebuano expressions. Her story was thus a complete surprise for me, who had all along wondered about and longed for a myth of origin. It was not quite the variant I expected, but it was certainly a legend concerning the origin of the name of the island. My wife and I were clearly the addressees of the story, but somehow the other spectating auditors stayed in and around our hut. They began reacting to this narrative as if it had been told at a most auspicious moment. They had neglected to tell it to us before; once uttered, however, it dominated the conversations.

As it turned out, everyone in the *barangay* knew the story of this limping man to whom the arriving Spaniards had spoken first (or at whom they had pointed). It was from him, or rather from his limp, that the island had acquired its name. The word *kihud* means "to limp"; it is preceded by the article *si* appropriate to a proper name; and Siquijor was thus imputed to the Spaniards' original mistake as they had confused a "Mr. Limper"—or at least his name—for the name of the island on which he lived.

That version of the story was in fact quite well known throughout the island, but it had an all-too-neat-and-clean aspect, as if edited for the local anthropologist. And indeed, another version circulated. More daring, it was not exactly meant for the edification of young children, nor was it easy for people to let us in on it. Although not considered proper, it was not any more or any less authentic than the other one. It was perfect material, however, to be buried in the depths of the subconscious.

Actually, the first time I heard this version, it was presented to me as a joke by someone who was far from sober, and it met with strong disapproval by his embarrassed immediate associates. The island indeed drew its name from that of a man; however, it is not so much that he was "limping" (*kihud*), but rather that he was "fornicating" (*kiyud*). The verb *kiyud* refers to the pelvic thrust movements of a man during coitus. It means at once "to mimic (by such movements) copulation" and, in a vulgar though common derivation, "to copulate."

Obviously, I had been wrong in my effort to obtain a myth of origin. Even when I asked explicitly for the origin of the island, I received what could be called a skewed answer, in fact a nominalist one. Instead of the origin of the island, I had gathered the origin of its name.

With the "limping" story, I had no difficulty turning to older informants, nor in asking them to tell it to me once more. Some obliged with visible pleasure, and sometimes with a raconteur's flair. Such was the case with *manang* Tibay Dagatan, who used to burst into laughter without restraint at the end of her narration. Such was also the case with *manang* Iyay Mahinay, whose advanced age had left her with only one front tooth. Older men and women liked to retell the story that they had heard in their long-gone childhood.

Waiting for the return of the fishermen or just enjoying the swift and spectacular setting of the sun before returning to their respective *balay,* neighbors often gathered on Auntie Diding's porch on a late afternoon. This was a propitious moment to ask questions. *Manong* Andres Sumagang, the oldest man living in Lapyahan, was likely to be there, often silent but endlessly smiling, his rimless straw hat deep on his head and his wrinkled hands closed on the handle of his cane.

On one occasion, they all entered into a debate as to whether it was Si Kihud himself who had answered the Spaniards, whether he had been alone on the beach, whether he had a *kauban* ("companion") who had answered in his stead, whether he was truly limping, or whether he had not in fact alluded to the way in which the Spaniards had had to hobble in their funny attire before reaching the dry beach. Clearly, even though it was taught in schools for the edification of the youngsters, the particular tradition that the old folks of the *barangay* interpreted right before me seemed to have an extraordinary resilience.

And yet the story—indeed, they called it *isturya,* a word obviously derived from the Spanish *historia*—that Virgie had told us and that I had taken as part of an oral tradition was in effect in the process of losing its orality, for it was about to become rigidified in writing. As performed, the "recitation" came straight from a text in English that was taught in the schools. I had transcribed in my notes less a bona fide, authentic, mythical account of a village truth (that which the oldest residents of the *barangay* could have given me) than a myth as fictitious narrative.

There was thus an interesting tension in the discourse of tradition between the vivacious interpretation the older residents of the *barangay* provided me and the presumption of death that schools made in transmitting to the younger generations a dead folklore punctuated with a few phrases like *kaniadto* ("formerly") and *sa kanhing mga tuig* ("in the days of yore").

Teachers, as the reader may discover later, were burdened with social meanings that they did not control, as they occupied a pivotal yet highly ambiguous place midway between a more or less urban bourgeoisie and a rural proletariat. Keepers as well as exemplars of an "official knowledge," they played a delicate role in the constitution of mythism in the *barangay,* especially since peasants let them—in fact, forced them—to arbitrate and validate most of their traditions and some of their conflicts. Being the referees of a peasant tradition, at once within and without that tradition, left them with a difficult part to play.

"By the way, nobody believes that anymore; all this, this is superstition," one of the teachers insisted in English, while several of her assembled colleagues nodded approvingly. For her, it was an authentic tradition at the very root of the island's cohesion, and yet it was a false story. But for most people in the *barangay*, it would have been much more difficult to play on this type of refined distinction. The existence of that Limping Man, of Si Kihud himself, was no more nor any less real or doubtful than that of Magellan or of Humabon, of Lapu-Lapu or of Legazpi.[33] They were all present in the same absence.

Many ideological currents converged at once and haphazardly on the inhabitants of the *barangay*. There was an oral tradition on the verge of becoming written; there were the school teachings; there was the Church doctrine; and the state had its own viewpoint. Each one exerted its ideological pressure on the minds of the peasants.

God—who else?—had created Siquijor; this was common knowledge on this most Christian island. But what of history, of geology, of all that was told and whispered and even proclaimed? The island had borne another name at the time of the Spaniards. Most people knew that, even though few of them could give that name. Confusion was certain, for different, competing traditions were playing on different, incompatible registers.

A quasi-official version of tradition existed. It had been codified in writing, the work of a teacher. She had produced it for the Souvenir Program published on the occasion of the inauguration of the Province of Siquijor on January, 8, 1972. This version further muddled the issue, especially in this remarkable paragraph:

> The Spaniards at the time of discovery gave this island a name, "Isla de Fuego" or island of fire. They must have seen fire along the coast while they were going to Cebu. Legend has it that the island was once under the sea. A big, big fire was seen. Thunder roared and lightning flashed. When all of these phenomena subsided, there arose an island. To corroborate this phenomenon, fossils of clam and other sea objects could be found on top of hills and mountain ridges even now. (Tumapon n.d. [1972]: n.p.[37])

From a rhetorical viewpoint, the fascination of the text comes from its author's efforts at reconciling the mythological contradictions of several overlapping systems of coherence. Tumapon starts with ob-

33. In 1521, when Magellan arrived in what is today the city of Cebu, Humabon ruled over the island of that name. Shrewdly, he accepted the Christian faith and recognized the suzerainty of the Spanish king, after which Magellan felt obliged to help him against his enemy, Lapu-Lapu, who ruled over the neighboring island of Mactan. In this most unwise venture, the Spaniards were trounced and Magellan killed. The Spaniard Legazpi took possession of the Philippines in 1565 and administered it until his death in Manila in 1572.

jectivist confidence. Her claim is descriptive, but she misquotes the usual Spanish name, *Isla de Fuegos*. The teacher's transformation of an "island of fires" into a "fire island," the passage from a concrete plural to an elementary singular points at the gap that separates her realistic intent and her ideological achievement. She presumes all the same that the Spanish denomination was empirically grounded. "They must have seen fire along the coast while they were going to Cebu." But why state so much or why say so little? Why stop there? Why Cebu? Whence do they come? What do they want? Who are they?

And yet the teacher's text reveals enough to acquire a quasi-historical tone. From the fact that the Spaniards indeed called the island "Isla de Fuegos," Tumapon transforms the attribution of this name into an historical event, a christening, which is immediately tempered with something else.

"Legend has it that the island was once under the sea." Here we are in fictive time, that of the legend of a submerged or submarine island. Big fire, thunder and lightning, all of these are elements in the grandiose décor of natural catastrophes, perhaps the volcanic eruption alluded to here. As for the supernatural presence of God, it is not mentioned, but He can be felt to be nearby. The arising from the sea of the naked island seems to owe a lot to the power of a mythical enunciation.

In a final rhetorical bouquet, the natural sciences are called in. Marine biology, geology, physical geography are all at hand. They provide the marine fossils that "could be found on top of hills and mountain ridges even now." One must admire such efforts at integrating what might otherwise appear incompatible information. Myth, legend, and history coexist and interpolate each other and even, ultimately, any lived experience—all assimilated in a gigantic just-so story.

Of course, teachers did not all share such a homogeneous conception of their common origin. In the *barangay,* people kept only the vaguest recollection of the Spaniards. If at all, they were remembered as nasty creatures, close to evil spirits. But many teachers reinterpreted in their own ways two distinct beliefs concerning the fires that the Spaniards were presumed to have noticed on the island. Some were committed to a rationalistic as well as to a realistic viewpoint. Any fire visible from aboard a Spanish ship could only have resulted from slash-and-burn cultivation (*kaingin*). Others had a more poetic turn of mind, or at least their familiarity with English prompted their linguistic imagination. For them, the fires referred to the luminescence of the *aniniput,* an insect known in English as "firefly."

Once more, the teachers, probably too closely related to the bourgeoisie, did not pretend to tell a story; they merely intended to mention in passing a "forgotten" belief. At the same time, they could not prevent themselves from mentioning it, as they were still too closely related to the *barangay*. Yet, no teacher probably would ever have placed us on the track of narratives that accounted for the ontological status of the island had it not been for an event which, entirely by chance, precipitated things, refreshed the teacher's memory, shattered everyone's daily routine on the island, and dramatically implemented our understanding of the local tradition. For this the reader will have to wait just the length of a chapter.

12

Of Fish and Men

S ETTLING INTO Auntie Diding's hut had
been a smooth process. It would certainly have been less so without
Ned Pasco. Not only did he come and visit us regularly but he spent
an inordinate amount of time seeing to it that my wife and I received
proper attention in the *barangay*. Whatever we needed and wished
for, we only had to let him know and he would help out. My eagerness
to begin my project was evident enough, and he offered encouragement, cooperation, and something else that was very reassuring and
that I would have been hard-pressed to put into words at the time.

Although our neighbors in the *barangay* were also accommodating, their lack of competence in English matched mine in Cebuano.
Exchanges, especially linguistic ones, were limited, as our neighbors
kept coming to visit us, asking questions and telling stories to which I
listened intensely without being able to understand more than the
general drift. This was not a surprise; I had chosen to live in a village
whose inhabitants were monolingual so as to be forced to learn Cebuano. Nonetheless, there were times, especially at the beginning of
our stay, when total immersion in our new cultural and linguistic environment felt overwhelming and frustrating.

Clearly, I perceived Ned as a sort of linguistic lifeline. He had less
command of English than his nurse wife did but more than most of
our neighbors. He dispelled our linguistic isolation. He usually had
an answer and a solution to propose for whatever we asked. Best of
all, he did not hesitate to admit his ignorance and direct us toward
someone who might know. My reliance on Ned's bilingualism obviously undermined my avowed desire to avoid the nearby town
where people spoke too much English for my own anthropological
good. But to the extent that I understood the vacillating character of

my irresolute resolution, I perceived it as an emotional as well as a linguistic necessity.

As for Ned, he had more than one reason for multiplying his round-trips from his home in town to our hut in Camingawan. Curiosity played its role, but there was more to it than that. First, he was trying in effect to renew with us the friendly relationship that he and his wife had established the year before with an American Peace Corps volunteer for whom Auntie Diding's hut—that we now occupied—had been constructed. The young American had lived only six months in Camingawan, as long as he had worked for the local small bank in town. Upon his departure, the hut was left—as had been agreed initially—to the owner of the land on which it was built, that is, to Auntie Diding. She had been more than happy to rid the hut of the fishnets that had encumbered it for a few months and even to make a small profit by renting it to us. After all, it was not just our charm that had secured us a shelter in Camingawan. In many other respects, as *Amerikano* whom Auntie Diding had declared *gwapo kay taas ang ilong ninyo* ("beautiful because of your long noses"), my wife and I fit into the shoes of its former resident, apparently a jolly fellow whose name was still vivid in everyone's memory and whose presence had been easily justified in everyone's eyes.

But Ned had a more compelling reason to visit Camingawan than entertainment. The people whom he referred to as "my fishermen" resided there. In this collective phrase, he included a diverse group of men, the composition of which confused me at first because of its fluidity. It never seemed to designate the same people, as "his fishermen" varied every day in number and in identity. This impression was not completely wrong. Although I had not yet acquired a thorough familiarity with everyone in the neighborhood, from day to day I was not seeing the same faces on the same fishing parties. Some men of Camingawan never worked for Ned, and others were only occasional participants, but there was nonetheless a core of people upon whom he could rely: Tropio Quilicot, Dadoy Quilicot, Ramon Quilicot, Leon Isoy, Filemon Lapinig, and Fidel Mahinay (see fig. 4).

Already familiar to the reader, Loloy Tundag belonged to the category of irregular participants, which did nothing to dispose Ned favorably toward him. Vis-à-vis Oyo and Berto Dagatan, Auntie Diding's two married sons, Ned had an opinion more accepting than the one he held with regard to Loloy, for while they had been core participants in his team, circumstances—their father's death and Auntie Diding's determination—had led them into other activities.

As an entrepreneur, Ned might have wished for regularity in the fishermen's behavior and reliability in the production of fish. But

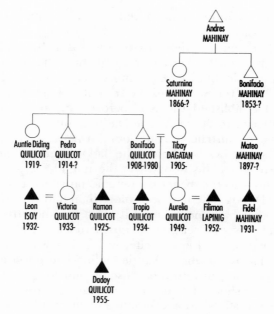

FIG. 4. Ned Pasco's core fishermen

even he knew that this could never be achieved; and so he continued to bemoan his fate and his fishermen's taste for drinking and gambling. According to him, these people were all *tapulan* ("lazy").

It was all too easy for him to point at Zosing Yano, a young man living right on the beach who insisted that he was *mananagat ra*, "just a fisherman," by which he meant that he had no land of his own, that he did not want to farm, and that he thought of himself and wanted to be considered by others as exclusively a fisherman. With his short and stout wife and their two-and-a-half rapidly begotten children, they lived on the edge of the shore, in a ramshackle, palm-thatched hut about half the size of ours in which all of them must have felt a bit cramped. But clearly this did not concern Zosing, who still preferred a card game, a jar of palm toddy, or just long hours lying on his mat.

Like most townspeople who seemingly had absorbed, with perhaps excessive zeal, the message of their colonizers, Ned blamed the economic and political problems that his country encountered on general Filipino indolence. And who else but "his fishermen" could offer a clearer, though ready-made, example of his pessimistic assertions? Thus, in the same statement, he could both excuse whatever laissez-faire they exhibited and castigate them all the while. Such ambiguity about *barangay* people was common among the town bour-geoisie.

After all, Ned was not here in Camingawan for the fun of it, at least not exclusively for the pleasure of diving and eating fresh raw fish. He came here to make sure that his capital investment was pro-ducing a return. The investment had been modest in the extreme, even though it represented a large sum to the fishermen. While Ned was discreet about it, the amount could not have been more than the equivalent of a couple of hundred dollars. He had simply acquired locally two new *baroto,* the traditional double-outrigger dug-out ca-noes, complete with paddles. Although meant for holding one or per-haps two adults, a *baroto* could accommodate—albeit in the most pre-carious and dangerous manner—up to seven people.

He had also bought a hundred-meter-long, one-meter-deep *pokot* net, which was often used for trawling by *baroto* working two abreast. Ordinarily, trawling in this way was done from larger inboard motor-boats, the ubiquitous pumpboats, which would have required a far greater capital investment. At the time, one could have bought a sec-ondhand pumpboat, with both the motor and the hull still in good shape, for about ten thousand pesos, but not for much less. There had been no pumpboat in Camingawan for a long time, although there were a dozen of them in another *sitio* of Lapyahan where the *barangay* captain resided. The fishermen of Lapyahan Beach tended to be better equipped, more successful and richer than those of Cam-ingawan, whose poverty seemed unsurpassed. Because the *baroto* had neither motor nor sail, effective trawling was out of the question. A more popular technique consisted in keeping one *baroto* still while paddling in a circle with a second one to which the net was fastened, so as to catch the encircled fish.

There was yet another technique, practiced very close to shore, which everyone both in town and in the *barangay* called "Japanese fishing"—although nobody seemed able to offer any reason for this designation. It required the cooperation and simultaneous efforts of several fishermen, a feat which was difficult to accomplish but which produced a general sense of festive excitement whenever it was undertaken. While the net was deployed between two *baroto,* a line of divers swam from the shore toward the net while pounding the coral reef on the sea bottom with a stick or a harpoon to which heavy rocks had been fastened. The intended result was that the fish hiding in the coral reef would be scared by the noise and flee, chased by the line of menacing fishermen toward the open sea and thus into the net. Fishing in this way was certainly a merry if infrequent social event for the swarm of noisy divers. It had also become, under martial law, an illegal activity because the pounding with rocks of the sea bottom was reputed—with reason—to damage if not destroy the coral reef, the very habitat of the fish. The law, however, did not seem to be too vigorously enforced.

Still, most of fishing activities were undertaken as more individual enterprises. Often two fishermen worked as a pair, from either the same or different *baroto*. The choice was then between angling and spearing fish. Every fisherman owned at least one *pasul*, a nylon "line with a set of hooks" for angling, and used locally crafted diving *antipara* ("goggles") and *pana* ("fishing spear").

Men took great pride in their ability to stay under water longer and dive to greater depths than anyone else around. Presumably this was an indirect measure of their productivity. In this area, the champions of Camingawan were a father and his son. Of the father, Ramon—precise in his gestures, meticulous in his enterprises, efficient wherever he participated, the quiet, reserved if not laconic dean of Ned's fishermen—I could be tempted to say that he fished with elegance, as one speaks of a surgeon who operates "elegantly." Despite his superb physical shape and graceful deportment, the wrinkles on his body, the pouches under his eyes, a special way of frowning, and his sustained gaze betrayed a rapidly advancing middle age.

His eldest son, Dadoy, in his twenties, liked to work and liked to play, both intensely. Gifted with a superb tenor voice and skilled with a guitar, sensitive and outgoing, the young man's good looks and charm made him extremely popular not only in his immediate environment but also in the surrounding villages. If he was not yet married, it was not because women did not reciprocate his interest in them. Unfortunately, however, as a child he had contracted *pulyu* ("poliomyelitis"); as a consequence, *nadaut iyang tiil* ("he had a bad leg"), which forced him to walk with a limp. But at sea he was in his element, and the handicap all but disappeared. Driven and gifted as a diver, he also had a sense of fish. While with his eagerness and stamina he was already a respectable angler, he was truly superb at spear fishing. This was certainly for him a way of compensating for his physical handicap, especially since the more successful he was in his fishing activities, the more attention he commanded from women. And I have every reason to believe that he relished such attention. With him, fishing was a seduction strategy.

The ability to catch fish was an expression and a measure of male success. He who caught fish in abundance could feed his family and was deemed to be an attractive party. Not only did little boys—like Arturo, Albert, and Sonny, Dadoy's three youngest siblings—learn at a tender age to swim and dive, but male teenagers, like Soy, knew how to appear in public wearing their goggles stylishly, for effect, either around their necks or up in their hair. They had also learned how to return from the beach by a circuitous path to make sure that everyone around, especially girls, took good notice of the fish that they had caught and were carrying back home.

Cause or consequence, fishing was an exclusively male activity, and there could not have been any surer jinx (*dimalas*) than the mere presence of a female in a fishing canoe. Only Tasing Dagatan, whom villagers, without ostracizing her, derided as a *lakinon* (literally, "boyish") or as a *tomboy* (the word had passed into Cebuano), could go fishing on a *baroto*. But no one would ever accompany her, and everyone, including those who would eat her fish, mocked her "countercultural" efforts. Had she caught any mermaid? Had she encountered any *enkanto* (a supernatural being who often takes the form of a handsome Caucasian)? Was her strength not exhausted?

Although Ned recognized and valued her entrepreneurial qualities, he also appreciated that she could never become one of "his" fishermen, not only because the others would not have tolerated her presence but also because she challenged some deeply engrained attitudes in their culture. And so, like most people of both sexes, while he did not make any disparaging remarks, Ned still could not speak of her with a straight face but had to release some of the unease, some of the tension her life style provoked in him, in giggles.

Except for his occasional participation in a fishing party, Ned had no specific interest in the technique(s) that "his" fishermen used, as long as they were efficient. Profit from his investment derived from the way in which the catch was distributed, a specific type of activity designated by the word *bahin:* as a verb, it means "to divide into shares," and as a substantive, it simply refers to "a share." The prescribed method was known as *tinulo,* literally, "into three" (from the root *tulo,* "three," combined with the infix *-in-*). Upon returning to the beach, a boat's catch was immediately apportioned into three equal shares. The first one belonged to the boat(s) or—local rhetoric notwithstanding—to whoever owned the boat(s). The second share was for the net, in reality, to its owner. If angling was involved, the owner of the line was the beneficiary of this share. As a consequence, whoever used Ned's *baroto* assured him at least one-third of his boat's catch. When both his boat(s) and his net had been used, he received two-thirds.

The third part remained for the actual producers. When, as was often the case, only one fisherman had spent the day angling or spearing fish, the division presented no further problem. Yet in a number of instances a *baroto* would take several fishermen, either to spearfish, or use the Japanese method. Once the boat(s) and net had received their shares, a secondary sharing took place. The last third of the catch was divided into as many parts as there had been participants.

At a time of abundance, and with luck, hundreds of fish could be caught. Such festive occasions were rare and occurred only two or three times during our stay. More frequent, alas, was the rather sad spectacle of a team of fishermen returning almost empty-handed after an entire day at sea. They had only poverty to share but always seemed to do so meticulously. We once saw the cutting into six equal portions of a single, pitiful fish, roughly the size of a trout, as the shares of an unlucky crew.

When the catch was adequate, a subsequent tertiary sharing was likely to take place, for fish was often used as a medium to activate or reactivate social links. Fishermen kept for themselves and their family only a minimal portion of their share and dispatched children to relatives, friends, and neighbors with sometimes modest, sometimes lavish gifts of fresh fish, thus supporting a dense exchange network. The division extended to us, and Virgie often arrived at dusk to prepare our dinner with a fish in her hands, exclaiming:

Gihatag ni Oyo, akong magulang, "a gift from Oyo, my older brother."

And if a gift from Oyo had been sent, it would soon be followed by a gift from Berto, Virgie's other older brother. Ned too never took fish home from Camingawan without bringing us some. Many other fishermen contributed to what appeared to us a constant chain of gifts of fresh fish, which arrived at our hut in ways that put a strain on our imagination. We knew all too well that we were involved in cycles of exchange and reciprocity, although we were quite blind as to the extent and intensity of that involvement, and we became increasingly concerned and trapped between offending someone by refusing a gift and receiving more than we could consume.

To some people—those we knew best—we tried to explain the guilt we felt by being overfed for free while everyone else was underfed, and our fear that we would be unable to reciprocate appropriately. As a Fulbright scholar, I could well afford a basketball for the *sitio* teenagers, but I would not be able to present them with a motorcycle. My arguments were sound but predictably ignored by all except the two or three persons with whom we had become intimate, Virgie, Ned, and Tropio. Clearly, if I could not reciprocate the gifts to us, it was not their problem but mine. We thus had to take a different tack. We accepted everything gratefully, and whenever there was a surplus we redistributed it as cooked food. This worked wonders. But let me return to my previous discussion.

To be *mahatagun* (derived from the root *hatag* for "gift"), that is, generous, was compulsory behavior for any fisherman; at least in theory, there were no shades of grey. One was either that or, contrariwise, *hakug*, that is, "greedy," "stingy," which was certain to bring as much, if not more, failure and bad luck as having a woman on board a fishing vessel.

After a fisherman had fed his household, after he had sent gifts of fish in all directions, only then could he dispose of the rest of his share as he saw fit. The fish could be either sun-dried as *bulad* or cured in salt as *ginamus*, which required the additional expense of buying *asin* ("salt"). Or the fish could be sold, and fresh fish always commanded a better price than processed fish. Men, however, did not retail their fish, as this was exclusively a female concern. The salable portion of a fisherman's catch was brought to town by a female relative who through time had established a regular steady commercial relationship, known as *suki*, with several town customers. Or the available fresh fish was sold to an intermediary, a *labasera* (from *labas* meaning "fresh" and specifically "fresh fish"), a "fish vendor" who held a municipal license to resell her fish at the town market. For some time, Feliza, Ramon's wife, sold her husband's and sons' catches to *suki* buyers in town but later in the year took out her own *labasera* license. As long as she was peddling only the fish produced within her household, she had no reason to obtain a license, since the profit of the sale remained within the household. When she began to resell the fish produced by fishermen other than members of her immediate family, being a *labasera* allowed her to assess a percentage of the sale price for her own benefit. From the viewpoint of the household in which the fish had been produced, she guaranteed that the fish would be sold.

In the end, no one was actually tempted by greed to keep too much for consumption or even to sell too much. For this there were two contradictory reasons: on the one hand, the sociality that fish could generate and entertain, and on the other hand, the pride that went into the production of fish.

Fish was at once food and discourse. Through the gifts of fish, something important was expressed. The indefinite number of exchange cycles that households maintained with each other through the medium of fresh fish generated and perpetuated, diffusely but endlessly, the very texture of the society—what I have called its sociality. The villagers showed an eagerness for smooth interpersonal relationships, and their gifts emphasized the conviviality and sociability of the villagers among themselves and with everyone else around them. Redistributing fish was a way to affirm social solidarity and cooperation. In other words, for the fishermen and their families, fish was instrumental in their perception and thus in the construction of their own society. It was their way of stating, but "in fish" rather than in English:

"Siquijor is an island of gentle beauty where we form one big happy family."

And yet, something entirely different was also expressed. Sotto voce perhaps, the obverse of that proposition could be heard, undermining the proclaimed—blissful but unrealistic—calm of a social environment deprived of jealousy, of envy, of hate, of conflict and other negative feelings, in short, of its weight of humanity.

While fish was food to eat—and good food at that—it was also food with which to play, to display, and to act out a fisherman's aggressive and competitive *buut*, his "identity." For indeed, sending fish here and there constantly to everyone and anyone, generous as it may have been, was in addition, in supplement, a subtle way of showing off, of bragging about the results of one's efforts. Clearly, if Oyo could afford the luxury of sending us a couple of *tulingan* (a sort of mackerel) or a *mulmul* (a parrot fish), was he not—in addition, of course, to the real and incontrovertible generosity of the gesture—putting pressure on his *manghod* ("younger sibling") and attempting either to force Berto's hand or to shame him for inefficiency or for stinginess?

Kun buut sa Dios, "God willing," Oyo had said before going to sea, meaning that with such help he would have a catch. But meanwhile, he had been able to give fish away. If he could afford it, God had manifestly wanted to let him catch it. And if he had sent one of his daughters to present some fresh fish to his neighbor Leon Isoy's household, it could only be because the latter had been *dimalas,* had had "bad luck," had not received God's blessing and bounty. And so fish materialized and objectified the *panalangin,* the "blessings," that this fisherman had received from "above," the positive rapport that the successful fisherman entertained, not so much with the Lord Himself but at least with some of His supernatural underlings who had taken his interests to heart and graced him with a substantial catch.

Furthermore, it was difficult to miss the psychoanalytical overtone of the meaning of fish, a phallic symbol if ever there was one. The *hatag,* the gift of fish, that is its "presentation" could not help but stand for a covert act of aggression. A surplus of fish to be given away already displayed a holier-than-thou attitude. In addition, the phallic aggressiveness—of which the presented fish was the icon—pointed up the keen competition that existed among the fishermen. They were, in their own eyes as well as everyone else's, only as good as their fish. In other words, the fish re-presented the fishermen who had caught it (and who had given it away), their identity, their very being, their *unud*—a word which itself has interesting connotations. In a concrete sense, it refers to the "flesh"; but it also conveys the meaning of "content," "signification," as well as that of "being" and "essence." Could the consubstantiality of fish and fishermen—or rather its figure—be traced with more discrete insistence?

Finally, surplus fish provided fishermen with the ability to engage in what could be described as networking. Because kindreds were very large and overlapped, choices had to be made and limitations introduced so that not everyone, but only a select few, received fish. Similarly, because the neighborhood was large and fuzzy in its boundaries, only a handful of neighbors could be given fish, but a few people in town could receive some, too. The reasons for giving to someone were always couched in terms of obligations—familial, social, religious, or whatever—but they always masked the true choice that had in fact been deliberately made. When Oyo gave fish to Leon Isoy, it was because he was his neighbor. Fair enough, but there were many other neighbors and some physically closer to Oyo's who received nothing from him. Or why did he give to my wife? Because I was the writer! Obviously this type of answer was not very satisfying.

Networking, as we all know, is selective and manipulative. It aims at the inclusion of a select few while condemning everyone else to exclusion. To choose recipients of one's gifts implies that one has also chosen to enter into a cycle of exchanges and therefore of rights and obligations with certain people. But it also implies ipso facto the exclusion of everyone else. Therefore fish exchanges served as symbols of recognition, whereby links between persons (and above all, households) were activated, reactivated and deactivated, thus constituting always unstable shreds and patches of connective social tissue.

But what of Ned's fish? His share—that which he derived from owning the equipment used by "his" fishermen, classic proletarians whose only possession was their labor—came to him in two obviously linked yet different forms.

In the first place, fish was food. Dried or salted, fish may have been available in town at all times, but in the absence of electricity and thus of effective refrigeration, fresh fish, although not exactly a treat, was certainly appreciated and well received. What arrived at Ned's house, hand-delivered from Camingawan, was not only part of his share but a steady supply of fresh fish. Since there was no formal accounting of the weight of landed fish (even though informally, everyone indeed kept tabs and knew that this fellow probably cheated or was suspected of doing so, while that one never would or would be deemed incapable of doing such a thing, and so on), on bad days he neither demanded nor received what would have been, from an arid arithmetic viewpoint, the share to which he was entitled. On good days, however, he received only the best and did not need to come to Camingawan: the choice fish had already been selected for him and delivered to his house. But he came there anyway, to keep an eye on the producers, on their productive efforts, and on his interests in the distribution of their products.

Secondly, fish was elusive—everyone knew that—and scarce enough to be a valuable commodity. In town Ned did not have the same redistributive constraints as the fishermen had in the *barangay*. Food exchanges in town were more likely to involve a much scarcer and more expensive product, namely, meat. Anyway, for Ned, fish was very ambiguous since it was "his" in that it was in his possession and yet not "his" in that he had not caught it himself. Only on special occasions, and if he had received more than he could consume, would Ned give fish away to a neighbor, although he did not "have to." In these conditions, the largest portion of his fishing share could be sold, not by him but on his behalf by a *labasera* or by the wife of any of "his" fishermen. Thus, whether return on his capital investment or appropriation by him of a produced surplus, fish could become cash.

Ned's venture was not yet a year old when we arrived in Camingawan. But when he spoke of "his" fishermen, it may not have been a mere rhetorical figure. In effect, in their mutual dependency, they may have been more his than his fish. Our presence had given him a wonderful pretext for showing up in the *sitio* at any time, ostensibly visiting us, but all the while managing his flourishing enterprise.

13

The Just-So Story of a Tilting Umbrella

WHEN WE ARRIVED on Siquijor in the middle of 1980, economically the Visayan island was—and for that matter still remains—a strongly depressed area of the Philippines. The late-nineteenth-century days when people came looking for economic opportunities from neighboring islands, mainly Cebuanos and Boholanos, had long gone by. Since the 1920s, a sizable proportion of Siquijor's children had steadily trickled out at first, then poured into Mindanao.

As a counterbalance, the islanders, in residence or in exile, clung to the idyllic image with which the readers are now familiar. The stock phrase prevailed:

"Siquijor is an island of gentle beauty where we form one whole big happy family."

It was echoed by equally frequently repeated statements, still made in English, to the effect that:

"We are all peaceful and law-abiding citizens."

And when, in the *barangay*, people spoke of something as being *linaw* ("calm"), it might have referred as much as to their *hunahuna* ("state of mind") as to the condition of the sea (*dagat*).

Nothing of earthshaking proportions ever seemed to occur there on the island. Even World War II had left it relatively unscathed. Perhaps the last newsworthy event had occurred on January 8, 1972, when Siquijor was inaugurated as "a separate and independent province." As for a great event in the municipality of Lazi, one would have to go back, I suppose, to 1897 when the *convento* ("priest's residence")—the largest one in the entire Philippines—was completed.

Yet something happened on December 6, 1980, that was obviously an ominous, momentous, portentous event to many. A slight but perceptible tremor briefly rocked our *payag* ("hut") on that night. I would have probably forgotten this modest manifestation of natural power, and I would have even forgotten to ask my neighbors how they felt about earthquakes, had they not volunteered an abridged piece of moribund, if not dead, folklore.

It was the ancient lore of olden times, still believed, they said, by old women in remote *barangay* in the mountains. Actually, it was not their own interpretation but a recitation, in one case practically word-for-word, of a tale identical to one drily collected in 1952 in a nation-wide historical data-gathering effort by public school teachers, from which I quote here:

> The flat world is supported by a single huge post. Sometimes a carabao tosses the post or rubs its body against it, thus causing the earth to quake. They [the old people] drive the carabao away from the post by shouting, "Br-r-r-wa!"[34]

Carabaos or water buffalos are the perfect draft animals for the cultivation of rice paddies, but rice paddies were not common on the rather arid lands of Siquijor. For the people of Camingawan, the cows that pulled their plows across their corn fields and the pigs that they slaughtered on festive occasions were closer to their daily experience. This is probably why, in the variants of the story that I would hear later from Tropio's mother, Tibay, from Auntie Diding, from Iyay and other *manang* (that is, "women older than me"), the carabao disappeared and was often replaced by a cow or even by a big pig.

Superficial as the school teachers had been in their old compilation, and despite their apparent lack of concern for context, they had echoed, transformed, and reinterpreted in the light of their own prejudices—at once Christian and rationalistic—a tradition that still had some currency at the time I conducted my fieldwork on Siquijor.

I had read the story indeed, but I could not understand at first why people were repeating almost *verbatim* a story probably learned at school. It was as if the earthquake, minimal as it had been, had been enough to jolt their mythical memory, although they did not seem to know or at least did not bother to tell us anything but the story that the teachers' project had discovered.

> It is still [in the early 1950s] believed by old folks that the earth shakes when pigs in heaven go astray. Their running here and there makes the world tremble.[35]

---

34. National Library of the Philippines, Historical Data Papers, *Historical Data of Negros Oriental 3, A Glimpse at Lazi (Lazi, Island of Siquijor[,] Negros Oriental) 1952–1953 (compiled by Lazi Elem[entary] Teachers)*, "History and Cultural Life of Barrio Catamboan," 1952: 5.

35. Ibid., "History and Cultural Life of Barrio Tignao," 1952: 4.

Anyway, the story was a resurgence from the past, and neither my informants nor any of the *barangay* inhabitants seemed overly concerned about the tremor we had felt that night or about its cause.

Two days later, however, a second and slightly stronger tremor rocked the town of Lazi, producing two visible cracks in the aging structure of the church and damaging the belfrey's third story, which forced the young bellringers to pull the ropes from the safety of the convent across the road. And outrage of outrages, the quake also shook several bottles of cola drinks off the shelves of a *sari-sari* store, sending them crashing to the cement floor.

In the meantime, a rumor began circulating. When exactly it originated and who started it, I could not determine. Had these facts been available, the "rumor" would be a piece of information, maybe of misinformation, but certainly not a rumor. At any rate, it was heard that someone had observed, off the coast of Lazi, white smoke, a phenomenon that, along traditional lines and under normal circumstances (but where was normality any more?), might have been interpreted as the mischievous intervention of a supernatural being (*balbal* or *enkanto*) by whom "fishermen are teased" (*gitiaw-tiawan ang mga mananagat*). It was taken instead to signal the birth of a volcano.

Rumors can spread pretty wildly, but they have one common property, namely the intellectual acceptability of the event that they purport to anticipate. In short, even an anonymous rumor is in itself a cultural interpretation which responds to a social demand for information. Not every wild statement is susceptible of becoming a rumor, for a rumor must touch base with cultural reality and have some degree of plausibility to those who receive it, reinterpret it, and more importantly yet, transmit it. The link, therefore, between earthquake and volcano was not just fortuitous.

And indeed, some people may have remembered the tremor that they had experienced on Siquijor just before the eruption of Hibok-hibok on Camiguin island in the 1950s, since, weather permitting, from Lazi shores this volcano is occasionally visible on the eastern horizon across the Mindanao Sea. But I am somewhat doubtful that this event was much more vividly remembered than the more awe-inspiring eruption of April 30, 1871, of the same volcano. Montero y Vidal (1887–1895:III, 555) reported it in eloquent terms:

> At three o'clock in the afternoon, a very high and thick column of black vapors began to rise, with a strong smell of sulphur. Suddenly bursting into flames, it set fire to the brush which burned completely, offering the most imposing and magnificent spectacle.

In the very last days of 1980 on the shores of Siquijor, the link between earthquake and volcano was a deduction, less empirically than ideologically grounded, as it appears from examining the chain of events that ensued. But let me begin with the obvious.

The rumor marked the transformation of a minor natural event into a cultural phenomenon of considerable magnitude. What people thus far had more or less ignored was now vividly recalled. And yet, now removed from the domain of physical reality, the tremor became disengaged from its actuality, and cultural reinterpretations then took over the entire scene. Surely tremors belonged to the domain of experience, but volcanoes belonged to the domain of social memory.

The next step, hastily taken indeed, was to pass from volcano to what was evoked as *dakong balod* in the *barangay*, as "tidal wave" in the town, and as "tsunami" by the precise but pedantic cognoscenti—a kind of event which, fortunately, no one in Lazi had ever experienced nor could even remember as having occurred on the island of Siquijor. If so, what exactly did people fear?

This was not entirely clear. Wild conversations grew about the volcano about to erupt practically under our noses. The island would be submerged by the sea, and so on. Accents of realism, surrealism, and hyperrealism seemed to color what Ned and Minay, Father Valentin, Justin and others in town, what Tropio, Filemon, Fidel and others in the *barangay*—some with a straight-face, others critically, others still unable to make up their minds—joked about in a way that indicated considerable hesitancy concerning what and whom they were supposed to believe. The general tone was nonetheless unforgettable.

According to these accounts, the island of Siquijor stood on a post and was just like an open umbrella. Earthquake, volcano, tidal wave, any of the three could and would cause its rod to lose its balance, and the island would then slip into the sea. And so, in town, several persons among the well-off and the most devout took the precaution of sponsoring masses, sung to quell the divine wrath. Meanwhile, in Camingawan, the members (only women were active members) of the religious voluntary association *Birhen sa Barangay* took the ritual initiative of moving their group's standard to the shoreline for daily prayer. Facing the alleged epicenter of the quake, they begged for supernatural clemency.

Heightening the general feeling of unease, the town's entire stock of candles had been sold out because, coincidentally, a printed leaflet originating elsewhere had circulated predicting three days of darkness for the end of the following month—a vain precaution, for neither fire nor candle would be able to burn in such a disaster. It was time to repent; the end was near.

The unusually inclement December (of 1981) added to the atmosphere of doom and mild panic which had begun to descend upon us. With the believed yet unreal imminence of death for all, it was more difficult to rejoice spiritually at the *misa de gallo* ("dawn mass") in these days of Advent. Some town people, more pragmatic than others, followed the municipal order not to spend their nights in their houses and began camping at the Lazi high school, where higher ground made it presumably safer, though not for long, for once the danger of the tidal wave had been dealt with, there was the threat of a landslide to fear, clearly a no-win case either *sa baybay* ("on the shore") or *sa buntod* ("in the hills").

Neither the provincial governor nor the town mayor could have been totally displeased by the turn of events. They were forced into action, and one of their first initiatives was to request from Manila a team of seismologists and volcanologists, some of whom kept round-the-clock observations in Lazi for several months. The assemblage of this swarm of scientists and technicians could only reinforce the power of those who had had it in the first place, even though a press conference, strategically staged at the marketplace on a Sunday afternoon right after the last fighting cock had bravely died in the *bulangan*, accomplished little to soothe the townspeople's volcanic emotions.

To the contrary, the press conference actually fanned them a bit because of the laudable and prudent reserve with which the PAGASA and ComVol scientists[36] predicted the future. It took more energetic measures to cool down emotions, as I discovered one day with dismay when my informants suddenly dried up on the volcanic topic, for fear of being jailed as "rumor mongers." Yet, there had definitely been success in the dispatch of Manila officials to this small town, demonstrating the ties that the local government had with the powers-that-be, not to mention with Imelda or Ferdinand Marcos.

On another level, it was a triumph; for the rumor had now escaped municipal and provincial boundaries and was making national, if not international, news, thereby decidedly placing Siquijor on the map—not a minor achievement considering that the strongest tremor experienced on the island had had an intensity somewhere between 1.0 and 1.5 on the Richter scale. The media's amplification

36. Both the ComVol and the PAGASA are official agencies of the Philippine government. ComVol is a plain and almost transparent abbreviation for Commission on Volcanology, but PAGASA is a more arcane and elaborate acronym that stands for Philippine Atmospheric, Geophysical and Seismological Administration. While ComVol has no further meaning, the very word *pag-asa*, meaning "hope," exists in Tagalog. However, the subtle, soothing invitation that the acronym conveyed was lost on Cebuano speakers, who use the word *paglaum* to express a similar concept.

of the issue gave an additional dimension. Inexactitudes and exaggerations were all alarmist. The palm in this respect should go to the Manila *People's Journal* of December 22, 1980. Its front page headline shrieked

EVACUATION

followed by

> Undersea volcano threatens Siquijor. Tremors have been rocking the island subprovince in Negros Oriental since Wednesday and its 70,000 people are being prepared for evacuation.

The word "evacuation" in Lazi had an instant popular appeal; it was on everybody's lips incessantly, as a catchphrase with powers of exorcism, uttered by people in the *barangay* who rarely used an English word, by people who had—some of them told us so—no intention whatever of making a move of any sort. For those like Auntie Diding, who saw all this agitation with some sane skepticism, *balhin ug baka, bunlay ug sagbot, pasaw ug baboy, pokot ug isda* ("pasture the cow, weed, feed the pig, catch fish") were still the order of the day. And yet, if there was not the total disruption that the press would have led its readership to believe, all was not the tranquil and resigned serenity programmed by Auntie Diding either.

Reluctantly, Father Valentin had to celebrate his Christmas Midnight Mass outdoors under the threat of imminent shower. By Christmas Day, it has become impossible to buy an onion, a box of crackers, or a kilo of rice. For this, there were two, contradictory reasons. On the one hand, townspeople with some cash reserves had begun to hoard as a precaution against the insecurity of the future. On the other hand, most shopkeepers, themselves uncertain of the future, had stopped maintaining their stock for fear of being unable to sell their goods. They had taken their cue from the number of people in town who were not cooking at home. In fact, kinship links hitherto dormant, if not practically extinct, had been hastily reactivated. Entire families had "evacuated" to the house of some kin on high ground or at least had sent their children there and begun daily commuting.

In various *barangay* a number of people found pressing reasons to visit relatives in Mindanao. Nobody was afraid, of course, but this man's uncle was sick, that one's daughter was pregnant, another woman's first cousin needed some help with her children, and so on. The weekly boat from Lazi to Plaridel (across the Bohol Sea, in the province of Misamis Occidental) was fully booked. Tiyong's widow, Angela Villaros, a woman from Camingawan, even managed to miss the *kwa-*

renta ("fortieth day prayer") for her departed husband, having gone to stay with her sister on the southern island. Children sent for vacation stayed unusually long among their Mindanao relatives. For a week or two kinship network transactions were highly intensified, with nuclear families moving out while others were beginning to return home. In short, people began "evacuating" still only halfway decided as to whether the situation was serious or not. They laughed and moved; they came back and laughed again.

On the one hand, there was the reassurance of the scientists. On the other hand, there was the belief, remembrance—what was it exactly?—of an island called Atlantis which had sunk somewhere. And could it not happen "to us right here?" It was hearsay, no doubt, but neither more nor less real from Siquijor than the too-actual and tragic earthquakes in Algeria and Italy that, a few weeks earlier, had been described in vivid and gory radio reports, likewise disengaged from actuality.

In the *barangay*, however, our neighbors had also laughed the situation away; they had given a forced laugh to something which, as Auntie Diding among others admitted on the spot, frightened (*hadluk*) them. Seeing that neither my wife nor I were particularly concerned by the situation, she pointed out with good sense that most of the inhabitants of Camingawan had no place to go, no money to escape, and felt stranded on a collapsing beach. It was clear to her that we took the situation all too lightly and that we did not appreciate the actual danger to the island:

> The island is an umbrella [*payong*] that is opened on the surface of the sea [*binukad ibabaw sa dagat*] and its handle [*pulohan*] lies there at the bottom [*sa ilalom*]. It is balanced [*natimbang*] there at the bottom. If there is an earthquake [*linog*], a volcanic eruption [*butu*], a tidal wave [*dakong balod*], we shall all drown right here [*dinhi sa baybayon ang malumsan nato*]. The island is already listing [*nagtakilid na ang pulo*]. If it tilts over, it is all over [*ug, kuan, mupaling, tapus na ug tapus na*]. That is the way it is [*mao gyud*].

Since we were located on an umbrella precariously opened on the surface of the sea, it was not difficult to understand the unease, if not the fear, of our neighbors. Auntie Diding puffed on her pipe, looked concerned for a while, and laughed as if to express disbelief in our disbelief. For her who stated it aloud, as for the rest of the population in the *barangay* who, instead, repressed the expression of their fear, the island was wobbly and rickety.

Many people in town had fled, all the while pretending that the traditional lore had no hold on them. The teachers, who had announced the forthcoming triumph of positive knowledge over antiquated superstition, were not in the least frightened, they said. In the same breath, we were told, "there is no danger" and then without pause, "still, it would be better to take shelter somewhere."

For all this turmoil, there must have been a cause. Science was useless. The experts were unable to find anything, at least anything convincingly soothing. In town as well as in the *barangay,* most people would have loved to believe in the presence of almost any reassuring scientific sign. But there was none. The mere absence of signs, which satisfied the experts, appeared to the public as the obvious refutation of the scientists' assertions.

Even religion, in which everyone sought solace, offered none. Masses and prayers had been said for naught, and the cracks in the belfrey appeared as a bad omen of the Lord's intentions. Prayers and sacraments should not have been neglected, but religious practice was evidently not enough. In addition, the alarmist leaflet was circulating, announcing that the end of the world was at hand.

Confronted with such generalized insecurity, neighbors from the village came to visit us, asking what we thought of the situation. More than a question, it was in fact an expression of their distress. The drama had taken on such proportions, with so much effervescent agitation among the bourgeoisie, that any authority conferred on us at a given moment was withdrawn the next, as soon as we opened our mouths. Whatever we did or said, our words as well as our silence, our assurances as well as our doubts, our denials as well as our prudent hesitations—all conveyed some ambiguity and were systematically interpreted as fodder for the drama.

This should not have surprised me, although it did. Why should we have succeeded where the available institutions, the church, the state, and science itself, all these authorities, had most lamentably failed?

Since there did not seem to be any other resolution to the issue that preoccupied everybody, the *barangay* people were left with their own symbolic resources. And it was in this climate of opinion that Auntie Diding—whose commonsense wisdom I used to trust—made, with the authority that her age and circumstances gave her in the *barangay,* an unexpected return to mythical thought in action.

As she used to do every evening on her way back from changing the pasture of her cow, she lingered a while in front of our hut or on our porch, exchanging quips and gossip with us and whomever else was at hand. I began joking with her and teasing her. Did she not look afraid? Was she not going to join the others? Was she not going to "evacuate"—that had become the sole theme of conversation—as many others had already done, to leave Camingawan and get away from the seashore?

Instead of taking it lightly as she usually did, she answered quite seriously that there was nothing to fear, that everything was normal (*nurmal ba*), that she was afraid (*hadluk*) indeed like everyone else, but that there was nothing serious (*walay kasu*).

Several women who had been waiting for the return of the fishermen on the porch of her house had now joined her at our hut. And she addressed herself to whomever would listen to her. What she said was of course meant for us, for anyone within earshot, for her whole family, for the entire neighborhood. But she was perhaps herself the main addressee of her own discourse, for her assertions and denials were attempts to regain some self-assurance.

Don't be afraid! It's nothing! You know why there are these earthquakes? The island lies [*gipahiluna*] on top of a post [*sa haligi*], like your hut [*pareho sa payag ninyo*], level [*lapad lang*]. Down there, lives [*karon dayon*] a big buffalo [*karabaw*] which scratches itself [*nangalut*] against the post because it itches [*kay gikatlan*].

The half dozen persons who constituted her audience began chuckling. A few teenagers followed. Children ignored everything and continued playing. Zosing's mother, *manang* Cristita, who in public rarely took anything seriously uttered a doubtful:

"*Uy!*"

Among Auntie Diding's audience, I was not the only one to be attentive. *Manang* Tibay—her advanced age gave her few privileges and being listened to respectfully was one of them—wanted to propose a correction to the narration:

"Not a buffalo but, *kuan*, pigs [*baboy*], very big ones [*dako kaayo*]."

With her toothless mouth, *manang* Iyay usually said very little. The smoke from her home-made cigar gave her eyes a perpetual glitter. With an enthusiastic movement of her head, she said:

"They were turning up the soil with their snouts."

"A buffalo," Auntie Diding insisted.

After a disapproving pause, Auntie Diding resumed with confidence. While she pretended to rub her shoulder against one of the posts of our hut, she proceeded:

Not so, it is a buffalo which itches much. It rubs itself hard. This is why the earth shakes [*mao nga mutay-ug ang yuta*]. It is nearly over [*hapit na*]. The buffalo is already tired [*kapoy na*]. After that [*sa pagkahuman*], no more earthquake [*walay linog*]. It is finished [*human na*]. Of course I am afraid [*hadlok ko, lagi*], but there is no reason [*piro walay kasu*]. I stay right here because the earthquake does not last long [i.e., will not reoccur; *sigi gihapon, diri ra, kay dili magdugay ang linog*]. The buffalo is already tired.

In telling this, Auntie Diding had indeed immersed herself entirely in an ancient mythical tradition. It was all too obvious that she was not simply reciting a text once deliberately committed to memory; it was not a legend about to disappear or pass from oral tradition to a written one. As I began to realize, it was a story of which the *barangay* people were very much aware. There was nothing secret about it. It had, over time, lost a bit of its currency. Superficially at least, it had exhausted its symbolic usefulness and become a tale hardly worth the effort of telling. Fossilized by the educators in their 1952 collection, it had become dry and cold. But told to me by a few *manang* in Camingawan, it now became warm, alive, full of the vigor of belief.

That story was indeed present in everyone's minds. The sort of panic that an insignificant tremor had apparently provoked had, in reality, more cultural than natural causes. Quite disproportionate to the strength of the tremor, the fear that followed had been generated within a particularly repressed belief system, of which no mention was ever made save for vague references that neutralized it either as survival of superstition or glorification of a bygone era.

And yet, Siquijor had apparently not lost its mythical charge. From it came the panic induced by a very small tremor. Neither science nor faith had been able to soothe minds, for the good reason that they did not share the same mythical language. Local tradition was thus still best equipped to solve the problem. According to that tradition, a water buffalo (or pigs) caused earthquakes. In the tradition that schools and science shared, earthquakes, volcanic eruptions, tidal waves, every one of them belonged to the same domain, that of geology. In the religious tradition, everything is subordinate to divine will. In reciting the local tradition, Auntie Diding had opened the door to an exegesis wherein a potential solution lay, namely the animal's weariness, which would allow people to recover their peace of mind and the island of Siquijor to stay flat on the surface of the sea, straight on its pole.

Whether it had been her intent or not, Auntie Diding had been entirely successful, transforming what had become no more than a just-so story into a partial and localized truth.

Unlike science based on knowledge outside the normal competence of most villagers, and unlike religion based on the unfathomable will of a divinity whom prayer could barely move, the recitation of the local myth was an act of faith, at once symbolic and effective. Through it, the island could be reasserted and reinvented, for it affirmed both the supernatural cause of the disaster and the probability of its happy resolution.

And thus in the *barangay* the reaffirmed and reactualized tradition fortified people's appetite for life and reestablished their serenity. The excitement passed and the routine of daily life resumed. In town, however, people were already alienated from that local tradition, which prevented them from taking refuge in it. People there lived with more or less discomfort, by habit and perforce in a twilight between knowing and not knowing. The rumors dragged on for a while. After a month or so, the threat began to subside—not the natural phenomenon, of course, which remained scientific material to be analyzed by the Manila experts—but the felt presence of this threat. It was as if its actuality had begun to wear out. The volcanic consciousness receded from the houses to the billiard parlor, entered the domain of private homes, and there soon vanished for good (or until next time) in general indifference. At its sharpest, the awareness had jolted the norms of traditional behavior among the Lazihadnon. When the intensity of its ephemeral existence began to dim, it lost at once all of its powers, the power to interpret, the power to move, and the power to set in motion. It faded away into oblivion.

The villagers as well as the townspeople had experienced all kinds of fright. At the same time, the event ended as a moral tale. In town, the members of the bourgeoisie returned to their profits as well as to an ideology that maintained a middle course between positive knowledge and religious belief. In the *barangay*, the villagers found the energy of reactualizing their own tradition. And I, for one, heard with my very own ears of the mythical status of the island.

Nonetheless, ultimately, everyone had been drawn in and taken in. Soon after, townspeople resumed their denial; nobody knew of any "tradition" whatsoever. And yet, aside from the empiricism professed in schools and the devotions performed in church, tradition exercised its ascendency on a great many persons. Who could pretend to be completely fearless, sheltered from, and indifferent to the *abat* (supernatural being), the *ingkantu* (apparitions), the *unglu* (possessed persons), the *balbal* (vampires), the *kataw* (mermaid), or the *wakwak* (bird of ill omen)? Still full of its own memories, the bourgeoisie burdened itself further with Western myths.

Among the villagers, the uttered myth, with its happily-ever-after ending had quelled fears for a while. It had forced a narrow and temporary passage between the ideology of an empirical knowledge that schools dispensed and that of an eternal salvation that the Church promised. The recitation of the myth would not always prevent the earth from quaking. Everything functioned at once in the cacophony of incongruous ideologies. The superposition of different myths—those of the school, of the Church, of the state, and of the local tradition all supplemented each other—brought its dissonances and produced its chords without resolution.

Who in this had absorbed what? Had the event triumphed over the structure? Or had the structure absorbed the event? Were the different mythical interpretations offered in town as well as in the *barangay* at all compatible? Was there a mythical structure or mythical structures? Were the townspeople ignorant of what they did not want to know any longer? Was the abandonment of a local tradition more than mere forgetfulness, the lay act of faith in a differing and deferring tradition? Had the mythical manipulation in Camingawan been the mere reassertion of parallel traditions from which, indifferently, pragmatic peasants drew?

Finally had I been the victim of my own anthropological naïveté? Even though I had started with different premises, I as much as anyone else had constructed the island of Siquijor. I had heard at last, as I had wished, a myth, "my" myth which, in the division that it implied between entangled traditions, subverted the pretext with which I had come. Whatever the mythical variant I heard—narrative or not—and whoever invoked it, the mythism of the island could not be apprehended in the closure of a text. On the contrary, it remained a discourse, open to a multiplicity of symbolic rearrangements. Born of a plurality of diverging traditions, it oscillated always between the efficient reality of a "little localized truth" and the pleasant lie of a "just-so story."

14

Big Bills

THE USE OF MONEY in the field—when to pay an informant and how much, what services to remunerate, and so on—has always been for me a problem with ethical and practical implications but without any really satisfactory resolution. I suspect that this unease is quite a common experience among ethnographers.

I hated to be taken by a pedicab driver who would make me pay ten times what the ride normally cost. But I derived no joy from haggling either, as I saw it as a form of cheating by mutual consent. In fact, it always made me feel cheap, insecure, and altogether inadequate. Relief came only when my wife, who did not suffer from the same distaste for bargaining, handled such delicate matters, while I would pretend, with less than virtue, to be hardly concerned.

When we arrived in Lapyahan to settle in Auntie Diding's *payag*, I had not the faintest idea as to what I should rent it for, especially since she had promised that her daughter Virgie would provide some cooking and laundry services for us. When I asked directly—in retrospect, a rather gross way of behaving—it brought a most noncommittal and uninformative *sa imung gusto*, "it's up to you," as an answer. I turned to Ned Pasco, whom at the time I barely knew but who had taken it on himself to oversee our installation. He echoed, uselessly from my viewpoint, the previous answer: "It is up to you."

After what appeared to me a lengthy hesitation, he ended up suggesting that perhaps I should consider paying a hundred pesos a month for the lodgings, including Virgie's service. Had I been less preoccupied with the practical aspects of our installation, I would have paid more attention to the fact that all this had taken place in front of a large group of Camingawan residents assembled there at the occasion of our arrival, for all to hear.

In his role as an intermediary, brokering between the arriving *Amerikano* and "his fishermen," he had been perfect. Although he gave all the appearance of being reluctant to do so, Ned had in fact negotiated publicly and seemingly to every party's satisfaction, the price of our stay at Camingawan. He had just secured an income otherwise unavailable locally, at a good city price, for a household central to the family relationship among all of "his fishermen," thus placing his clients further in his social and moral debt. Needless to say, he was also helping me greatly in my settling in. Since no relative of Auntie Diding had raised any objection, and since I had remained silent, it was a deal.

The suggestion that Ned made had, in fact, the character of a directive. Accordingly, I offered Auntie Diding such a monthly payment. But it was Virgie who pocketed it with a large smile. It was obvious that from her viewpoint this was a coup. In the *barangay*, one hundred pesos constituted a sum of consequence: its roundness enhanced its appeal, and its promise as a monthly salary, combined for some people with the largely imagined attraction of city life, would be just sufficient to lure young, enthusiastic, but unskilled persons— mainly women—to other islands. Ned's rationale for the proposed sum was quite clear. It was the ongoing salary rate for waitresses, salesgirls, and other "domestic helpers" in Dumaguete or Cebu City, as well as in several cities of northern Mindanao such as Plaridel. Virgie would have very little to do for us, and she would have a city salary without having even the expense of coming and going, so it would be "pure savings, pure profit" for her. In addition, she was neither entirely free nor inclined to move around and abandon Auntie Diding.

The one-hundred-peso bill that I had handed to Virgie as a first payment (the 1980–1981 equivalent of $13.33 at the official exchange rate of 7.5 Philippine pesos to the U.S. dollar) was the biggest available banknote in the Philippines. It was so big that it was practically useless even in town where finding change for a twenty-peso, even a ten-peso bill, was an occasional challenge. It would have been difficult to shop at the Lazi market with such a bill, where a single peso could buy a handful of tobacco leaves for Auntie Diding's pipe, an avocado pear, a couple of tomatoes, or even a tricycle ride back to the *barangay*. Our most extravagant yet regular expense in town was filling the gas tank of our motorcycle and acquiring kerosene for our Petromax lamp. The combination of both operations could be done with less than twenty pesos, but my presenting a "big bill" as payment was almost certain to prompt the merchant to extend credit to us rather than look for change on the spot.

But Virgie, at least for the time being, did not consider such a bill something she could and would eventually have to spend. It was an object then disengaged from the practicality of its exchange value. As she explained later, she had hoped to accumulate many of these bills to be stored preciously in a box. More than mere savings, money in that denomination had a different quality, as if its mere contemplation reassured her.

From her viewpoint there were two distinct spheres of exchange. She handled smaller denominations separately, as well as loose change with which to meet her ordinary, daily expenses. The one-hundred-peso bills were stored by themselves, in principle at least, untouched and untouchable. Disengaged from their exchange value, or reserved for the extraordinary monetary symbols marked for the exceptions of life, they were the illusory guarantors of her dreams and ambitions, of escaping the grip of the dire poverty that prevailed in her *barangay*. That she did not seem to convert her own accumulations of one hundred pesos into single "big bills," while she expected us to give her every month the agreed amount in one single bill, only reinforces such an interpretation.

Throughout the Philippines but mainly in cities, a lively black market for American dollars flourished. It largely involved people who received remittances from relatives who had emigrated to the United States and people who were eager to acquire dollars as they planned a trip or dreamed of emigration to America. While it was a concern of the local bourgeoisie, emigration was of little concern to the Siquijor peasants. They might, in their respective *barangay*, have had altogether equivalent, though vaguer, dreams of escaping their poor condition, but they did not have the means—other than symbolic—to act upon their liberating fantasy. Instead, they joked about their permanent poverty; they mocked the Chinese merchants whose thriftness and successes in town they at once envied, resented, and despised; they contemplated with a mixture of awe and jealousy the expatriates and *balikbayan* whose economic and social achievements seemed so much beyond the common peasant's reach. On top of it all, they also scoffed—and both Auntie Diding and Virgie were certainly prompt to do so—at the inappropriateness and vanity of their own entrepreneurial efforts.

And yet Auntie Diding and Virgie, both members of the same household, were certainly not the worst off in the vicinity. Their entrepreneurial efforts were not completely in vain, but their very success, modest though it may have been, was suspicious even in their own eyes; hence there was a certain amount of disingenuity in their self-deprecation. *Pinobre ra kay tapulan man mi sab,* "we are still poor because we are also lazy," one or the other had said, but it was not clear whether the personal pronoun *mi* designated just their household or the entire *barangay*. Also the giggle accompanying that sentence somehow belied its authenticity of feeling. Whomever *mi* designated, it would have been difficult to characterize either of the two women or the residents of their *barangay* as "lazy," especially when compared to the richer and more leisurely town residents.

Datu sila, tua didto, announced Auntie Diding. "They are rich over there." The *tua didto,* "over there," was always accompanied by a move of the head and a protrusion of the lips pointing with manifestly ambiguous feelings in the direction of the rich others. Jokingly but pointedly, defiant and amused by her own wit, she would turn her head rapidly and point next in the direction of our hut: *tua didto pod,* "over there, too." To indicate people in town in the first gesture and my wife and me in the second, she had used interestingly the same phrase marking a maximum of distance, even though the town was a few kilometers away and our hut was only a few yards away. Clearly, it was not just geographical but social distance that she was thus indicating.

She did not reserve such an "othering" just for members of a richer social class. There were people right in her vicinity who were much worse off than she was, some poor and others even lazier. She designated Zosing with the same *tua didto,* with the same tilt of the head in the direction of his minuscule, poorly built, and badly maintained *payag* on the beach a few steps away from her own house, with the same, almost despising protrusion of the lips toward the young man's abode. His was perhaps an extreme case of virtually accepted poverty to which I will have occasion to return.

Suffice it to say at this point that the consciousness that Auntie Diding and Virgie, like most *barangay* residents, had formed of their economic and social status on the island were a triumph of ambiguity.

At one level, most people in the *barangay* had internalized the domination to which they were submitted. As peasants, resignation to poverty was their lot. They knew from firsthand experience that they stood collectively at the bottom of the social hierarchy; but the emergence of class-consciousness seemed blocked, as if they were much too accepting of the ideology proposed/imposed by the ruling class/ party. They were religious and prayed to the Roman Catholic God as they believed in their salvation in the Other World, but ultimately they were too this-worldly to turn to the imagined solution of a millenarian movement. They were led to believe (by the radio stations as well as by their town patrons, to which and to whom they listened at times indiscriminately) that then president Marcos and his gubernatorial spouse were national heroes; and dissatisfied with their fate though they might have been, this did not cause them to switch political allegiance—and a fortiori they did not feel pressed to rebel. They seemed to accept economic failure as an incontrovertible occurrence with such conviction that it seemed to acquire the force of self-fulfilling prophecy.

But there was, at the very same time, the exact opposite tendency, without which there would never have been such incessant fibrillation of doomed entrepreneurial activity. Despite their actual but variable poverty and their repeated failures, they always seemed ready to launch themselves afresh into a new enterprise in a manner unwarranted by their abysmal record of past failure.

All happened as if they, the *barangay* peasants, carried within themselves at least two contradictory traditions. The dominant culture told them of the doom that was to be theirs and reinforced in its depressive/repressive aspect their submission and conformity to the social order imposed upon them. And yet there was something else, something radically different, a cultural countercurrent that pushed them to take initiative, to act with light-hearted enthusiasm, and to throw themselves again and again into novel enterprises. Between hope (*paglaum*) and its absence, despair, they did not choose. They just took both, if not with grace, at least in stride. To be sure, everyone's personality and circumstances differed greatly; but as nonchalant entrepreneurs, they seemed programmed to fail, that is to say, to diffuse their efforts and ultimately to remain, generation after generation—as the dominant ideology demanded—poor and dispossessed peasants in their own *barangay*.

THE RENT WE PAID Auntie Diding, which turned out really to be a salary for Virgie, was not the only verbal contract facilitated by Ned. We had another practical problem to solve. What was now "our" *payag* stood so close to the beach that, until the end of September, the southwestern wind, the *habagat,* carried enough seaspray to keep the inside cool but continually damp and salty. From October to December the northerly wind, the *amihan* of the northeastern monsoon, often threatened to blow us into the sea. Access to fresh water, however, was problematic. We could store water in a big plastic bucket, but a daily supply had to be trundled in from the well down the trail from Auntie Diding's, two jerricans at a time on a rudimentary wheelbarrow that Auntie Diding owned. Ned was certain that a daily supply could be brought to us, suggesting that Zosing Yano be given the job. Once more, it was "up to us," but the hint was that one peso would guarantee, to mutual satisfaction, a trip a day. Zosing acquiesced and began his daily deliveries.

A young man in his early twenties, Zosing was taller than most men in Lapyahan. It was he who had suggested that I bring a basketball back to Camingawan with which the young men of the *sitio* would play endlessly. At the tip of his chin, unlike most his age, he grew a long but sparse goatee, which he constantly stroked, visibly pleased with the effect he produced. Not infrequently, a soft hat—protection or style?—that had been worn for years and had faded in the sun completed his appearance. Proud and often defiant, he thus asserted with affectation his independent personality.

With the young wife whom he had not so long ago brought back from northern Mindanao, he had had two children in rapid succession, and she was already pregnant again. She had no relatives at all on the island of Siquijor and, further, was at the time the only Protestant in Lapyahan. Within a year or two her visits, even to her in-laws' neighboring house, had become less and less welcome as she had developed the habit of "borrowing" *bugas* ("husked rice or corn") from them to feed her household. Thus, she was quite isolated and had little else to distract her than strolling between her dilapidated *payag* and Auntie Diding's front porch, where she would sit still for hours before returning to her own hut. The apparent monotony and boredom of her life, her seeming solitude and unhappiness, explained why I never saw her smile.

Her life with Zosing cannot have been an easy one, either emotionally or economically. Zosing was a relative of Auntie Diding's late husband, but this affinal link was tenuous. Remote enough for the parties concerned to be unable to trace it step-by-step, it nonetheless existed not only for me who could reconstruct it through parish records (see fig. 5) but for them as well. Only because of its existence had Zosing's presence been tolerated—on a temporary basis threatening inexorably to become permanent—amidst Auntie Diding's palm trees on a beach recognized as hers. Zosing was otherwise landless.

Purportedly, Ned had chosen Zosing to be our water-carrier because he lived close by. This was certainly the case, but he was not the only possible choice. More importantly, he was one of Ned's irregular fishermen and an excellent, although at times moody, one. Although Ned relied on Zosing's technical skill, he could not always trust him to follow Ned's wishes and join a fishing party, especially if Zosing perceived it as an imposition or a constraint. For Zosing, the problem was that he had no other source of income, and consequently, even by local standards, he was extremely poor. Except for his goggles, his harpoon, a fishing line, and a couple of hooks, he owned nothing at all.

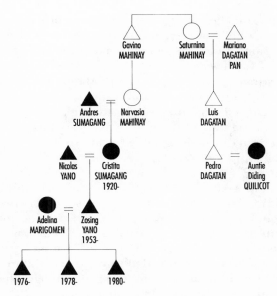

FIG. 5. Kinship link between Zosing Yano and
Auntie Diding's late husband

Although Zosing could have made a peso an hour working at agricultural tasks for someone else in the *barangay,* especially at plowing
or harvest time, to supplement his most modest earnings, this was not
his temperament, and he always refused. As he convincingly explained to me, he was

a fisherman [*mananagat*] and just that, not a farmer [*magdadaru*]. The others
[*ang uban*] could do as they pleased, but [he had] enough [*igo*] with fishing.

In enlisting Zosing as our water-carrier, Ned, the good patron,
was giving his needy client an extra push and an extra chance to earn
a fistful of pesos. As I later realized, the arrangement satisfied almost
everyone. Ned had shown his command of the situation, which he
saw almost exclusively in moral terms as encouragement toward self-
sufficiency. Zosing's neighbors and relatives in Camingawan, who too
often had lent *bugas* to his wife, greeted Ned's "suggestion" with approval. His wife herself—but this is conjecture on my part—must
have hoped that this unexpected income, small as it was, would go
toward feeding the family. As for Zosing, because we were a novelty
in the *barangay,* he was amused and began collecting his daily peso.
And we had a steady supply of fresh water.

For a few days, everything went well. Zosing delivered the water
just after dusk while we were eating dinner. In addition to collecting

the promised peso, he often stayed to chat with us and share our meal. Soon enough, however, the novelty wore off. Collecting the shiny peso became an insufficient enticement for him to deliver a reliable supply of fresh water.

Auntie Diding was prompt to identify the problem, attributing it to his incorrigible laziness. Far from bringing his daily earned peso to his wife, she blamed him for using it to drink *tuba*. If he was tired, it was not from too much fishing but from too much drinking. And what had not been drunk, he gambled away. Auntie Diding also identified the cause of his behavior:

"*Nasayup si* JP."

She had addressed me with a laconic as well as ironic accusation. It sounded funny, and she intended it to be so; otherwise, in talking to me she would have used a grammatical construction with the personal pronoun for the second person singular, *ka* or *ikaw*. As it stood the phrase could be translated as: "JP goofed." I must have expressed some puzzlement, for she proceeded with a detailed development in which she displayed her astonishing sense of ethnographic accuracy, proving that little we did escaped her attention.

First, I had lent—in my mind given—Zosing a couple of extra pesos one day, then five pesos at another date in response to his request. When too few days later he came back wanting ten more pesos, I refused because I felt—in retrospect rightly—that the situation was getting out of hand. The conclusion of her first point deserved punctuation, so she repeated:

"*Nasayup si* JP."

Second, if and when Zosing arrived at our hut with his supply of water while we were eating, we offered to share with him—and for that matter with any other visitor—our modest meal. This was strictly in keeping with the local code of etiquette. To the invitation *kaon ta* ("let us eat"), the formal answer was for one to pretend to be *busog pa* ("still full," not being hungry yet) or *busog na* ("already full," having just finished eating). But Zosing was hardly reluctant to munch with us. In Auntie Diding's judgment, we should not feed him, nor should we ever have offered him a shot of local rum; and once more it was evident that: *Nasayup si* JP.

Third and worst, my wife and I had a deck of cards that Zosing had once seen. I could not comprehend the fascination he had for this deck of cards. A week or so later, he asked to borrow the deck. Naïveté prevented me from anticipating what would follow, so I loaned him our cards. A fury of gambling developed right in front of my eyes on Auntie Diding's porch, where Zosing and other fishermen from the *sitio* began playing *piyatpiyat*, a local version of poker. They played ceaselessly, late at night and again during the day; they were

The anthropologist's residence in *sitio* Camingawan.

Lazi *munisipiyu* (Municipal Hall).

A burial party on its
way to the cemetery
walks through the town's
main street.

Jeepneys waiting for
passengers in front of
the market place.

This formal traditional costume has all but disappeared.

A Camingawan fisherman patronizes a toddy shop in town.

The only successful convenience store in *barangay* Lapyahan.

On weekends, women gather at the spring for laundry—and more.

Preparing and drying copra.

Teeny-boppers' combo
in *sitio* Camingawan.

Woman and child in
front of the family *altar,*
by the standard of the
prayer group.

Fishing at *sitio* Camingawan.

Ned Pasco's fishermen sink a fish trap in front of *sitio* Camingawan.

Labasera waiting for the fishermen's return.

Fisherman mending
his net.

In 1983, fishermen in
sitio Camingawan began
to use makeshift sails.

A *dalaga* from *sitio* Camingawan.

Manang from *sitio* Camingawan.

Manong from *sitio* Camingawan.

so passionate about their game that they stopped fishing altogether. Auntie Diding repeated: *Nasayup si* JP.

And that was the reason that our supply of fresh water had evaporated. Even more unreliable than expected, Zosing only came occasionally, when he desperately needed a fresh peso for gambling. More importantly, however, the men of the *sitio* had stopped fishing. The women, who at first had been amused by the men's gambling, became furious at them. They had become *nabalaka* ("worried," "concerned") as they had been all of a sudden deprived of any fish. Their concern was so great that Auntie Diding, under the pretext of reporting a funny little story about me and my mishandling of Zosing, spoke not only for herself but for the group of women as a whole, who wanted us to retrieve our deck of cards and thus force their men back to their fishing. In short, it was my fault that there was no fish. Had I not given in too easily to Zosing's monetary demands, had I not fed him too easily, had I not encouraged his laziness?

What Auntie Diding really meant she could not say directly, but I understood clearly that taking back my deck of cards was the only solution to the problems of the *sitio*. What she actually stated was that I need not be concerned for Zosing. He would stop being our water-carrier, and instead Soy Duhaylungsod would bring us fresh water every morning at daybreak, just before going to school, for the same price as Zosing.

Soy, as the reader will remember, was Auntie Diding's grandson who lived with her. Zosing, however, squatted on her land and was only her late husband's distant relative. For Soy, still a teenager in school, the earning of a daily peso did not have the urgency it had seemed to have for Zosing. Water-carrying or not, Soy was being fed by Auntie Diding and even though he had household responsibilities, he did not have a family to take care of. His daily peso meant that he would be able to satisfy some of his desires for small luxuries.

I could not ascertain how much the fact that Soy was a member of Auntie Diding's household influenced her in advocating the plight of the women who had remained fishless while their husbands gambled. I can state with some sense of certainty that in securing the services of Soy for us, not only did she provide us with much-needed fresh water, but she also had reaffirmed her leading role among the women of Camingawan: she was a successful intermediary between them and us, even concerning all that we represented of strange otherness. Furthermore, she had been a perfect intermediary between her grandson and us. She had advanced the interests of another member of her household in the same way—discreetly and efficiently—as she had volunteered Virgie to provide laundry and cooking services for us.

Soy, as it turned out, delivered his water every day at the crack of dawn, with the precision of a clepsydra. Day after day, he poured the water in our bucket, examined both sides of the peso that we handed him, and hastily retreated. Virgie saved the peso coins for him, which were meant for short-term accumulation. Soon, he bought himself a pair of blue jeans, which he came to model at our hut before inaugurating them at a *barangay* dance, and of which he was particularly fond. The jeans were only the first item of wardrobe with which he meant to attract the attention of young women. Soy also had to save money to pay the fifty-pesos he needed to go to visit his mother in Mindanao.

Auntie Diding never objected when we occasionally gave him an extra peso or two. From that day on, Zosing kept his distance from us as well as from Auntie Diding, in whose eyes he was unable to redeem himself. He fell even lower when, one day, under the pretext that she had refused to turn the radio either on or off, he battered his own mother so brutally that for days to come she exhibited facial bruises and two black eyes.

IN A WAY, Auntie Diding kept Zosing at the edge of her social periphery. Perhaps he had contributed to his own marginalization but, even though she still recognized him as "sort of related," she preferred to think of herself as belonging to a different social milieu—hence the performative rather than indicative character of her *tua didto,* the "over there," with which she pointed less at Zosing's dwelling on the beach than at the distance which, in one single pursing of the lips, she would have liked to maintain.

And yet, I still wonder whether the strong aversion she expressed toward him did not express as well the threat that he represented to her own self-image. Auntie Diding was able to perceive her social surroundings in less than flattering terms. She did remark how "lazy" *barangay* people were, how vain were their and her entrepreneurial efforts, how peasants were meant to be poor, how it was the standard state of affairs. But there was obviously a limit to this pessimistic tableau. Zosing's reality, his laziness, his unreliability, his irresponsibility, in short, his display of failure overwhelmed her, as if he were too close to her—and too real, too—not to challenge her own social order and sense of social identity and those of others as well.

Despite—or in addition to—what she claimed about the doom and gloom of life in the *barangay,* her own life indicated that she herself had been able to take a different, perhaps even opposite, path. She had certainly inculcated in her children an enthusiastic and optimistic taste for enterprise.

Her own daughter Virgie, whom I have left contemplating her static treasure lying in a box of one-hundred-peso bills, displayed a strong, active sense of responsibility (she belonged to every possible civic organization in the *barangay*) and optimistic enthusiasm. Her youth gave her the energy to match. Many of her projects, however, had an eerie, unreal quality that augured poorly for their chances of success.

For several months in a row, there had been no reason, no family emergency, no project sufficiently worthy or attractive, for Virgie to break her determination to save the "big bills," although she had told us several times of her desire to go and visit Marilyn, her older sister on Mindanao. On a shoestring budget, this could not have been accomplished for any less than a hundred pesos. Boats came to and left Lazi while Virgie saw fit neither to take her projected trip nor to break any "big bill."

One day, however, without any forewarning that I can remember, she decided to supplement her income by becoming a *labasera* ("dealer of fresh fish"), which consisted of going to sell in town the fish caught by fishermen in Camingawan.

When I asked her why she wanted to do so, she answered that she wanted money to buy food and clothing. With a small profit on the resale of fish, after some time she could buy a pig from which she would have piglets, fatten them, then resell the pigs and buy a cow from which she would have calves; and then she too would be rich. She was half-seriously, half-jokingly reinventing La Fontaine's famous fable of which she did not know the end or at least did not care to follow through to its unpleasant conclusion.

Her chances of even starting on this enterprise were extremely slim because, even if she "forgot" to obtain a municipal license as a *labasera*, not only was there very little fish to peddle in town, but there were already at least two other women in Camingawan, closely related to her, with whom she would have been at a strong competitive disadvantage, since they had been *labasera* long before she even thought about becoming one.

Her immediate project soon changed direction, while her general pursuit of ever-elusive wealth remained a wishful constant in her actions. Instead of handling fish, she decided to "operate" rather than "open" a *sarisari* store, right from her home at Auntie Diding's. At least such a venture had a greater chance to take off than the previous one, for there was no *sarisari* store in Camingawan, and the closest one was way beyond the well, in the vicinity of the Lapyahan chapel. Finally, one of our hundred-peso bills disappeared with her venture into penny capitalism. She had gone to town and hired a pedicab to drive her back to Camingawan, where she disembarked amidst a variety of cardboard boxes. From a town merchant, she had bought, cash-and-carry, a supply of *edible* ("cooking oil"), cartons of cigarettes, soaps, and a few other items which were to constitute her local retail operation.

Like most, if not all, *sarisari* store operators, she did not buy from a wholesaler but from regular shops in town. The only way she could make a profit was by retailing a minimal quantity of goods at significantly inflated prices to satisfy the needs of a convenience-store clientele. Cigarettes, for instance, bought at a discount in cartons, could be resold for almost twice the purchase price as "sticks," that is, by the cigarette. Such fragmenting of goods was the current practice in other stores, and, of course, it was profitable. Virgie only implemented a system that prevailed in other *sarisari* stores, and her prices were identical to theirs. Customers who wanted to smoke but could not afford a whole pack were still able to acquire one or even a few cigarettes, but at a higher price.

Apparently, this was sound penny capitalism, and the system worked for a week or two until it ran against the grain of economic practices in the *barangay*. As Virgie explained herself, almost at the same time as her operation folded, far from making profits, she was falling behind. Since everyone in the *sitio* was related, even closely related, to everyone else, it was difficult for her not to extend credit to any potential buyer. Three at a time, five at a time, or one-by-one, Virgie's supply of cigarettes, aspirin tablets, containers of cooking oil, was swallowed up by buyers, all friends and relatives, who declined to pay on the spot. When the time came for Virgie to resupply herself, she tried to collect from her debtors what they owed her. Nobody could pay: they just did not have the money right then or had other priorities, such as buying *bugas* in town with their limited supply of cash, rather than repaying Virgie for what she had in effect lent them. Each one had a perfect excuse; this one needed to buy some medicine for his wife, that one had a gambling debt, this other one had not caught any fish for a while.

Sensibly, Virgie realized that her retail operation was doomed, and rather than sinking more money into it, she took her loss. One "big bill" had been enough. *Samu lang,* she would hasten to pretend between smiles, "it does not matter." For a while, she spoke of buying a sow, at a minimal cost of 125 pesos, as if resuming her interrupted dream of economic felicity. Wisely, perhaps, she did not pursue this idea further.

15

Forgetting Relatives

WHEN VIRGIE PONDERED her entrepreneurial options, she was so tentative that it was difficult to know whether she was not simply daydreaming. She might as well have been, for her chances of changing her place in the social class organization of her society were quite minimal. Despite Auntie Diding's modest ease and small privileges in the *barangay,* her immediate and extended family were essentially poor peasants; and as anyone could declare without prompting: *Dinhi pinobre mi, pinobre ang tanan* ("here we are poor, we are all poor"). There was no stigma attached to being a Dagatan, but neither was there any particular advantage to carrying that family name. In the immediacy of a *sitio* in which everyone was a Dagatan or else directly related to one, it was respectable. As soon as the *barangay* limits were crossed, however, such a family name only indexed its bearer as an unknown, poor peasant. The name itself encapsulated the likelihood of a modest destiny, for there was no network associated with it, no help one could expect to receive, in short, no future outside of the *barangay* itself, only continuing membership in the rural proletariat, generation after generation.

Education, for those very few privileged persons who might have access to it, perhaps gave a chance of escaping what was a tradition of poverty. But education implied a move away from the *barangay.* There was still the possibility of marrying "up"—another way of marrying "out"—but that too was certainly as chancy a route as getting an education. For the majority of *barangay* residents, the *barangay* of their birth or that into which they would marry—each with similar if not identical limitations—was likely to be the place within which their future would be circumscribed. Once born in the rural proletariat, one could expect little in reality to change that destiny. Although very few people escaped from the rigidity of such social class determination, it stopped no one from dreaming.

Paradoxically Virgie's entire person emanated an inexhaustible enthusiasm for novelty, manifested as part of her explicit desire to escape the poverty that life in the *barangay* entailed. She could see Zosing's fate as an example of that which she wanted to evade. She would speak of a new project with animation, if not impatience. Her eyes would twinkle. In a sharper than usual voice, a flow of words would rush out, punctuated by giggles when she felt that she had been too assertive and thus needed to place her ambition in perspective. She was going to undertake this or that, associate with a friend from her *barkada* ("peer group") or a cousin, get money from her elder sister, and then go for a stint to Mindanao, no, even to Cebu City, if not to Manila itself.

But in the end she stayed in Camingawan with Auntie Diding, and her sense of purpose usually foundered. She drifted into the pleasant fantasy of daydreams, showed a solid reserve of displayed optimism, and managed to keep herself very busy with a flurry of neighborhood tasks. She was indeed active at raising pesos for a community project, organizing a Saturday night dance, participating in a daily prayer group, and more. But her successes were at the same time her doom, for the deeper she got involved in and excelled at such *barangay* activities, the more bound she was to this rural life of poverty. The contradiction that this entailed, of course, struck me more than Virgie, who did not link rural environment and poverty as inexorably as I did.

Escaping poverty first of all involved escaping from the *barangay*. Many former *barangay* residents had taken that route. Most had failed and found themselves as poor "over there" (*tua didto*), in Mindanao, in Dumaguete, or even in Manila, as they had ever been "right here" (*dinhi ra*). A few success stories constantly played back provided sufficient fuel for the outmigrating energy of some dreaming and ambitious young people. Ultimate success had been achieved by one *barangay* resident who had reached the United States, but nobody in Lapyahan expected to duplicate this feat. Northern Mindanao was the only frontier zone that realistically remained open to an unskilled, uneducated laborer from the *barangay*. Most people would have preferred to resettle in the nearest local town on the island of Siquijor itself had there been any serious prospects for lucrative employment there.

Virgie of course knew all this and yet expected—or just hoped against all odds—that "with the help of our divine God creature," as she used to say with all the fervor of which she was capable, an exception would be made for her. She relied overconfidently (in my own cynical view) on the power of her prayers instead of her own actions: moving out and severing once and for all the profound attachment that kept her at her mother's, as well as the multiplicity of more tenuous but no less real links that kept her where she was. And what was Camingawan if not a *sitio* in which all its inhabitants were in one way or the other related to her? And what of Lapyahan, the *barangay* where she had grown up, where she knew everyone face-to-face, where she was so popular? To leave her mother would perhaps have been disloyal; but to leave her *sitio* and her *barangay* would have been to cut herself off from her own social anchoring. To the town, as she knew all too well, she did not belong, since she had neither the education nor the political pull to overcome her class origins.

Only marriage, with its expectation of virilocality,[37] could have forced this teenager to venture beyond her present horizon. Short of it, and despite her energy, despite her vitality, despite her dreams, the ambiguity of her goals prevailed. In a way, without being yet resigned to her fate, she had already accepted it, maintaining all the while a façade of youthful optimism despite her ever-losing luck in her passionate involvement with penny capitalism.

And yet, the very ambiguity that Virgie seemed to cultivate marked her life more than the life of most of her fellow *barangay* residents. Unlike Zosing's, her economic circumstances were not desperate, and her family commitments were such that she still had options, some room to maneuver. But unlike so many whose ambition was crushed from the onset by their poverty, she still had no grand plan either revealed or hidden, no real ambition—in effect, no desire to leave the precarious situation in which she nonetheless felt comfortable and secure.

In many respects Auntie Diding's youngest daughter avidly participated in the social, economic, religious, and political life of her surroundings. And yet, she, who had neither profited much nor greatly suffered from the conditions and constraints of her life, whose last name indexed her with the lower confines of the Siquijorian peasantry, went about her life largely undisturbed by the status quo and blind to the likelihood of her own future in both rurality and poverty.

If Virgie had such a comfortable sense of social insertion in the *barangay* of Lapyahan, it was due in large part to her being a Dagatan. The combination of two factors had produced a concentration of Dagatans in the *barangay*. There was a strong propensity to follow a virilocal rule of postmarital residence. In addition, under ordinary

37. "Virilocality" refers to a rule of postmarital residence whereby a wife, at marriage, moves to her husband's whereabouts rather than the reverse.

circumstances last names were transmitted patrilineally, that is from father to child. As an unsurprising result, the Dagatan family name was strongly concentrated in Lapyahan. Although there were many fewer Quilicots, there were enough of them in Virgie's immediate vicinity of Camingawan to make her social surroundings completely familiar.

Furthermore, the bilateral reckoning of kinship generated huge personal kindreds, so that in effect Virgie could claim to be related one way or the other to everyone in the *barangay* and certainly to each of its numerically dominant families, the Gahob, the Jumawan, the Mahinay, and so on. Since everyone around her was actually or potentially a relative, how could she discriminate practically among them and set limits to the size of her kindred? This was smoothly accomplished by entering, mostly unconsciously, into the business of forgetting relatives.

I BECAME AWARE of the importance of social amnesia very early in my fieldwork.[38] My understanding did not come from a flash of intuition but from the slow pace of my progress in deciphering the local who's who. Ned had been prompt to point out that he was related to everyone on the island, here in the *barangay* as well as there in town. He was manifestly proud of his connectedness and amused at my puzzlement. I often asked him about someone's identity. Before or instead of giving me the name of that person, he would often declare:

"And this is one of my relatives, too."

I would follow up with,

"And how are you both related?"

But I learned to expect disappointment.

"We are just related."

He would pause and make a visible effort at searching his memory. He would think about it overnight, more often than not, in vain.

In the *barangay*, with Auntie Diding and people of her age and entourage, it was an even worse struggle. I had realized that I could not understand much, if anything at all, in the life of the *barangay* until I could figure out who was related to whom and how. I expected this would be a routine procedure, as soon as I had acquired some fluency in Cebuano. I would just have to ask, or so I thought. I was to be disappointed in my attempts.

Repeatedly and more often than I could have anticipated, different informants answered my questions about their relatives with the same frustrating and laconic *wa ko kahibalo* ("I don't know") or *naka-limut ko* ("I have forgotten"). At first, I blamed the answers on the

38. A preliminary formulation of this development can be found in Dumont 1981.

informants' old age, on their indifference to my work, or on their reluctance to help me. But I had to realize that Auntie Diding, as well as her relatives, friends, and neighbors, meant just what they said— they did not know or they had forgotten—because their lack of co- operation contradicted so radically what I knew otherwise of their graciousness and their memories.

Even so, I still found the imprecision that punctuated almost every statement disturbing to the extreme. *Si kuan,* a phrase made up of the article *si* and of the filler *kuan,* could be rendered in English as "what's his/her name." It was the answer I drew most often to my queries. When to my relief a less vacuous answer was forthcoming, it was almost systematically followed by an expression of doubt, such as *tingali* ("maybe"), which ruined all too hastily any sense of achieve- ment I might have felt.

Frustrating as this experience was, it forced me to pay attention to what people remembered and knew and why, or more precisely to the reverse: what was it that people did not remember, and what was it that people did not know about their own personal and family his- tory?

On the positive side, rural Siquijorians could accurately recount the places of origin and residence of their own parents, grandpar- ents, and in-laws. Everyone knew one's parents' and parents-in-law's complete names, by which I mean all three: the *apelyido* ("last name"), *ngalan* ("first name"), and *angga* ("nickname").

Thereafter, startling gaps occurred. A number of parents whose children had outmigrated were unable to state in which municipality these offspring lived. Independent of gender, approximately one child-in-law in three could be recalled neither by *ngalan* nor by *apelyi- do.* Several grandparents who housed visiting grandchildren or who raised them on a semipermanent basis (as *binuhi,* i.e., "who live-in") had to ask the child, first, in order to answer my questions about members of their own household. Some parents, both the old and the young, both male and female, either completely forgot a child or were unable to recall a child's *ngalan* when listing their children in birth order, while remembering scrupulously the birth order itself.

That older individuals had difficulty keeping track of their grandchildren and a fortiori of their great-grandchildren was not particularly surprising. More strikingly, however, a sizable number of my informants, especially but not exclusively persons over sixty, could not remember accurately the full names of their four grandparents. Frequently, one *apelyido* might be mentioned, only to be immediately retracted and another one proposed, in turn retracted, and so on until a *dagway* ("perhaps") brought about an ultimate sense of unreachability of the elusive ancestor. By then, of course, neighbors and relatives had already assembled and interjected their own opinions and further muddled the apparently irretrievable information.

The greatest imprecision of all concerned the age of people who declared to be *tigulang na* ("old already") without having any idea about the year of their birth. In general, people seemed at odds with years. Mothers, for instance, could often state correctly the day and month of birth of their children but remained unable to recall the year. When pressed for an answer, with discursive perfection they routinely spaced their children every two years.

While I found all that puzzling at the time, it was also clear that here the unsaid, the unknown, the forgotten were not just nothing. Quite to the contrary, they provided in their very absence a sort of negative image of the way in which the *barangay* people pictured their own society. In fact, no silence could have been more eloquent.

When information was missing, it concerned most frequently the identity and the age of people. Such suggested agelessness of some people here indicated less a disinterest in personal history than a different understanding of duration on the part of my informants. This was further underlined by the radical difference expressed between absolute age, which was often forgotten, and relative age, which was systematically and consistently remembered. In effect, year of birth and age could only refer to a mechanistic and altogether Platonic conception of time, since they were markers in a succession of equivalent instants, a most un-Visayan way of apprehending reality. In other words, dates were as irrelevant as time of the day. What was relevant, however, was a Bergsonian sense of duration, which gave its value to events.

This sense found expression in daily interaction. When we announced a short trip away from Camingawan, Virgie did not ask us when we planned to return but how long we planned to stay away. It was this same duration that was memorized and expressed in the relative age of individuals.

Similarly, if it was said of someone that *patay, dugay na* ("he has been dead for a long time"), as I was told of Luis Dagatan, Auntie Diding's father-in-law, the occurrence of that person's birth could still be traced without too much difficulty because a whole web of social signification could be derived from the age of this person in relation to others. Indeed, this was the case with Luis. Whether he was older than, younger than, or of the same age as his sister, *manang* Tibay, as his late brother-in-law, Bonifacio Quilicot, or as Auntie Diding, who was at once his daughter-in-law and his brother-in-law's sister (see fig. 6), remained of import inasmuch as this information provided a charter for interpersonal interaction.

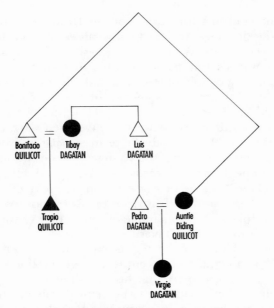

FIG. 6. Dagatan-Quilicot intermarriages

Within the domain of social interaction in general and of kinship in particular, relative age determined the familiarity or the respect with which two persons were supposed to conduct their daily transactions. Since relative age had such relevance, it was something that people noticed and remembered. Since there were no other kinship groups than overlapping, ego-oriented kindred, the more closely related people were, the better they remembered each other's relative age. Furthermore, genealogical distance and geographical distance had similar effects, since transactions with a distant relative living far away came practically to a standstill and thus either decayed or needed regular reactivation.

In import and in scope minuscule, the following incident documents nonetheless how historical events can rapidly disrupt any traditional pattern of behavior. Ned arrived one day at our hut, smiling as usual. But he was also red-faced, breathed rapidly and shortly, and his eyes rolled in fury. He was visibly upset.

"You know, *kuan*, Fidel Mahinay [one of his fishermen]. I met [one of] his nephew[s] at [*sitio*] Caliguwan at the spring [where we washed close to the provincial road on the way from town] with his *barkada* [his gang of friends]. He is just a kid. You know what he said? He said '*gabii, Ned*' ['evening, Ned']. Just no shame, *kuan*, no shame at all, *kuan*, "*bii* Ned.' He does not show respect."

Ned could continue for a while on the troubles of the new generation, on the disappearance of family values, and on the good old days of his own youth. What had shocked Ned so much was that someone who was his junior, and his junior not simply by a few years but by more than a couple of decades, had addressed him in an impolite, disrespectful way. For someone of the same age as Ned or older, it would have been appropriate to call him by just his name. But here, the age difference between the two men warranted, in fact demanded, the use of the honorific term *manong* in front of Ned's name. For reasons of his own, the youngest of the two men had not complied thus neglecting to recognize the age difference. Was it youthful rebellion? Was it provocation on the part of a rebellious teenager? Was he showing off in front of his friends? Whatever the answer, he was following the example of some other youngsters in the *barangay* in their dealings with Ned.

In deploring Fidel's nephew's misbehavior, Ned denounced the collective lack of manners of an entire new generation who did not address him with the respect that his age should have guaranteed. But was the break with tradition to be blamed only on these youngsters? Perhaps not, because, in a way, Ned had already slipped away from the traditional mode of interaction based on kinship and residence relations. To a large extent in the *barangay*, he was no longer perceived as a relative but as a town entrepreneur who controlled the fishermen's means of production. As such, he had entered in a social class relationship with the inhabitants of the *barangay*. Inasmuch as the actual relations of production were systematically blurred by an egalitarian ideology, the kinship relations were redefined and the system of address changed. Even lip-service respect was fading.

And thus the mis-apprehension of relative age by Siquijorians can be understood as the result of two radically different types of attitude, either neglect, by plainly forgetting, or manipulation, by just ignoring.

TO INTERPRET the missing identity of people I understood to be close relatives poses a more formidable challenge. I would have expected gaps to be a rarity, given not only the kinship ideology but the pervasive function of kinship behavior, in such a peasant society. Without minimizing in the least the importance of class relations in such a market economy, kinship remained to a large extent the idiom through which the units of production and consumption were organized. In fact, this had to be the precise meaning of the statement "one big family on this island" that had been hammered into our heads over and over again from our very arrival. Even though grossly

overdrawing the smoothness and harmony of social relations in Siquijor, and even though the serenity of family life was here as elsewhere all but wishful thinking, still the valued image of kinship bonds
was ever-present in the consciousness of most islanders. If so, then
how could my informants possibly have forgotten some of their relatives? How on several occasions could some children's names, if not
their very existence, have been obliterated from the consciousness of
their parents? How, even more frequently, could grandparents suffer
a similar fate?

When I inquired about this, I was struck by the consistency of the
commonsensical answers that different informants gave me. The
grandparents had not exactly slipped out of memory. They had died,
instead, "long ago, in a faraway place, when I was very young, before
I was even born." In other words, such grandparents had never been
known in the first place. This was straightforward enough, but the
total lack of curiosity this implied struck me at the time. No interest
was ever expressed and no effort seemingly made to know any of
these ancestors. And I have yet to find one person who could tell me
who one of his/her great-grandparents were. When I myself traced
that type of genealogical information through the parish church records, it raised more eyebrows than interest among the living. It was
almost as if time, in its historical dimension, had been abrogated or
narrowed down, if not flattened, to the span of one's own generation.
One generation below, there were already some memory gaps; more
than two generations away, and everything and everybody had disappeared.

This apparent structural collapse of time strongly contradicted at
least one other element in the kinship system on Siquijor, namely the
determination of marriageable partners. As in any other complex
structure of kinship, there was no positive rule of marriage, only a
negative one. With a bilateral principle of descent, the extent of the
kindred determined the degree of prohibition. But people were at
odds as to the extent of such prohibited kindred. All agree to include
fourth cousins (*igagaw igtagupat*) as members of their kindred, but
they hesitated as to the status of fifth cousins (*igagaw igtagilma*). Third
cousins (*igagaw igtagutlo*) were definitely prohibited as marriage partners, but fifth cousins would have been permissible. As for fourth
cousins, it depended, and I shall return to this below.

For the moment, it is necessary to brace for a short but informative detour through the domain of kinship. Two individuals who are
related as collaterals by definition share at least one common ascendant. In the same way as siblings (*igsoon*) can be defined as individuals
sharing the same parents (*ginikanan*), two fifth cousins must share

one set of great-great-great-great-grandparents. In other words, among the sixty-four people who are my blood relatives in direct line and stand six genealogical levels above me, there must be at least one who is also one of the sixty-four people related to you in an identical way, for the two of us to be fifth cousins. As a matter of fact, this is implied by Visayan kinship terminology, which is rich in generational terms, so that first cousins share at least a common *apohan* (grandparent), second cousins a common *sungkod* (great-grandparent), third cousins a common *sungay* (great-great-grandparent), fourth cousins a common *sagpo* (great-great-great-grandparent) (see fig. 7).

That no equivalent term can be mentioned for the common ascendant of fifth cousins does not necessarily set formal limits to the extension of the kindred, but at least its functionality stops at the level of fourth cousins. It is also understandable that the same informants who agreed on the marriageability of fourth cousins seemed to have forgotten about the existence of the term *sagpo*, which was only mentioned by those who denied the acceptability of such marriages. At any rate, for marriage purposes, the prohibition was supposed to be determined by the sharing of a common ancestor, whether he or she stood four or five genealogical levels above Ego.

No matter how we look at it, it seems that Siquijorians could not afford to luxury of ignoring the identity of their grandparents, unless of course they did not follow the rule of kindred exogamy to the letter. In order to check this, my wife and I undertook to follow twenty-two family names through the church records of Lazi, from its constitution as a parish in 1857 up to 1980. A rather predictable fact leaped to our eyes: not only was the rule of kindred exogamy frequently violated, but it was done so in the shortest possible time span, to the point where we could find, throughout the entire history of the parish, several cases (exceptional though they might have been) of first-cousin marriage.

A second rule of exogamy, repeatedly and emphatically stated by Siquijorians, deserves some examination. Two individuals who bear the same family name, even though their actual relationship was unknown or forgotten, are considered to be *partido* ("related") and therefore could not possibly marry. Since names are transmitted patrilineally, this results in the maintenance of virtual patri-clans, the exogamy of which I found violated only exceptionally since 1857. In and of themselves, these two rules of marriage prohibition and their transgression begin to offer a functional clue to the interpretation of kinship amnesia.

In effect, grandparents were not forgotten in just any old way. Maternal grandparents were more often forgotten than paternal

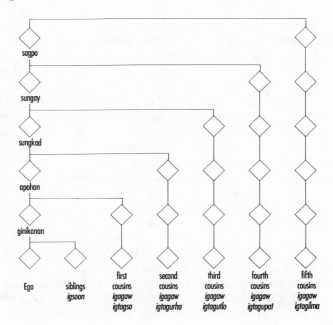

FIG. 7. Model of Visayan cousin terminology

ones, an easily understood phenomenon. With a pattern of virilocal residence, grandchildren were likely to have interacted more and thus to remember better their father's parents than their mother's. Second, what was forgotten was more often the last name, if nothing else, of the grandmothers and the first name and often nicknames of the grandfathers.

This seemingly innocent fact had a momentous consequence. It effectively eliminated a number of people from one's kindred, with the additional advantage of multiplying one's child's potential spouses. In forgetting the last name of my two grandmothers, I had amputated a portion of my children's kindred. Similarly, in forgetting my two grandfathers' first names, I prevented myself from transmitting to my children the knowledge of who the siblings of these ancestors had been, and I further reduced the size of their kindred. The extreme case of total grandparental amnesia would be absurd in practice, although it serves to express the logical tendency of the system. Although none of this was consciously manipulated, the loss of memory thus involved seems to have had singularly functional overtones.

But there was a third and final rule at play concerning marriage prohibitions. In addition to being the big family that they claimed to be, several young people in the *barangay* complained that they had difficulty finding marriageable partners on their own island. In fact, they emphasized this reason for moving to Mindanao rather than what seemed to me more compelling, the depressed economy of Siquijor and the economic opportunities that Mindanao could offer.

From the *barangay,* the larger island to the south looked like the land of promise. And indeed, since the first marriage with a *Mindanawon* recorded for Lazi in the early 1920s, the number of such matrimonial exchanges has grown regularly, as reflected in the parish records. Out of the some three hundred households that constituted the *barangay* of Lapyahan in 1980, few were those which did not have at least one member on Mindanao on a more or less permanent basis. The degree of interaction between the departed member and the rest of the household varied greatly. Only those children who had been "adopted away," raised and permanently settled in Mindanao without ever coming back to Siquijor, could have been forgotten.

Parents of Siquijorians who had moved to Mindanao might have seen their children's spouses only at the time of the marriage arrangements and the wedding and could since have forgotten the children-in-law's identity. But coming back to exogamy, there was, according to my informants, still another modification of the rule of kindred exogamy, which concerned geographical distance.

Some people asserted that fourth cousins could actually marry if they had been born and raised "far" (*layo*) from each other, if their respective parents had not been "neighbors" (*silingan*), and if they did not bear the same family name. As can be appreciated, this left ample room for convenient interpretation. Tropio even told me that, truly, if the distance were as great as that between Siquijor and, say, Zamboanga del Sur, it would be acceptable—though not desirable—for someone to take some liberty with tradition and venture to marry a third cousin. Most people, evidently more bound by tradition than this man, balked at this idea.

I became intrigued by the notion of proper distance for social comfort and learned that Mindanao, and for that matter any other island, would do. Furthermore, any of the other five municipalities in the province of Siquijor would really satisfy the geographical distance requirement. The truth of the matter was that it was not pure geographical distance that made the difference, but how it was experienced by people. And thus, for Lapyahan, a seaside *barangay,* other sea-oriented *barangay* within the same municipality were considered closer than any *barangay sa buntod* ("in the hills," that is landlocked), even if the latter were geographically closer.

The dialectics of ideology and behavior in terms of marriage thus appeared to be predicated on the notion of distance. And such distancing occurred at three different levels: historical, geographical, and behavioral. All three were evidently subject to the prevalent cultural hermeneutics. It was not who one's grandparents truly were that was important here, only what historical importance one granted them. It was not how many kilometers away one's children lived, but how much ease of access one had to them. It was not how closely related two persons were, but how much they activated or refrained from their kinship relationship. Obviously if all three negative rules of marriage were followed rigorously, if fourth cousins could not marry, if people who lived too *duol* ("close by") could not marry, if people who were *partido* could not marry, the whole island of Siquijor would indeed be "one big family," and there would be no marriageable partners available at all and, paradoxically, no social life at all. What forgetting relatives thus accomplished was to create distance, to forget history, to ignore relatives, to turn distant and vague relatives into potential affines, and to transform *kaubanan* (relatives) into plain *tawo* (people).

I am not suggesting here that people were deliberately or consciously engaged in the act of forgetting. As I witnessed it, individual informants tried hard to remember. But there were many blanks in their memories, at any rate too many not to perceive a pattern in these lapses that informed their whole social life. In contradistinction to lineage societies whose members have to memorize their genealogical past, here on Siquijor, social amnesia seemed to have been called forth so as to forget, to ignore, to lose relatives—serving as a retardant to the pervasive extension of social life, so that ultimately a minimal endogamy might reemerge, precisely that which allowed the island of Siquijor not to dissolve but, to the contrary, to maintain its cultural identity.

16

A Name of Repute

MEANWHILE, from an immediate and practical viewpoint, Virgie, as a young single woman in the *barangay,* understandably showed little patience and even less interest in my kinship pursuits. Altogether, Auntie Diding was a better informant in this domain, but in large measure she had already lived her life.

Ned and Minay, on the other hand, who had committed themselves to each other, were more detached than I could have expected and would speak freely about kinship. They even joked about the unthinkable, about being perhaps, somehow, distantly related to each other. They were more intrigued, if not amused, than troubled by this possibility, although they did not make any great effort to discover a grain of truth in it. As members of the educated town bourgeoisie, they might have found themselves less constrained by tradition than Virgie and Auntie Diding were.

And so, not only were they quite informed about their own past and the ways of the town, but they were altogether excellent intermediaries in my exploration of kinship relations in the *barangay* because they were sufficiently close to its residents without feeling directly concerned. They may have had *barangay* origins, but they were now townspeople. Even with Ned's fishing involvement in Lapyahan, even with Minay's nursing in the neighboring *barangay* of Tagaw, they did not live in the *barangay* but belonged and lived "over there, in town" (*tua didto sa lungsod*). Despite the pathetic sincerity of their efforts to reach and keep in touch with the *barangay* folks, Ned's and Minay's education, their manner of speaking, their social class, their income, their life style, their general social being, everything betrayed their town orientation to *barangay* residents. And for the townspeople a different sort of social amnesia was at play.

Everywhere, in the *barangay* as well as in town, everyone had a stake—although each had perhaps a different one—in restricting the extent of their kindred. Virgie as a young single woman in the *barangay*, just as much as Minay as a successful matron in town, each remembered their respective relatives in a selective way; so did Auntie Diding, and so did Ned. For the rural proletariat, however, the issue was almost exclusively matrimonial, while for the town bourgeoisie it involved recruitment into and membership in the elite group as well.

Virgie and Minay in effect shared, almost a generation apart, fairly similar *barangay* origins. In sharp contrast to Virgie, however, Minay had made radically different choices. In so doing, she had proved to be a vigorous player in the shaping of her own destiny. She responded with the will and determination to take advantage of and profit from the opportunity of education. She had also successfully joined the ranks of the town bourgeoisie not just by virtue of her residence in town but because she had managed a successful career in health care and now patiently awaited her transfer to a more prestigious and more convenient assignment in town. Most importantly, her membership in the town bourgeoisie followed from her marriage to Ned, whose name she now bore. It would be difficult to overemphasize the importance in town that being a Pasco conveyed.

Names—last names—tended in the *barangay* to index quantity: being a Dagatan indicated that Virgie belonged to a family whose members were aplenty, while Auntie Diding, who had been born a Quilicot, had a much smaller network of relatives around her. In the town bourgeoisie, last names tended to index quality. As such, they were all-important if not essential attributes in defining a person within the upper echelons of the social hierarchy. It required less effort to inherit a name than to make a name for oneself. But in and of themselves, names were insufficient to guarantee one's membership in the ranks of the town bourgeoisie, conceived of as an elite. With the passage of time and the succession of generations, collateral branches of the same family tended to have different fates. Some managed to maintain themselves in the elite du jour; others fell by the wayside and lost their position in the social hierarchy.

Given a bilateral kinship system which "failed" to discriminate in terms of status and property transmission either by gender or by age, it was in the interest of individual families to "place" as many of their members in the elite group as they could. There were practical limits to this, however, since any notion of social hierarchy was necessarily based on a principle of discrimination. If a majority of members of the society at large belonged to the elite, it would not be an elite at all: the fewer, the merrier. The occurrence of a wobbly process of social amnesia and social memory allowed for a wild selection that strongly contradicted the notion of bilateral equality.

Just as in the *barangay*, a limit was imposed on the actual size of the kindred. The townspeople had the same matrimonial constraints as *barangay* residents. In addition, however, in an oxymoronic manner wherein activity and passivity failed to contradict each other in the same way unconsciousness and premeditation did, members of the town bourgeoisie were able to purify their entourage of misfitting rural cousins.

"Same name, no relation" could have been an appropriate translation of the Cebuano phrase "*partido ra*," which literally meant "just related" or "just of the same group." For two otherwise unrelated people, the very fact of bearing the same name created a bond and thus instituted the relationship. Depending upon the context, the word *partido* was used to emphasize that there was between two persons indeed a relationship, such that, for instance, they could not get married. Or, to the contrary, the word served to emphasize the absence of actual relationship between people who, seemingly by accident, bore the same name.

"Not related," Minay had echoed her husband in English. Ned had said "*partido*." Despite his—economic and sentimental—attachment to Lapyahan, he had used the expression to refer to two brothers, one of them a regular on Auntie Diding's porch. The elderly Jesus Pasco lived on the roadside behind Auntie Diding's under a thatched roof in need of repair. It may have been home for him and his wife, but lack of money and energy made it look miserable, more a *payag* ("hut") than a *balay* ("house"), especially in comparison to that of Loloy Tundag, his immediate neighbor. The sexagenarian had an older brother, Leoncio, in a different *sitio* of the same *barangay*. I had separately asked Jesus and Leoncio if they had any kinship relation to Ned and, although they knew perfectly well who he was, they denied having any, offering me the same answer Ned had: "*partido ra*." Neither of them was Ned's relative. The relations between Ned and Jesus were formal. Ned addressed Jesus as *manong*, appropriately considering the age difference, while Jesus shied away from any interaction with Ned, whom he saw, equally appropriately, as a town entrepreneur. The relationship between the two took place at a social class level: Jesus could have been one of Ned's fishermen.

My own records indicated that in fact they were second cousins (see fig. 8). This information had more interest for me than for any of the persons concerned. Neither Leoncio's nor Jesus's ignorance of kinship matters surprised me, but I was certainly intrigued by Ned's inconsistency. How could he not know—or how could he pretend not to know—the existence of such a relationship, when he had been the one to insist so strongly that everyone on the island was related and when he constantly pointed at everyone in the *barangay* as being "another of my relatives"? Had he not forgotten a bit selectively and eliminated from his consciousness an unfitting branch of the Pasco family?

It seemed clear that Ned had little use for Leoncio and Jesus. Both were too old to fish for Ned and had never done so, so that no concrete, actual link with them had ever been truly activated. Jesus had no children and was thus structurally useless. With Leoncio the matter was slightly more complicated. Of his three adult sons that Ned did not recognize as members of his own kindred, none fished

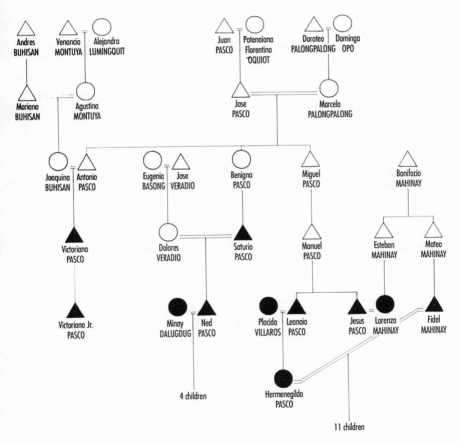

FIG. 8. Ned Pasco, his origins and some of his namesakes

for Ned. Like Leoncio they lived in a different *sitio* from Auntie Diding. Rarely had Ned or I any occasion to interact with them.

But what complicated the matter was that one of Leoncio's
daughters, Hermenegilda, lived in Camingawan, where she had married one of Ned's fishermen, Fidel Mahinay. Although the step-by-
step link between Ned and Hermenegilda could be traced by neither
of them, the relationship was constantly activated because of the interaction between Ned and Fidel. As such, it was a tenuous link, invoked on occasion when the interaction was smooth and easy when
fish were aplenty, denied on other occasions when, for whatever fishing reason, the two men became cross with each other.

The interaction between Ned and different Pascos in the *barangay*
illustrated how entire collateral branches of a family could thus be—
passively or actively—forgotten, and equal status within a set of siblings could be at once claimed and denied, whenever convenient for
whatever purposes. In these circumstances, kinship tended to lose its
substance—but not its function(s)—as it became a mere form, an
idiom through which other social relations could be expressed.

But for the members of the town bourgeoisie, there was a supplement of kinship activity. Not only did the extent of personal kindred
tend to be limited, amputating excess relatives, but the reverse was
also taking place in a selective and delicate effort to maximize the
scope and importance of one's kindred. No example can illustrate
better these remarks than an understanding of the importance of the
last name that both Ned and Minay bore after their marriage. This is
best done by placing the name of the Pasco family in historical perspective.

IN TOWN MORE THAN in the *barangay,* last names were convenient social markers; they were considerably more troublesome when I tried
to push for deeper genealogical inquiry. Despite the good nature of
most townspeople, I undoubtedly taxed their patience in direct interviews from which I obtained hints more readily than precise information.

A second difficulty came from the fact that last names as they are
known today resulted directly from the implementation of the Superior Decree of November 21, 1849 (see *Catálogo Alfabético de Apellidos,*
hereafter C.A.A. 1973 [1849]), promulgated by then Governor-
General Narciso Clavería y Zaldúa, who took that position on July 16,
1844, and left the Philippines on December 26, 1849. A translation
of the particulars of that decree is well worth quoting here at length:

> During my visit to the majority of the provinces of these islands, I
> observed that the natives in general lack individual surnames which dis-
> tinguished them by families. They arbitrarily adopt the names of saints, and

this results in the existence of thousands of individuals having the same sur-
name. Likewise, I saw the resultant confusion with regard to the administration of justice, government, finance, and public order, and the far-reaching
moral, civil and religious consequences to which this might lead, because the
family names are not transmitted from the parents to their children, so that
it is sometimes impossible to prove the degrees of consanguinity for purposes of marriage, rendering useless the parochial books which in Catholic
countries are used for all kinds of transactions.

For this purpose a catalogue of family names has been compiled, including the indigenous names collected by the Reverend Fathers Provincial
of the religious orders, and the Spanish surnames they have been able to
acquire, along with those furnished by the vegetable and mineral kingdoms,
geography, arts, etc. In view of the extreme usefulness and practicality of
this measure, the time has come to issue a directive for the formation of a
civil register, which may not only fulfill and ensure the said objectives, but
may also serve as the basis for the statistics of the country, guarantee the
collection of taxes, the regular performance of personal services, and the
receipt of payment for exemptions. It likewise provides exact information
of the movement of the population, thus avoiding unauthorized migrations,
hiding taxpayers, and other abuses.

Having heard the testimonies of the Most Reverend Bishops, the Reverend Provincials of the religious orders, and the Honorable Assessor-General
of the Government, I hereby order . . . (Abella 1973:x)[39]

A list of more than sixty thousand available last names was thus
published, and general registers (*padrones*) were to be established.
The mid-nineteenth century thus represents the maximum geneal-

39. The original Spanish is written in the traditional style expected for this type
of official document: "Habiendo notado en mi visita á la mayor parte de las provincias
de estas Islas él que la generalidad de los indigenas carezcan de nombres patronímicos
propiós que los distingan por familias, y el que arbitrariamente adopten el de Santos,
de lo que resulta encontrar miles de individuos con uno mísmo: vista la confusion que
esto produce en la administracion de justicia, Gobierno, Hacienda y Policía, y las tras-
cendentales consecuencias morales, civiles y religiosas á que puede dar lugar, por no
transmitirse debidamente los apellidos de padres á hijos; sin que á veces puedan pro-
barse los grados de parentesco en los enlaces matrimoniales, quedando inutilizadas las
pruebas que en los paises católicos suministran los libros parroquiales para todo género
de transaciones: Formado al objeto un catálogo de apellidos en que figuran las coleccio-
nes de los indígenas reunidas por los RR. PP. Provinciales de las órdenes religiosas y los
apellidos Españoles que han podido adquirirse, aumentados con los que ha suminis-
trado el reino vejetal, mineral, geografia, artes &c.; y visto, que emprendida esta me-
dida de notoria utilidad y conveniencia es llegado tambien el momento de dictar las
necesarias, para la formacion de un padron, que no solo cumpla y asegure aquel objeto,
sino tiene los de servir de base á la estadística del pais, asegure mas el pago de los
impuestos, la regularidad de los servicios personales, el ingreso de los arbitrios que de
ellos resultan, y produzca un conocimiento exacto del movimiento de la poblacion,
evitando las translaciones sin autorizacion, las ocultaciones, y otros abusos: Oidos los
Ilmos. Sres. Diocesanos; los RR. Provinciales de las órdenes religiosas y el Sr. Asesor
general de Gobierno; vengo en disponer . . ." (C.A.A. 1973:xix).

ogical depth attainable. A *padrón* for the parish of Lazi would be most invaluable, but so far no archive either in the Philippines or in Spain has yet yielded this precious document.

A third difficulty stemmed from the fact that, even when the Filipinos took or received last names that insured their identity, a number of them began to resist Spanish authority, moving around without authorization, evading taxes, dodging the draft, and doing so with relative impunity by hiding, lying low, and assuming entirely new and fictive identities. For instance, I learned that I could not find out more about a *gobernadorcillo* of Lazi in the 1890s, Mariano Paglinawan, also known as *Tan* Anong (*Tan* was an abbreviation for the Spanish title *Capitán*) because he himself or his father had been a draft-dodger from Cebu who had assumed a completely new identity on Siquijor. It follows that people today whose last name is Paglinawan could be either fictive Paglinawans or real Paglinawans. In today's consciousness, except for one or two very old informants, the distinguishing memory has been lost.

Fortunately there were also some written documents, among which the parish records of Lazi stood out as a source of uninterrupted documentation going back to 1857. When used with prudence, this superb tool allowed some reconstruction of families.

Finally, a unique private record beginning in the 1880s had been kept in town. Two couples from the island of Bohol had moved to Siquijor, and their migration had been successful. More importantly, some of their descendants had also prospered, even becoming influential in local politics. Some were literate and articulate. With the passage of time, part of this hyperextended family, constituted by the immigrants' descendants, had become the backbone of the local town elite.

Under circumstances that I could not exactly reconstruct, a genealogical tree of all the descendants of these original settlers had been kept. A retired teacher, former principal of a town school and former mayor of the municipality, was the proud guardian of this document, which was "complete," or so he assured me. By the 1980s, the interpolation of American culture had taken such root that there were talks of a family reunion, even though the impracticality of such a monstrous affair would surely have tempered the enthusiasm of any potential organizer. With characteristic flair for acronyms, the "Society" of descendants was referred to by a name made up of the initials or first syllables of the original immigrants to Siquijor.

Ned in his own right, Minay by virtue of her marriage, and their children in turn through descent, all were members of the "Society," the very existence of which so blatantly contradicted what I had understood to be a dominant trend of social amnesia. With its inscriptions preciously kept in a jealously guarded notebook, the "Society" was an attempt at preventing anyone among the original settlers' descendants from being forgotten. In writing down the "Society" notebook data that were sketchy but to the point (although they added little to what was already inscribed in the Church records), a process of selection had occurred. It instituted the original settlers and their bilateral descendants as an "us" and separated the same from the anonymity of the rest, from a "them" of undistinguished Siquijorians.

Despite the all-encompassing nature of bilateral descent and the apparently scrupulous registration of all descendants in the "Society" notebook, the actual inscription was not entirely devoid of bias. Consciously or not, memory tended to be selective, even when the point had become to enlarge, rather than to restrict, a network of kinsmen. While the ideology was to establish solidarity among equals in this distinguished group, the notebook established a sort of hierarchy.

First of all, in practical and individual terms, everyone's main concern was to find out, to know, or to prove how he or she was related to the apical ancestors. This amounted to demonstrating one's relationship to power in town. To be written down in the notebook affirmed and validated one's connection with and insertion into the local power structure. The notebook was the archival piece that objectified and authenticated such status, perhaps explaining why the object itself was willingly produced, if not brandished, almost on demand—as if the very materiality of the notebook itself insured the legitimacy of its content. I had greater difficulty discussing the details of its content with its guardian. In general, the notebook was used to establish one's connection with the elite and not to determine whether two living persons were related. Although there certainly were members of the town elite who did not belong to the distinguished "Society," registration in its notebook almost guaranteed membership to the bourgeois elite.

Second, avowed intent and effort notwithstanding, the records, either by omission or by commission, kept some distant relatives locked out. Such people were mainly on the periphery: interaction with them was minimal, and they were not sorely missed, so no one had prompted the notebook's guardian to make an entry for them. The greater the distance—geographically, socially, and in degree of collaterality—the more likely someone would have fallen outside the domain of the "Society."

Conversely, dormant relationships between collaterals could be reactivated, and the more successful—politically, economically, or in any other respect—someone was, the more others were likely to make demands on that person. As a consequence, while belonging to the core of the "Society" was a matter of private pride which could be taken matter-of-factly, its least fortunate members were often eager to emphasize their membership by displaying their link with this successful entrepreneur, with that former mayor, or with that lawyer who had the proper political credentials. In the absence of money, of education, of influence, and of prestige, the glamour of their origins may have been the only mark of their threatened membership in the local bourgeoisie.

Contrary to what was asserted, contrary in particular to an ideology of equality, this allowed for the introduction of invidious comparisons. Full siblings had not had the same fate or the same luck, so that entire branches of the "Society" were treated differently.

Beyond what occurred within the "Society" itself (and little did, since the "Society" rarely if ever acted as a group), the town bourgeoisie behaved in similar ways. Its members consistently downplayed, deemphasized, deactivated, and sometimes even severed their personal and social links with the lowest strata of the society, the proletariat of the rural *barangay*. At the same time, an incipient historical memory emerged whereby the members of the town bourgeoisie, insecure in their achievements, registered their membership and consolidated their links with the powers that be, with the rich and the powerful, i.e., with each other. In other words, registration and inscription were attempts to counterbalance the fluidity and fragility of their own class membership. In claiming links that otherwise would have remained dormant and thus disappeared, the bourgeoisie in the effervescence of a multiplicity of competing claims established its own solidarity, that is, constituted itself as a social class.

OTHER THAN THE FACT that they shared the same last name, Ned, who lived four generations below Juan Pasco, knew absolutely nothing of this great-great-grandfather. And as far as that ancestor was concerned, the parish records yielded only the faintest and most indirect traces (see fig. 8).

By 1874, Juan Pasco was dead. His widow lived at that time in the town of Canoan (now Larena) in a different Siquijorian parish from where most of his descendants are found today. Née Potenciana or Florentina—the records are inconsistent about her first name— Oquiot, she survived him until at least 1885. I was unable to verify any of this because the parish archives of Canoan had burned a few years before my arrival on the island.

Both husband and wife in fact were natives of the island of Cebu. Juan had been born in all likelihood around 1810 in the town of

Danao, where the two had married, subsequently lived, and raised their children.

Before 1840, Juan Pasco and his wife begot at least one son, Ned's great-grandfather, José.

The first in the family to migrate to the island of Siquijor, José was also the oldest Pasco to be remembered by his descendants. As a first settler, he had acquired the relevance of an ancestral eponym. Anyone on Siquijor today by the name of Pasco appears to have descended from José in direct line.

José settled in Canoan at first probably as a trader, but nobody could tell me what exactly his occupation had been. And soon (before 1858) he, the *homo novus,* joined the local establishment by marrying a woman from a prominent family in Lazi, Marcela Palongpalong. He had no real, or at least no strong, attachment to Canoan, and she was very well connected in Lazi. Instead of having his wife move with him to his residence as was customary, he moved to live with her in Lazi, just at the time when its first priest took possession of the newly erected parish in 1857. José obviously joined the ranks of the *principales* and eventually—but I do not know exactly when—became, under the jealous authority of the Spanish priest, *Tan* José, the political leader of the town, the *gobernadorcillo* of the *pueblo.*

His eldest son, Miguel, was baptized in Lazi in 1858; his last child, in 1885. In the course of twenty-seven years, his wife gave him some fourteen offspring, twelve of them baptized in Lazi. The discontinuity in the records between Antonio's birth in 1867 and Timoteo's birth in 1874 suggests a temporary change of residence more than an interruption in the impeccably regular rhythm of pregnancies.

José's children did not all lead the same life, but all had some opportunities denied to ordinary islanders. Under the Spanish colonial regime, not only were there some tax advantages in being close to power, but also the children of the *principalia* had relatively easy access to whatever education was available in town. All of José's and Marcela's children could thus read and write at a time when such an achievement remained rather uncommon.

José died in 1899, while Marcela lived until 1908, not quite long enough to see her youngest child, Victorio, married, an event which did not occur until 1910. But this was long enough for her to have known some of her great-grandchildren in Lapyahan, the grandchildren of her eldest son, Miguel; long enough also to have known the first children of her fifth child, Antonio; and finally, long enough to have known Ned's father.

Most of the Pascos who lived at the time of my fieldwork in Lapyahan were Miguel's direct descendants. Born in 1858, married in

1877 in Lazi, he begot, between 1880 and 1901, ten children with his wife née Dolores Tuastumban. When their third child, Manuel, born in 1883, settled in what would later become the *barangay* of Lapyahan upon his marriage to Vicenta Baguio in 1904, he had lost any power and influence in town. The fate of his descendants—to be poor struggling peasants—was already sealed. Manuel was Leoncio's and Jesus's father, and we have met these aging characters above.

Antonio, one of Miguel's younger brothers, whether by choice or by chance or by some combination of luck and determination, assumed more of his father's adventurous and ambitious character. Taking advantage of his connections in the local society of Lazi and of the little education he had received, and treading on the path already cleared by his father, Antonio in turn became the *gobernadorcillo* of Lazi. His best move, however, was marrying Joaquina Buhisan in 1898. For anyone with any social and political ambition, she was indeed a catch.

At nineteen, she had the radiance of youth. But the thirty-three-year old Antonio, who already enjoyed the maturity of a man with a head for politics, could not have failed to be sensitive to the social qualities, the economic success, and the political clout of the family into which he was marrying.

Joaquina had been born on the northern coast of Bohol, in Paminguitan (today Cortes), a parish near the provincial capital Tagbilaran, shortly before her parents decided, around 1880, to migrate to the island of Siquijor and settle in Lazi. There, until 1901, her parents, Mariano Buhisan and Agustina Montuya, were to produce eleven more children. They also flourished. An indirect measure of their success comes from the parish records themselves in which— and this is unique in the early baptismal registration of that parish— Mariano was not listed as a mere "plowman" (*labrador*) but as a "tradesman" (*comerciante*). Other markers in the records indicated that Mariano had a status superior to that of "native" (*indio*). Mariano's father, Andres, who died in Bohol before his son moved to Siquijor, was "half Chinese," (i.e., *meztizo sangley*) and passed that status to his son, while Mariano's mother was herself of Spanish ancestry (i.e., was a *mestiza*). At a time when the parish priest was the only Spanish-born person in town, a small circle of relatively well-educated and wealthy *mestizos* controlled the local economy and the town elite. Joaquina's mother, Agustina, and her maternal grandparents, Venancio Montuya and Alejandra Lumingquit, were all Boholanos. Despite more traditionally *indio* origins, they also seemed to have enjoyed some commercial success.

Antonio thus married for success, or so I suspect. Before their respective deaths (his in 1954, Joaquina's in 1963), they brought some eleven children into the world, among whom was Victoriano, born in 1910, who was, in time, to become mayor of Lazi. Victoriano in turn fathered nine children, among them Victoriano, Jr., who was born in 1946 and who, by the time I arrived on the island, had already obtained an important official post in the municipality. It is specifically this branch of the family, descending in a straight line from Antonio, which managed with considerable success and little cost to maintain its hold on local politics.

Ned and his branch of the Pasco family needed desperately to maintain a link with them, especially since Ned did not belong to that branch of the family. If anything, Ned and his father and siblings had to be careful not to be detached from the family, not to be merely forgotten by the members of the politically more successful branch of the family.

Ned actually bore the name of his paternal grandmother, Benigna Pasco. She had been born in Lazi in 1882 and was the penultimate of José Pasco's legitimate offspring. She died in the 1960s. In 1903, she had married Juan Gahob, a man from Lazi who was her elder by five years. She did not bear him any children. Nonetheless, some fifteen months after the wedding, she gave birth to her first child, Saturio, whose baptism is recorded in a separate book specifically devoted to the illegitimate children of the parish. Within and without the family itself, it seemed to be common knowledge that the child had in fact been fathered by Francisco Buhisan, one of Mariano's sons and Joaquina's younger brothers who was not yet married.

All this information concerning the turbulent life of Benigna came from two different sources, the Church records and the scattered souvenirs of different descendants. They corroborated each other and were remarkably consistent. Nobody missed the fact that Saturio's birth had in its time a rather scandalous nature. The circumstances of Saturio's birth even today were mildly shocking and that type of information was still spoken of in hushed tones.

What was perhaps more surprising was the reverse tendency, namely, that the family made so little mystery of its irregular origin and practically volunteered the information. All happened as if Ned and his siblings drew some evident pride from a behavior that emphasized the liberty that their grandmother had taken with the expected mores of her era. They whispered the information, but they did not refrain from giving it. Of course, the event had occurred long ago, and the mere passage of time had lessened the likelihood of any possible tarnish to the family pedigree.

Furthermore, a supplement of information was conveyed by revealing the unorthodox filiation. Since the name of Saturio's absconded biological father had been stored in memory, it was the absence/presence of this genitor that was displayed with some pride, for it maximized the social insertion of Saturio and consequently of his descendants. On the one hand, the incident of this birth comprised the link that existed between that branch of the Pascos and the rest of the family. On the other hand, it linked, though perhaps not in a socially optimal way, that same branch of the Pascos with the Buhisan family. Had the grandmother behaved according to the social norms and expectations of her day, the social and political visibility of Ned's family would have been entirely different. It would not have been directly related to the Buhisans, and although its members would still be related to the Pascos, they would bear a different name, an honorable though frankly less prestigious one, that of Gahob.

The hushed proclamation of the grandmother's "failing" had two contradictory effects. First, it affirmed genealogical links with the best families in town and thus served as a means to insure membership among the happy few that constituted the town elite. Being performative, it was thus remedial, as it emphasized less the forbidden aspect of the liaison than the political strength that it might have entailed had she married a Buhisan. Second, it marked the distance that nonetheless separated Ned's branch of the family from the politically influential trunk. And indeed, while Ned and his seven siblings each had access to relatively flourishing commercial activities (Danny, for instance, had a seashell business and Mick continued his father's transportation operation), they had a very modest involvement in the political affairs of the town.

In addition, Ned, who in this respect was no different from his father and brothers, had little immediate political ambition for himself. But that in itself was perhaps a wise adjustment to the dissimilar fates of the descendants of old José. Far from having been treated equally, sets of siblings had been submitted to an array of different fates. All those who still lived in town were active members of the local bourgeoisie and interacted as such with each other, while many *barangay* cousins had already lost importance and relevance. As for those who shared the same town setting, forcing mutual familiarity upon them, a strong sense of hierarchy had already sanctioned inequalities.

With Victoriano, the former mayor and a cousin much older than himself, Ned had little choice but to be formal, restrained, and to show deferential respect. With the older man's son, who was a town official at the time, a more relaxed relationship could prevail. They could joke and drink together. Manifestations of "respect" (*tahud*) need not be displayed. And yet, it was more to Ned's advantage than to the municipal officer's to remember the kinship relationship that linked them both, and both knew exactly where they stood in the local hierarchy. The civil servant, scion of the most powerful branch of the Pascos, was strongly entrenched in his official status. Ned, who had been stripped of actual power by fate and the vagaries of birth, had a heritage full of rich kinship credentials. With the success of his commercial ventures, he perhaps had a future. But it was his present that was weak, since he was always under the double—economic and political—threat of slipping from the ranks of the town elite. Only a spectacular and unlikely economic success—which Ned pursued relentlessly in project after project on land and at sea with entrepreneurial doggedness—could have recentered Ned, bringing him and his immediate family the political position and influence that his past may have warranted.

If Ned and Minay had been looking for social climbing and political glamour when they married each other, they had probably failed. Although they led a respectable and happy life and resided in a house in town that was both spacious and comfortable by local standards, Ned's business could barely maintain itself. It was almost stagnant; he complained bitterly about it and about the repeated breakdown of his equipment. Ned and Minay's success and strength came from other sources.

Minay had married "up," albeit into a relatively powerless branch of a prestigious family, to a man who on all accounts was generous, certainly considerate, and even affectionate, who neither drank nor gambled, but who was also thoroughly devoid of political ambition. Ned, on the other hand, had also married "up," but in a different sense. His wife was a beautiful, fun-loving, outgoing woman, who had given him four healthy children. She was also an ambitious career woman, and without being in any way aggressive, she had unusual poise and assertiveness. Her strong will matched perfectly his gentleness. Above all, they cared for each other.

17

Good with Numbers

A T THE AGE OF FORTY-SIX, Tropio Quili-cot was a mature man whose life had been in shambles for what seemed like forever. Small in stature with a receding hairline but in remarkable physical shape, he had an engaging personality. Serious in his enterprises, he was also thoughtful and intelligent. Above all, he had the rare quality of being totally reliable. Perhaps what I appreciated most in him was his unique patience.

"Say that again, Tropio, please (*ibalik nu*)," I asked, again and again, and Tropio never tired of repeating the same utterance until I, ever so slow and clumsy, had a chance to transcribe it or repeat it.

Providing me with an orientation in the subtle labyrinth of his culture seemed to interest him as well as to amuse him, for in the process I also gave him ample occasion to exercise his wit. For instance, he remembered without hesitation the number that, in a survey, we had assigned to each of the three hundred households of the *barangay* Lapyahan. Weeks later, when I asked him where a certain character lived, he answered with a straight face:

"In house 167, behind house 94."

He was obviously gifted with an excellent memory. Accurate as his reply may have been, I was slightly surprised to hear him quip in this manner, for he had only heard these numbers a few times when we completed our census. But he knew he had me, and now laughing, he continued:

"His younger brother so-and-so lives in 156 and his older sister over there in 230."

His answer was perfect in its precision but contained little information for me, since I was way behind him in learning by heart, if

170

ever I had even tried committing to memory, the numbering I had myself imposed on the dwellings of his *barangay.*

"I have told you before. I used to be good with numbers."

He began flipping the pages of my notebook, as if searching for the page on which I had made a note of his taste for figures. He had indeed told me of his childhood and of the promise that it had held.

THE QUILICOTS had only recently settled here, which explained why there were so few of them in the *barangay.* He and the other members of his kindred claimed the municipality of San Juan as the cradle of the family, and they had all forgotten that the family in fact had more distant origins. The Quilicots had not always been Siquijorians but, like many others on the island, had come originally from the neighboring island of Bohol.

Tropio's paternal grandfather, Julian Quilicot, and his brother, Antonio Quilicot, had both been born around 1885 in Calape, a town on the northern coast of Bohol. Their parents, Jose Quilicot and Nicolasa Batbat, were each in their second marriage. A previous union had left Jose Quilicot a widower and the father of a young daughter, Rita Quilicot, who died in Lapyahan many years later. As for Nicolasa Batbat, a previous liaison, or a previous common-law marriage, had left her the mother of a son who bore her name, Bonifacio Batbat. Shortly after the birth of their own sons, the Quilicots, complete with their entire set of children and stepchildren, moved to Siquijor for reasons that remain unclear. Was Jose Quilicot trying to avoid the Spanish draft or dodge the head tax or had he had a conflict with the local parish priest? The family's real motivations now seem irretrievable. In any case, the Quilicots settled in a coastal *barrio* of San Juan, a municipality adjacent to Lazi, and fished for a living. Eventually Julian and Antonio, the two sons, married two sisters, themselves of Bohol origin (see fig. 9).

Soon after, in 1908, Bonifacio Quilicot, Tropio's father, was born. He was the first Siquijor-born child of Julian Quilicot and Telesfora Sumandang. By 1914 Julian Quilicot and his family had moved to Lapyahan in search of farming acreage in fact to the very land on which Tropio and his siblings were settled when I arrived on Siquijor. Resettling the family in Camingawan at the time had seemed a smart move. Local fish resources had not yet been depleted, and few people had settled in that *sitio,* a raised coral reef which was stony indeed but nonetheless could be cultivated.

By 1928 Julian and Telesfora had expanded the size of their family considerably with eight more children, all born in Lapyahan. Epi-

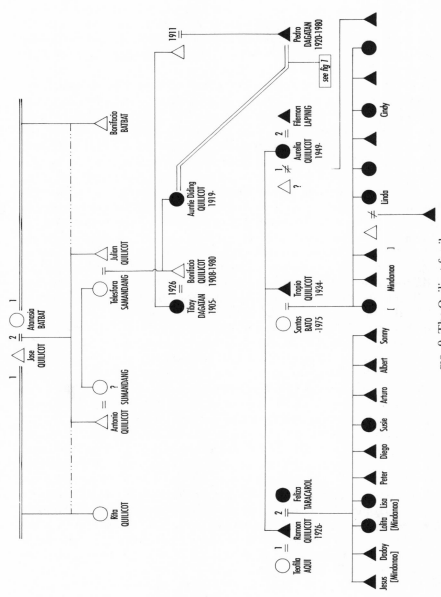

FIG. 9. The Quilicot family

demics took their toll, and several of the children did not reach puberty. The daughters married away, even though one of the daughters had married into one of the two most numerous families of Lapyahan and thus had moved very little, perhaps only one kilometer away, to a different *sitio* of the same *barangay*. All in all, only three siblings within that rather large set—two men and one woman—continued living in *sitio* Camingawan.

The parents lived there the rest of their long lives. Although Julian kept his social verve until his demise in 1972, he lost the physical stamina necessary either to fish or farm the land that he and his wife had first cleared with their own hands. The land still belonged unambiguously to him and his wife and had remained undivided, facts that his children understood better than anyone else. For all practical purposes, however, since about the 1940s, the land had been cultivated by the three siblings who stayed in Camingawan, as if they had never grown up, married, nor acquired separate interests. Progressively, however, a de facto partition took place, for these three siblings came to work on parcels that were contiguous and more or less equivalent in size. The parcels were distinct, however, so that the net effect of that situation was an actual, though anticipatory, tripartition of what was still Julian's and Telesfora's land. The parents had in effect relinquished the control over their land to their children.

This particular land-use pattern was the result of a long process which affected the family configuration and in which those who had departed played a role as significant as those who had stayed home on their parents' land. When Bonifacio Quilicot married in 1926, followed by his younger brother Pedro in 1932, each settled in his own house on his parents' land and began cultivating a part of it, that is, his own parcel, adjacent to that of their parents, while both continued helping cultivate their parents' parcel.

Only one of their younger sisters stayed in Camingawan in their immediate vicinity. That was the woman whom we know as Auntie Diding. A half-generation separated her from her eldest brother. Born in 1919, she was eleven years younger than Bonifacio, and exactly eleven years after his marriage, she married Pedro Dagatan in 1937. For the time being I shall continue to focus on Auntie Diding's older brother, Bonifacio, Tropio's father.

In contrast to his parents who had often moved, seemingly in search of the ideal setting, Bonifacio Quilicot remained in one place during his entire life. Remarkably sedentary, he cultivated roughly the same acreage: his father's parcel and, adjacent to that one, his own. He planted corn where his father had—it was the staple food for his family—and also added peanuts as a cash crop. Because copra promised additional income, and following in his father's footsteps, he planted coconut trees for the future, his own and that of his children.

All his life Bonifacio Quilicot struggled with some success to make a living on about one-third of his parents' unyielding land, enlarged by the small lot that his wife brought in dowry. Partly because of his charm and suavity (I was told that Tropio had acquired his engaging personality from his father), partly because of his political savvy, partly because of his popularity, partly because of farming and fishing successes that favorably impressed his neighbors and underlined his entrepreneurial qualities, partly because he was literate (he had gone through grade school), and partly because he had married into an already well-established local family, he bore the title first of *teniente del barrio* (i.e., *barangay* lieutenant) and then of *barrio* captain for over twenty years until after the end of World War II. This status conferred on him and his family the maximum level of respectability that residents of a rural *barangay* might possibly hope to reach. Any greater ambitions could have only been fulfilled in town.

Respectability was something, and something desirable; but it did not mean wealth. Being *teniente del barrio* was a very low-paid position, the compensation he received being a meager complement to the income from farming and fishing. The whole was barely sufficient to feed an immediate family that included the thirteen children to whom his wife had given birth between 1926 and 1949.

Shortly before my arrival in Camingawan, Bonifacio Quilicot died, in the early days of July 1980, not quite a year after the passing away of his brother-in-law, his *bayaw*, Pedro Dagatan.

WHEN I MET Tropio's mother, *manang* Tibay, who was born Primitiva Dagatan, she was over seventy-five years of age. Still visibly affected by the recent death of her husband, she at first remained as reserved with me as her culture commanded. She was alert but also moody and quick-tempered. I addressed her as *manang* Tibay, as Auntie Diding did. This was an appropriate way of showing the old woman the respect that I owed her relative age, but she did not inspire any of Auntie Diding's pleasant, relaxed, and jocular style of interaction, and thus my relation with her was at first confined to cautious and formal politeness.

She could have been a superb informant about the history of the Quilicot family, since she was the last survivor at the highest genealogical level, had she had inclinations similar to Tropio's. But, as she put it:

"I have forgotten everything."

She added a palm frond to her cooking hearth and blew on the embers. Silence settled for a while. I was about to leave when she added:

"I was the youngest (*ang kinamanghuran*) in the family. I was very young at the death of my parents."

How to interpret that statement? Was it really an explanation or, as I suspected, just an excuse, a way of marking the end of our conversation, of discouraging my probing into her family history?

A month or so later, however, our mode of interaction changed. She warmed up to my presence in Camingawan. Alert and sharp-tongued, *manang* Tibay began to pick on my shortcomings.

She did not speak or understand any English at all. My efforts at communicating with her in her own language were clumsy, but their very inadequacy curiously forced her attention and made her change her attitude toward me. For whenever I spoke, it provoked an explosion of hilarity, which started with a radiant twinkle in her eyes, evolved into a sharp muscular contraction from her forehead to her chin until, unable to contain herself anymore, she buried her head in her lap or turned away to avoid the mutual embarrassment of laughing straight in my face. My accent, my difficulties with stresses, my solecisms and barbarisms, all of my more or less inept utterances, all seemed now to delight her.

On her way from her house near Tropio's to Auntie Diding's, she needed only a few extra steps to reach our *payag*. She often took this detour for comic relief, as she came and went and almost daily stopped for a brief visit on the porch at Auntie Diding's house. There she used to take a quick glance at who had stayed around and throw an inquisitive gaze after those who had gone fishing. She also conversed and gossiped when someone was there, but she often stayed by herself, quiet in her searching contemplation of the sea as she busily pondered her own thoughts and memories.

Eventually, she turned out to be an invaluable kinship informant. As far as her own or even lower generations were concerned, she was an authority, and little of what went on in the *barangay* seemed to have escaped her attention. She had a remarkable habit of describing relations between persons in two steps. In the first step, the understated unsaid triumphed, with its accumulation of pause words. She could say without batting an eye:

"*Siya si kuan ang kuan ni kuan, kuan ba!*"

The meaning was perfectly clear to her, and it was not as empty a statement as the translation suggests:

"He you-know-who is the, well, of what's-his-face, you know!"

She could converse easily and fluently in this way with Auntie Diding, because both women knew intimately their social setting, and allusions could deal with everything. They did not seem to need the referentiality of words to understand each other. With me, who knew so little and who had no choice but to take statements literally, such discourse was a disaster, and I was grateful that Tropio never talked with me this way.

In the second step, *manang* Tibay realized that I did not follow her and marked this by a hardly flattering *kulangkulang,* which thoroughly revealed the low opinion she had of my intelligence. The adjective derives from the root *kulang,* "lacking" or "deficient," and in its reduplication qualifies anyone who is slightly "mentally retarded" or "slow for the age in understanding." Then he or she who a minute before was "just a neighbor" (*silingan ra*) turns out to be so-and-so's *bayaw* ("sibling-in-law") or that one's *bilas.* This latter term has no exact equivalent in English; it extends an affinal link laterally one step further to designate the spouse of someone's spouse's sibling. Quicker than her son, the articulate Tropio, she could trace endless lateral links between *barangay* residents. He or she who could not be thus related clearly did not exist.

And yet, as pleasant as her change of attitude was, she could not recover the memory of her family origins. I had to confront reality. When it came to time and depth, her knowledge was minimal. She did not think "vertically." With her, all happened as if the past were quite devoid of presence and the long dead had lost their existence yet a second time.

"There are many Dagatans here, many more than Quilicots."

In itself, this was not a shattering observation. In terms of quantity at least, the Dagatans easily outnumbered the Quilicots.

"Wait (*isa pa*). Long ago (*sa una*), the Dagatans came from *kuan* (*taga-kuan kuan sila*)."

Her expression *sa una* that I have translated as "long ago" did not just measure the passage of time. It also involved a change of quality. "Once upon a time," with its eerie quality, is perhaps a more exact rendition of her words. This is further emphasized by the use and repetition of the pause word, *kuan,* as if the very hesitation in revealing what has come back to memory reinforced the unreality of the past. Only after several *kuan* did she risk, sheltering herself behind the hearsay that *kono* implied:

"From San Juan, I was told (*taga* San Juan *kono*)."

Tropio repeated what his mother said, but did not know either. If they had kept a very faint memory of the distant origins of the family, older adults in the *sitio* had a coherent memory of the relative seniority of families in relation to each other, and so did Tropio. The Mahinays, the Gahobs, the Palongpalong had "forever" (*kanunay*) been in Lapyahan. At any rate, they had been there longer than the

Quilicots and the Dagatans, who were dominant in *sitio* Camingawan. With great lucidity, Tropio added:

"Otherwise (*kung dili man*), they would not be in Camingawan where the soil (*yuta*) is so poor (*hupas*)."

And indeed, prior to this century when there had been little population pressure on the land, the particularly stony soils of Caminga- wan had been left uncultivated. By the 1980s, the Gahobs, Palong- palongs, and Mahinays had acquired the reputation of being indigenous to Lapyahan, while the Quilicots and the Dagatans were in the process of losing even a faint memory of their migratory ori- gins.

Once more, the Roman Catholic church records, though laconic, proved a priceless help in efforts at reconstruction.

THE EARLIEST RECORD I was able to find concerning the Dagatan fam- ily referred indirectly to a married couple, Antonio Dagatan and his wife, Matea Bacsal, who were both probably born between 1810 and 1815 in the territory of the present municipality of San Juan (see fig. 10). They lived there most of their lives and between 1834 and 1854 brought to life at least eight children. Matea Bacsal lived past 1883, but I have been unable to track down either the date or the place of her death. As for Antonio Dagatan, he died in Lapyahan in 1876.

Their eldest child was a girl. They called her Bernarda. And all the Dagatans of Lapyahan descended from her. By 1861, she had already moved into the parish jurisdiction of Lazi, for two events con- cerning her are recorded in that year. On March 18, 1861, she gave birth to a baby girl, Monica Dagatan, who, as an illegitimate offspring (*anak sa gawas*), bore the name of her mother.

Legitimacy and illegitimacy were understood quite differently by the parish priest and his flock. The Recollect Fathers who succeeded each other almost uninterruptedly from 1854 to 1953 in the shep- herding of Lazi souls, the secular clergy that followed, the Spanish friars, and the native clergy, all believed in the sanctity of marriage (*kasamintu*). Without a wedding rite (*kasal*), there could not be legiti- mate procreation.

Their parishioners also distinguished between married couples (*ang mga magtiayun* or *ang mga minyu*) and those who were not who thus produced illegitimate children. But there were two different ways of being married. Either people had gone through a marriage ceremony (*kasal*) and they were *kasadu,* or they had not and they lived in socially recognized common-law unions (*mansibadu*).

As often in the past as at the time of my fieldwork, a couple might postpone their wedding celebration for a variety of reasons, without

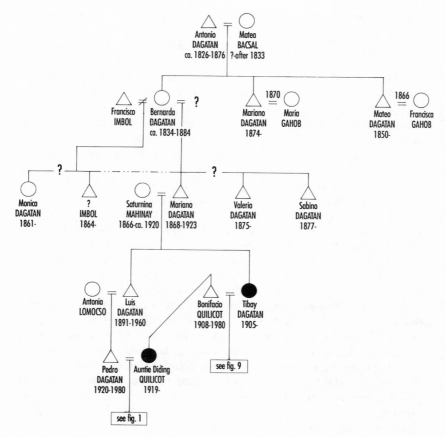

FIG. 10. The Dagatan family

postponing cohabitation. Lack of money, food, or other goods for the sumptuary display and consumption that a full-fledged ceremony and the ensuing celebration entailed sometimes forced endless delays. On occasion, a cheaper and convenient alternative was to postpone weddings until the day of the town or *barangay* fiesta, when ritual consumption had been planned a year in advance and the guests were certain to be present.

The second event in the life of Bernarda Dagatan that was recorded that same year in Lazi was her wedding. On June 1, 1861, she married a widower, Francisco Imbol, who may or may not have been the father of her first child. He was from Cangtugbas, now a *barangay* of Lazi, bordering on the municipality of San Juan, and the couple settled there, begetting at least one legitimate child in 1864. This child of course bore his father's name. But the marriage does not seem to have lasted long, for Bernarda's next child was baptized under her own name. By 1868, not only was Bernarda already a widow, but she gave birth to Mariano Dagatan, Tropio's maternal grandfather.

Mariano was born in Cangtugbas, but within a few years of his birth, probably around 1873, his mother moved with her children to what was to become *barangay* Lapyahan. Two of Mariano's maternal uncles had already married there into the Gahob family. And they must have lived there for some time, since future sons-in-law (*umagarun*), before being accepted, were supposed to perform services (*pang-agad*) at the house of their prospective parents-in-law (*ugang-anun*). They could not have failed to make some observations: Lapyahan at the time had readily available fish, as well as good, flat, arable land. At the end of their obligations as sons-in-law, instead of returning to their own parents in San Juan, they settled in Lapyahan.

Their own parents had then reached their sixties and decided to resettle in Lapyahan. They brought in tow three or four of their younger children who were still unmarried teenagers; Bernarda, then unattached, joined them. She never remarried in the formal sense but gave birth to two more boys in 1875 and 1877 respectively.

And so, some forty years before the Quilicots were to settle in Lapyahan, the Dagatans started cultivating several acres of reasonably arable though stony land that neither the Gahobs, the Palong-palongs, the Mahinays, any of the oldest families, or anyone else had thus far claimed. It also stopped short of what the Quilicots would later claim as theirs, which was left then uncultivated.

Bernarda Dagatan died in April 2, 1884, leaving Mariano an orphan (*ilo*) of sixteen.

"And so, *manang* Tibay, you do not know who raised your father after his mother's death?"

She did not. Mariano's fate for the next seven years thus remained unclear to me, whether he joined the family of one of his uncles or aunts or stayed with his mother's latest companion. *Manang* Tibay only made a vague gesture pointing at the back of her house, away from the sea, in a general movement that encompassed most of the *barangay*, asserting only that her father had been raised "here in Lapyahan."

By 1891, however, Mariano Dagatan married a woman who was two years his elder, Saturnina Mahinay. If he had ever suffered from being poorly linked to the social network that dominated the *barrio* of his residence, he could not have made a better marriage to remedy the situation. The marriage linked him to the Mahinays, who had, it

seemed, "always" been residents of Lapyahan, the oldest one on record being Saturnina's grandfather, Juan Mahinay, who had been
born at the very beginning of the nineteenth century. It linked him
as well, on Saturnina Mahinay's mother's side, to the Gahobs, who
were thought to have had as much local seniority as the Mahinays and
in addition were already the most important local family, given the
relative power that size and number conferred (see fig. 11).

The very year of their wedding, they also begot their eldest child,
Luis, who was followed in turn by nine more children appearing
every two years with relentless regularity until 1910 (only the last two
are separated by three years). Born in 1905, *manang* Tibay was the
eighth. Since the two last children died respectively in 1911 and 1912,
she considered herself the youngest (*ang kinamanghuran*) of that set
of siblings. Fourteen years—in other words, a half-generation—separated her from her eldest sibling. In effect, with such an age difference between the oldest brother and the youngest sister, Luis Dagatan

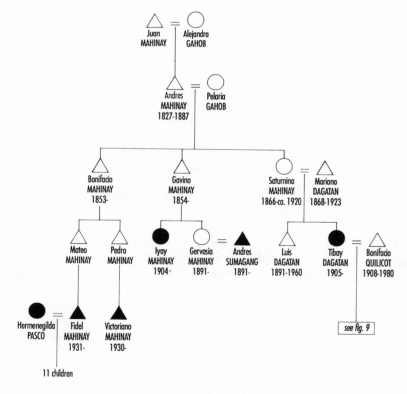

FIG. 11. The Mahinay family

played as much the role of a surrogate father for *manang* Tibay as Bonifacio Quilicot had played for Auntie Diding. When Mariano Dagatan died in 1923 shortly after his wife, *manang* Tibay was only eighteen years old. She blamed her lack of knowledge concerning the life of her parents on the rank order of her birth.

"All that happened long ago when I was a child. This is why (*mau ra*) I cannot remember."

Three years after her father's death, she married Bonifacio Quilicot in 1926, bringing with her the seventh part of her parents' land she had inherited, a meager plot indeed after the division among all the surviving children. Adjacent to the land that Bonifacio considered his own, it formed in effect a new lot. It was precisely this new lot, still undivided after Bonifacio's demise, that fed his widow *manang* Tibay and three of their thirteen children: Ramon, the eldest, Tropio, the sixth-born, and Aurelia, the youngest, all with their own respective families. By then all the other children of Primitiva and Bonifacio Quilicot had either passed away, married away, or moved on.

By marrying Bonifacio Quilicot, *manang* Tibay had become Auntie Diding's sister-in-law (*bayaw*). The two women were intricately related for *manang* Tibay was also Auntie Diding's husband's paternal aunt ("*iyaan*"). Again, a half-generation of fourteen years separated them. The accumulation of age differences was such that *manang* Tibay's nephew—Luis's son, Pedro Dagatan—was the same age as Auntie Diding, which made them acceptable marriage partners. Auntie Diding, just like *manang* Tibay before, had conformed to the virilocal rule of residence, although neither of the two women had to move very far, since the land of the Quilicots and the land of the Dagatans were adjacent.

The plots of land controlled by the two women, however, were of different sizes. From the Quilicot family division, each had received equally. From the Dagatans, Auntie Diding's plot was very small because Pedro's father, Luis Dagatan, had married a woman from the adjacent municipality of Maria, Antonia Lomocso, who had brought no land at all with her; and their land had eventually been divided among the children. Eight of their eleven children survived, and Pedro Dagatan could thus only claim one-eighth of his parents' land.

TROPIO WAS GENERALLY soft-spoken when he reminisced about the past and particularly his own. It was his habit to pass by our hut before going to sea or on his return—to borrow rubber flippers and goggles, to bring fish, to have a cup of coffee, or most of the time just to chat with us, he speaking softly and I taking notes as best and as fast as I could. His inquisitive smile punctuated the end of each sentence, as he made sure that I was following what he had said. This gave me time to frown. With such a prompt, he repeated or rephrased his statement:

"My oldest sibling (*ang akong kinamagulangan*), *manong* Ramon, our oldest brother, cannot read or write because he was not sent to school."

"How come?" I asked, but Tropio had not finished his train of thought and ignored my question about his brother Ramon, the dean of fishermen in Camingawan. Instead, he continued his exposition in his own rhythm:

"None of my older siblings (*magulang*) went to school for very long. I was the first one."

His father, Bonifacio, had understood the benefits an education would give his children, who thus would be able to move to town and become eligible for an array of positions. One of them could even have become a civil servant, which could not fail to be seen in *barangay* eyes as a desirable sinecure in the government bureaucracy. There were however several obstacles to this plan, not the least of which came directly from Ramon and Tropio's other older siblings, who apparently had very little inclination for study. An even greater constraint perhaps was their father's predicament, for he was trapped between two contradictory demands, between the desire to see his children move up in the world and the economic necessity of using their labor in his farming and fishing activities.

From his birth in 1934, Tropio's circumstances were slightly different. Being the sixth-born (and fourth son) immediately freed him from the constraints which tied his older brothers to domestic production. In addition, as a child he was intelligent and seemingly eager to learn:

"I was able to go to school, but just a little. Up to fifth grade only. Dersen Buhisan was my companion in first grade. He now lives over there in America."

Tropio moved his hand in the general direction of the United States. Any comparison between his fate and his former companion's situation was discouraging. Understandably, Tropio exhibited, ever so slightly, some envy at Dersen's presumed achievement.

"I went to school in town for the first grade. After that, right here, in Lapyahan. They built a school in Lapyahan. Lapyahan took me in second grade, since I am from Lapyahan. Until fifth grade."

"So you were in school during the entire duration of World War II, were you not?" I asked.

"No. I was already big when they sent me to school, maybe about twelve years old then. It is really after the war that I went to school. I did not even go to school during the Japanese occupation (*panahun sa Hapon*, literally, "at the time of the Japanese"). They had a Japanese school before; I know, because they even had a song, 'Odoro, Usahino Hikare.'"

I must have frowned deeply.

"What does it mean? I do not know. Maybe, that is 'Good morning' [in Japanese]. That is what I heard, you know, when other sang. I cannot tell you because I was not able to study Japanese."

Tropio kept his solid sense of humor in all circumstances, as if to prevent bitterness from setting in. That he could still manage to laugh about himself and his entanglement in the world, to show concern but no resentment, and to take his fate in stride never ceased to amaze me. He certainly had fallen short of his early ambitions.

"Engineer *unta*, *kay* bright *man ko*. I wanted to be an engineer, because I was bright. You know this arithmetic, I felt so comfortable (*hayahay*, literally, 'the feeling of being comfortable and refreshed') with it. All these damned (*yating*, literally, 'devilish') problems and all these *kuan* topics, they were easy topics for me when I was studying. But now, if I was sent back to school, well, I would manage, but it would not be like before, because my brain (*utuk*) has been muddled (*nalibug* from *libug*, literally, 'to confuse') by a lot of problems."

He had kept vivid memories of his scholastic achievements:

"My grades were good. I was bright. My average was 92. To the end, I was always the best. But in fifth grade, at the closing program, I did not show up. I was to receive 'first honor' [for the student with the best record in a specific grade]. They had already shown me my ribbon [i.e., the ribbon I was supposed to receive], because I was even ahead of Dersen [Buhisan]. Dersen and the others, they had to play catch up with me. I was tops in class before. But I stopped going to school on March 10, I think."

Even though he had forgotten the year in which this occurred, the date itself at the very end of the Philippine school year, only a few days before the prize-giving ceremony, had stuck with him. He must have been about sixteen at the time.

"I stopped [going to school] because of a Boy Scout uniform. It was such a small thing. I was supposed to be the Boy Scout Master, but then my parents did not buy me the uniform. I am [sic] embarrassed because I was to be the master and I had no uniform."

In using the present form "I am embarrassed" (*ma-ulaw man ko*) instead of the past "was embarrassed" (*na-ulaw*), did he mean to emphasize the persistence of that feeling and its dire consequences for the life he had led afterwards? At any rate, Tropio was never to return to school and, unwilling to compromise his public reputation but frustrated in his ambition, he settled for the much harsher life of a regular *barangay* dweller.

"Now you understand why I am good with numbers."

A few years before these events, in 1946, his older brother, Benedicto, married a woman from the town of Siquijor, moved out, and remained among his in-laws in a *barangay* of that town. About the time when Tropio quit school, another of his older brothers, Gregorio, moved to Dapitan in the province of Zamboanga del Norte, where he subsequently married. One of his two older sisters, Felicisima, had died in infancy, but the other one, Teofila, was then "already a teenager" (*dalaga na*) and still at their parents' home. Although the oldest brother, Ramon, was still a bachelor living with his parents, Bonifacio needed help on his farm (*baul*) and help with his fishing. Tropio had now come of age and his presence was required at his father's side.

The need for Tropio's productive involvement at his parents' was directly related to the extent to which Bonifacio's family had grown. In 1949, about a year before the incident that resulted in the abortion of Tropio's career, Aurelia, his youngest sibling (*kinamanghuran*), was born. Without even counting the two younger brothers who died in infancy, Tropio still had four younger sisters. The production of fish for the entire family thus fell upon three men, Bonifacio and his two sons, Ramon and Tropio.

Upon our arrival at *sitio* Camingawan, Tropio certainly had rivals—among them Ramon, his own elder brother, and Fidel Mahinay, one of his second cousins—who could pretend to be better swimmers, better divers, or even better all-around fishermen than he, but none could rival his popularity. Other fishermen would trust him blindly, and so did Ned.

In fact, Ned's own involvement in fishing the waters off *sitio* Camingawan, an operation that was already several months old when we arrived, would never have occurred without Tropio's initiative. Both men, who were practically the same age, had known each other since their childhood as Boy Scouts.

"When I encouraged Ned to throw his fishtrap off the coast here, I thought that it would be good for all (*sa tanan*)," Tropio said.

"For all?" I asked.

"For all here (*para sa tanan diri*), for everyone here in Camingawan (*para sa mga tawo dinhi sa Camingawan*)," Tropio said.

Auntie Diding cut in:

"For his (extended) family (*para sa iyang kabanayan*), for the neighbours (*para sa mga silingan*), for his household (*para sa ila*), for me too (*para sa ako*)."

She got up, brandished the fish that Tropio had just brought to us and said:

"For you too (*kanimo sab*). You understand? (*Sabot ka?*) Because, well, we are all relatives (*kay paryente ming tanan*)."

In this neighborly fellowship, I was, in the very same breath and at Auntie Diding's mere whim, included as beneficiary of Tropio's fishing talent as well as excluded by the use of a "we" (*ming*) that rejected my wife and me as outsiders in Camingawan.

"I told you," said Ned the following day, "we are all one big happy family on this island."

18

Feeling, Dreaming, Remembering

T HE DEMISE OF Auntie Diding's brother, Bonifacio, despite the social vacuum that it created, did not lead immediately to any noticeable reorganization of the Quilicot housing cluster in Camingawan. A few yards from what had been Bonifacio Quilicot's dwelling, the eldest son, Ramon, in his mid-fifties, had his house. His own eldest son and eldest daughter, Jesus and Lolita, both already married, had moved to Mindanao in search of economic opportunities that neither the *sitio* of Camingawan nor the *barangay* of Lapyahan nor even the island of Siquijor could ever give them. Ramon's home seemed modest, especially in size, but it was apparently sufficient to shelter him, his wife, Feliza, and all nine of their remaining children, from Dadoy, the twenty-five-year-old son whom poliomyelitis had crippled at an early age and who charmed everyone with his songs, to little Sonny, who had just turned seven and already knew how to recite some poetry (*balak*).

A very few steps separated them from the house where *manang* Tibay lived with her youngest daughter, Aurelia, who was in her early thirties and had a ten-year-old son from a broken marriage. Mother and son had the same radiant smile. As long as the husband who had deserted her was still alive, she could not remarry formally but only enter into a common-law relationship, which she did. When Filemon Lapinig, another of Ned's fishermen and one of Tropio's friends— and in addition, a very handsome man—moved in with her, it reestablished the gender balance in *manang* Tibay's household that Bonifacio Quilicot's death had disrupted. From a Siquijorian viewpoint, to live by oneself for long without the benefit of a companion of the opposite gender presented a rather scandalous picture. Since a respectable, normal man did not cook, and a respectable, normal

woman did not fish, it followed that everyone needed the multiple
services that a spouse, be it a common-law one, should render.

From their house, it was barely necessary to raise one's voice to
reach Tropio's modest abode. Although it was not dilapidated, he always apologized when I came to visit him:

"*Pasayloa kay pubrihun man mi*" ("I am sorry that we were meant to
be poor").

I could understand the referential aspect of his comment, namely
that he regretted being poor. But I had more trouble with its performative slant. Why did he do that? Was he "ashamed" (*ulaw*) of the
modesty of the house? Did he apologize for not maintaining the
house properly? For the interior being in less than tiptop shape? For
not having any food to offer to his visitor? Or was it just the general,
usual, and formulaic expression of humility, the self-deprecation that
his culture required him to express? With Tropio, it was probably a
combination of all of that, but given his sensitivity I knew that he felt
particularly embarrassed (*ulaw*) by being poor, by being a widower
(*balo*), by not having lived up to the ambition of his youth.

In 1954, a few years after Tropio left school, he had married Santas Bato. Three of his twelve children had died in infancy, and his
three eldest children had married and moved to the northern coast
of Mindanao, so that at age forty-six he already had more than ten
grandchildren (*apo*). This left him with six children at home. The
eldest one, Linda, was barely eighteen and had already been married
and abandoned pregnant; she was now the only adult female in the
household to take charge of her five younger siblings.

SANTAS BATO HAD DIED in 1975, leaving Tropio with a large family
and grieving memories.

> "We had the same age. My wife was from Taligsik."
> (*Pareha ra mig idad. Taga-Taligsik ang akong asawa.*)
> [Taligsik was a *barangay* of Lazi adjacent to Lapyahan.]
> "We got to know each other while we were weeding on a
> mutual help party."
> (*Nagka-ila mi sa nag . . . nag-alayun ba mi ug bunglayay.*)
> [*Alayun* or *hunglus* refer to cooperative work exchanges in which
> people work together, spending equal amounts of time on each
> person's land.]
> "Then we were not engaged for a long time. A year maybe."
> (*Unya, wala pod muagi kog dugay-dugay nga panagtrato. Usa
> ka tuig tingali.*)

[The semantic range of *trato* goes from "sweetheart" and "fiancé" to "lover" or "mistress."]

"She pitied me, that is why we got married."

(*Nalu-oy siya nako, busa nagkaminyo mi.*)

[The notion of "pity" or "mercy" expressed by the verb *lu-oy* tends to indicate that Santas Bato in the end "gave in" to Tropio's supplications. In many ways, this is indeed the opposite of our notion of "se-duction."]

"Then, at our wedding, they all attended, even employees from town. My parents were well known in town."

(*Unya, pagkasal namu, nanambong gani ang tanan ug hangtud mga empliyado sa lungsod. Ilado man ang akong mga ginikanan sa lungsod.*)

[Tropio's parents' reputation in town derived from Bonifacio Quilicot's unusually long tenure as a *barrio* official.]

"My wife died in 1976. Giving birth to Judith, the youngest. The child survived a week."

(*Namatay akong asawa sa 1976. Pagpanganak niya ni Judith, sa kinamanghuran. Buhi pa akong bata, sulod pa sa usa ka simana.*)

[Tropio's memory is off by one year. The child died of pneumonia on the seventh or eighth day.]

"When the child came out, then the placenta did not come out, the midwife could not bring it out, so I got a doctor and a midwife."

(*Paglugwa sa bata, wala man dayon moguwa ang inunlan, di man madala sa mananabang, so gakuha ko ug doctor ug mid-wife.*)

[The verbs *lugwa*, *guwa*, and *gula* are not only synonyms but are variants of the same form. The noun *inunlan*, "placenta," derives from the word *unlan*, "pillow," which in turn derives from the verbal root *ulun*, "to rest one's head on something." The *mananabang* are "traditional midwives" who often have a good practical experience, although little if any formal understanding of Western-style hygiene.]

"But the physician was unable to come because he had gone to the town of Maria; only the midwife could come along with me."

(*Pero ang doctor wala maka-uban tungod kay mi-adto sa lungsod sa Maria; ang* midwife *lang ang naka-uban nako.*)

[Tropio left the midwife at his wife's side and managed to reach the physician; the pronoun *namo* that he used in the next sentence is an inclusive "we" that referred to himself and to the physician.]

"But when we arrived home, my wife was already dead, because, I was told, the midwife had [tried to] pull down [the placenta] with her hands; at least that's what I was told."

> *(Pero pag-abot namo sa balay, patay na ang akong asawa, kay gikuot no ang, kuan, bangag sa iyang kinaiya sa mananabang sa gawas, matud pa sa estorya karong gitu-igan na.)*

[The causal clause can be translated literally as: "because her woman's hole had been reached from outside (and grabbed) by the midwife." The context makes clear that the midwife tried to reach and to grab the unreleased placenta rather than the parturient's genitalia per se. The cause of death was the ensuing hemorrhage. The last words suggest that Tropio learned exactly what happened "only now, a year later." Tropio did not perceive the death of his wife just as the result of a faulty manipulation by the midwife, but he placed it in the larger context of what he understood to be his multifaceted and generalized *dimalas*, "bad luck."]

"Before I was married, I sold fresh fish, I was into small business, I slaughtered goats. For business, with small profit. And more, whatever I could think of to make money, I did. But I am still not rich, because poor is my luck."

> *(Sa wala pa ko maminyo, manglab-as, negosyog ginagmay, mag-ihawg kanding. Para negosyo, ginansya pog gamay. Kaalo pa, bisag unsay akong mahuna-hunaang maka-kwarta ko, ako gyong buhaton. Pero wala gihapon madato kay pobre man ug kapalaran.)*

[Tropio illustrated this idea by listing the problems that inhibited his productive activities.]

"My canoe is broken into pieces. My fishnet is old. My cow is fed by the *barangay* captain."

> *(Ang akong baroto na-buak na; ang akong pokot kara-an na; ang akong baka, kuan nilalug na na kang barangay* Captain *Victor Saplot.)*

[The verb *lalug* means "to feed," but *maglalug*—from which *nilalog* derives—refers to a system of exchange concerning a female domesticated animal, a buffalo, cow, or pig. The owner entrusts the animal to someone else who feeds the animal in exchange for half of the future offspring. This involves a great deal of trust between the people involved in such an exchange and is a frequent source of conflict. Here, the person supposed to keep the animal alive (the *gabuhi*) was Victor Saplot, not only the *barangay* captain but also one of Tropio's distant relatives. Neither Victor nor Tropio could trace the exact links that existed between them, but in fact, Victor was Tropio's father's fa-

ther's half-sister's son's son's son, as well as Tropio's father's father's half-brother's daughter's son (see figs. 9 and 12)]

"Before, I had a cow; my wife died, that's what I spent for
her death."

*(Sa una, duna koy baka; namatay akong asawa, ma-oy akong
gasto sa kamatayon sa akong asawa.)*

[When someone dies, the mourners have to be fed by the be-
reaved family. A wake is often the occasion of slaughtering a
cow.]

"I had one more cow. My son got married six months later, it
was also spent. . . . I ran out of cows."

*(Unya diha may sobrang baka, nangasawa akong anak abutan
ug unom ka bulan, gigasto pod. . . . nahutdan ko ug baka.)*

[The only cow Tropio had left at the time he uttered these sentences was the animal that had been "mortgaged" to the *barangay* captain.]

"We were members of this . . . um . . . this devil of a life insurance, but at the death of my wife, I asked someone to do
the claiming for me regarding my wife's death; but then
nothing doing because the insurance company gave nothing;
since then, I have not taken any insurance, no matter which,
because I had wasted my money."

(Membro mi sa kuan, kining yating . . . life insurance; *pero
pagkamatay sa akong asawa, nagpaklim ko kabahin sa kamatayon sa akong asawa, unya, kay wa may nahimo kay wa man
taga-i sa* Insurance Company; *gikan adto di na ko mo en-
trag* insurance, *bisan pag unsang klase sa* insurance, *kay na-
biya na man tong akong kwarta.)*

[A swindler had been collecting the life insurance policy premi-
ums throughout the island and, having collected, vanished.]

FOR TROPIO, the flow of his memories had its strain of contradictions.
He could dream of his deceased wife and lament the fate that separated them. He also remembered her with what appeared to me as
genuine fondness. But he also remembered that his wife had only
been a sort of third choice at the time he had married her. He did not
say it that way but in the following terms:

"As a bachelor, I was able to travel for three weeks, to Baliangao. I was brought there, you know, by my friend Victoriano Mahinay."

(Pagka-ulitao nako, naka-langyaw tulo ka simana, didto sa

> *Baliangao; gidala lagi ko ining akong higala, si Victoriano*
> *Mahinay.)*

[Baliangao is a municipality in northern Mindanao. The two
men were not just friends but second cousins, since Victoriano
Mahinay was Tropio's mother's mother's brother's son's son [(see
fig. 11).]

"He said: let us go there because you have many relatives
there, fellow Quilicots; so, I went there."

> *(Ingon siya nga mu-adto ta didto kay tu-ay daghan nimong*
> *parinti mga kaubanan nga Quilicot; so, hing-adto ko didtu.)*

[Locutors frequently use the Spanish borrowing *paryinti* or *par-
inti* to designate a relative instead of the more strictly Visayan
term *kabanay.* The attraction of having relatives in northern
Mindanao was a powerful argument, because if need be they
provide hospitality as well as companionship. Siquijorians, inde-
pendently of age or gender, rarely if ever travel alone, but always have a "companion" or *kauban.*]

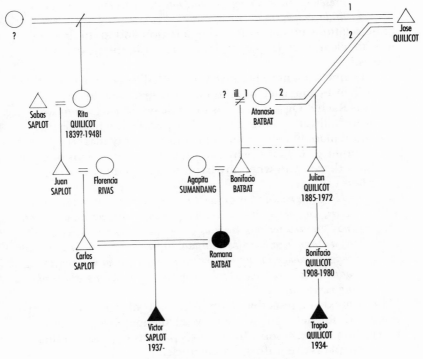

FIG. 12. Kinship links between Victor Saplot
and Tropio Quilicot

"When I got there, he took me to his boss, because he was working in a printing shop."

(Pag-adto nako, gidala ko sa iyang agalon, kay nanarbaho man siya sa printing.)

[The word *agalun* meaning "master," "boss," has the same root, *agad*, as *alagad* meaning "servant," "employee," and as *umagarun* refering to a "prospective son-in-law."]

"Now the Chinese man appreciated my work; that's why they brought me to Nasipang."

(Karon hing-angay man nako ang Insik sa akong buhat; ma-o tong gidala ko nila sa Nasipang.)

[Nasipang is another northern Mindanao locale where the Chinese printer had another shop.]

"Then, there was a beautiful woman, Sofia Quilat; I declared my love; we became sweethearts; so, I stopped working."

(Unya, may babaye man nga gwapa, Sofia Quilat; hing-presentar ko sa akong gugma; natrato man mi; so, hing-undang kog trabaho.)

[The relationship between having a liaison and quitting a job was not clear, and Tropio explains himself in the next sentences.]

"I came back here because we decided to get married. When I came back here to Lazi, my first sweetheart, that was Rachel Ogoc—she was my first sweetheart when we were still very young. I asked her permission to marry in Mindanao, but she would not consent to my marrying another girl. This is why I did not pursue my plans of going back there. And when my parents criticized my marriage plans . . ."

(Hing-uli ko diri kay gasabot magminyo; pag-uli nako diri sa Lazi, ang akong unang trato nga kana si Rachel Ogoc—mau nay primiru nakong trato ug sa batan-on pa mi; nananghid ko nga magminyo ko sa Mindanao, unya di man siya musugot ug magminyo kog la-ing babaye. Mao nang wa ko mahinayon ug adto didto. Pero, ug sa gihagit nako, ag, sa akong ginikanan ug minyo, ag . . .)

[The context suggests that Tropio's parents objected to his marriage with Rachel Ogoc, since they "challenged" *(hagit)* her to marry him. The reason why Tropio's parents objected to such marriage plans are unfortunately unclear.]

". . . I still was unable to marry the one who held me back because she fell ill. Since I had several sweethearts, I married another one, my now departed wife, Santas Bato."

(. . . Naghawid nako, wala pa gihapon nako himinyo-i, kay na-
atol man pong gadaut siya. Dili, ag, usa na pod ka trato maoy
akong gipangasawa, kanang akong asawa karon nga namatay,
si Santas Bato.)
[The realism of the previous narrative, especially its ending,
may hurt our contemporary Western sensibilities, but we should
beware of projecting our own cultural standards onto the Siquijorian ethos, lest we distort it beyond recognition.

WHEN THE LOCAL parish priest, Father Valentin—undoubtedly a bon
vivant, judging by his corpulence, but also, unlike a number of his
peers, a most virtuous man without any live-in maid, niece, or even
female cousin—spoke of *amor,* he collapsed two languages into one,
Latin and Spanish. It was difficult to know from which vocabulary he
had drawn the word, because he could use the word *amor* with equal
ease within a linguistic context that was neither Latin nor Spanish
but, rather, Cebuano or even English. Though born on the neighboring island of Negros, he insisted on the Spanish ancestry he could
claim and was most proud of being a polyglot, functional in four languages. Cebuano was his mother tongue. Spanish matched the ethnic
feelings he professed. English, the language of the Americans and
the successful bourgeoisie, reflected his affiliation and aspirations in
terms of social class. As for Latin, the pre-Vatican II language of his
trade, it emphasized, as his *embonpoint* did, his bygone youth. *Amor
Dei* or *amor de Dios,* whether Latin or Spanish, *amor* was *amor.* More
than translatable, more than equivalent, the two words were in fact
identical.
    Certainly, his mention of *amor* had obvious and immediate reli-
gious connotations. The reference was to God, to Christ, even to the
Holy Spirit, to the Virgin Mary, to the love they had already given
and continued to give us, as well as to the love we owed them. Perhaps
even more importantly, he used the term with wider connotations. He
thus designated "love" in several different senses of the term, such as
parental, filial, and so on, but whatever sexual content it might have
had was meant to remain latent. It was not that in his view *amor* could
not be sexualized; it could, but then it had to be tempered by conju-
gality.
    Fortunately, unlike so many of his predecessors, he had an alto-
gether compassionate sense of social realities, which prevented him
from coming down too harshly on many of his parishioners who, in
the eyes of the Church, were living in sin. A good sense of nuance
allowed him to distinguish between common-law relationships—they
could always be regularized—and the premarital impatience of teenagers or the extramarital indiscretions of consenting adults. Nonethe-

less, despite his practical tolerance, from the pulpit as well as in conversations with me, he deplored all of them. There was no *amor* in any of them.

And so it was that *amor*, if and when reduced solely to its sexual component, just could not be *amor* at all but was something else, its flip side. Since it was not *amor*, what was it then? To answer that question required of him more than a mere lexical change, more than a new tag. It demanded a complete linguistic code switch. He would dismiss this non-*amor* by referring to it both in Cebuano as *gugma* and in English as "lust," or more rarely as "love," almost indifferently. One or the other made little difference to him, as each one remained blurred in the emotional greyness of his surroundings. The words were not totally confused, because his rural *barangay* flock was made up almost entirely of Cebuano monolinguals who in his view were thus susceptible of falling for *gugma*, while it was the more sophisticated and partly bilingual town bourgeoisie whom he saw as prone to "lust" and to "love."

Of course, Father Valentin's command of English might not have been that of a native speaker, but it was good enough for him to know that "lust" and "love," though related, were not synonymous. Independent of the difficulties inherent in the plain exercise of translation, *gugma* was an acceptable approximation for "love" but not for "lust," at least not in its traditional sense of sexual desire, which is expressed in Cebuano by such phrases as *kabiga* or *kaulag*. Since the priest's failure to distinguish between the two could not be imputed to his lack of linguistic competence, it follows that he meant to confuse the terms and to have their respective meaning merge into each other. If he deliberately confused "lust" and "love," it was to condemn both.

Among the town dwellers, "love" could be an interesting topic of conversation. Everyone knew the word and used it, even those whose formal education had been minimal and whose command of English was negligible. But it was another matter with the word "lust," which belonged to a more sophisticated linguistic domain. Some members of the town elite, such as the medical doctors and the lawyers, had an excellent command of English, but most people did not. Their vocabulary was thus limited, and the word "lust" was unavailable to them. Consequently, whenever they used the English word "love"—and it came up often in conversations—the word had a semantic extension which largely overflowed what any native speaker of English would have expected.

When people in town used such an apparently strange expression as *iyang* love *kaniya* to say what should have been in Cebuano *iyang*

gugma kaniya and in English "his/her love for him/her," it was not immediately clear what was meant, especially since the word could be
used with positive or negative connotations depending on the context.

On the one hand, "love" was perceived as something valued, a
sort of superior sentiment of which the locutors and their immediate
kin and friends were capable. It would have been a reasonable equivalent of the priest's *amor* had it not acquired also a performative aspect. In that sense, love, here valued, was differentiated from something else that was looked down upon in town, namely *gugma*.
Although—or better, because—*gugma* had currency in the *barangay,*
it was the sentiment of the rural proletariat and so was manifestly the
inferior version of bourgeois "love." To evoke "love" was, of course,
to show one's emancipation from one's rural anchorage, as if, in the
domain of sentiment, the local bourgeoisie could deny or transcend
its origins. Succumbing to "love" was thus a pretense, whereby *gugma*
and whatever it entailed of inferiority, backwardness, and poverty
too, could be denied or relegated to the never-never-land of all-too-
near *barangay* origins.

While there was an element of exclusivity in this "love," which
rejected the excessively rustic feelings of the peasantry, there as a con-
comitant effort at inclusion, for the sentiment also modeled itself on
an American pattern. This was in fact what the English word illustrated, as this American orientation represented an escape from the
island and an aspiration to transcend its limitations. As such, it could
only be an imitation of an American style of "love" informed less by
direct experience—only a handful of people in town had visited the
States—than by vicarious knowledge, drawn from the testimonies of
former town dwellers who had more or less permanently emigrated
to North America, as well as from comic book representations, *Play-
boy*-like imagery, and melodramatic radio renditions, not to mention
all sorts of standard characterizations in love songs. If "love" was a
beautiful ideal, it was also asymptotic, hence its evocation every time
it could sizzle or flourish, whichever image applied. It was evoked by
women a propos of elusive husbands, penpals, and all remote males
who for one reason or the other remained aloof as marriage partners.
It was evoked by men a propos of unavailable women, who, for one
reason or the other, were unable or unwilling to become compliant
lovers.

On the other hand, "love" was also used in an entirely different
context: it could also be perceived in town as something devalued and
even ridiculous. The townspeople laughed at the "love" displayed by
a merchant who used the pretext of extensive trips to the neighboring

town to visit his mistress, leaving his wife and children behind. They giggled at the "love" that "hospitality girls" peddled in the city brothels. They also sneered at the "love" displayed in the marriage between a senescent yet wealthy man and an attractive woman still in her teens. In these contexts, "love" carried the connotation of nonconformity to the social norms, in other words, marginality, the very exterior of received ideas. As used here, "love" was deviant and derisive. "Love" was also conceived in opposition to *gugma*, although not to escape from its peasant connotations but on the contrary to emphasize the validity of the norm. Laughing, giggling, and smiling at "love" were ways to condemn its excesses in all their aspects: romantic, venal, adulterous, or simply socially unacceptable. Here, by using the English word what was emphasized was the disruptive aspect of change. "Love" thus represented the side effects of modernization. On it, the disappearance of *gugma*, of family values, of kinship ties could be blamed.

Consequently, whether considered a desirable tension toward modernity or a lamentable degradation of tradition, "love" in town, however twisted and ambiguous, was indeed a bourgeois sentiment par excellence, striking in its inauthenticity; and for that very reason it is incomprehensible without a further exploration of that from which—by promoted design or regretted slip from tradition—it deviated: *gugma*.

WHEN MY WIFE and I met Tropio for the first time, he was still a widower. There were good reasons for this. Auntie Diding had her own explanation which she summed up in two words, *delikadu na*. In using this expression, she expressed more than its etymological sense of being "delicate." It expressed also that Tropio would need to handle any prospective marriage very carefully. As she pointed out, after all, could an older man, "rich only in years and in children," be that good a marriage prospect? The word *delikadu* could also be read as "finnicky," "choosy," and her choice of words implied this as well.

Virgie concurred with her mother, seeing the remarriage of her older cousin unlikely:

"Difficult because of his many children" (*lisod na kay daghag bata*).

Manang Tibay preferred, wisely, to say "*ambot lang*" ("I do not know") rather than to offer unsolicited advice.

Ned thought that Tropio's situation was abnormally stressful. Why did I not ask Tropio directly? I did. The answer(s) I received varied greatly from day to day and even within the same day because, according to his younger sister's unflattering yet beautiful expression, Tropio was "still indecisive and hesitant" or *madilidiliun pa*—the expression is derived from the root "*dili*," "to refuse," but the redu-plication of the radical attenuates the refusal.

At times, Tropio answered: "It would be difficult. I still have sev-eral small children. If I remarry, my children may suffer, because there may be something about the new wife that we would not know about, she may be bad and fight with my children, they will pack up and leave. You will be embarrassed in front of other people. People will say, um . . . , the parent with a wife has become strict. So, I'll just remain a widower forever because, for my children's sake (literally, so that my children do not sin)."

> (*Lisod na. Daghan man kog anak nga gagmay pa. Ug manga-sawa ko pag-usab, makasala akong mga bata kay naa may batasan sa asawa unyang bag-o, di man nato mabaw-an ug dautan; awa-yon nang akong anak, di mangarya. Ka-ulawan na ka sa mga tawo. Mo-ingon tong mga tawog, kuan, na-isog nang ginikanan nga na-ay asawa. So, magpabilin god kong balo kanunay kay, aron dili makasala akong mag anak.*)

But Tropio could also speak in another voice, one perhaps more personal and less dominated by his fatherly responsibilities, that gave freer rein to his desires. His phrase was all too brief, just a two-word statement, the quotation and translation of which we must defer for a moment.

GUGMA WAS —as everyone in the *municipio* as well as in the *barangay* agreed—at the core of rural life on the island. It was the people's love, *gugma sa tawo*, which was said to hold the social texture of the island together. And *gugma* was most unproblematic. Despite the density of population on Siquijor, and despite the centrifugal tensions that per-meated the island, its inhabitants liked to present and represent an edulcorative image of themselves as a whole. In repeating incessantly, as Ned did, that they constituted "one whole big happy family here," the Siquijorians gave an ideal—and thus at least partially unfaith-ful—collective representation suffused by universal *gugma* for their fellow islanders. If there was supposed to be happiness (*kalipay*) everywhere and for everyone, it was because of the extension of fam-ily links to everyone on the island; each islander was bound to every-one else by a general feeling of *gugma*. And *gugma* was the agent that bound individuals to each other within actual families, parents to chil-dren and vice versa, siblings together, and spouses together. In this sense, *gugma* could not be invoked in vain. It was a feeling which went straight to the root of the Siquijorian experience.

In addition to being inherent in social life on Siquijor, a diffuse feeling of quasi-organic solidarity, *gugma* presented itself most frequently within a less integrative and hence a more "romantic" feeling. While a whispered *gihigugma ko ikaw* ("I love you") could draw such a response as *ayaw, nanglinbaut ang akong balhibu* ("don't, it gives me goose pimples"), I was not usually privy to such intimate conversations. When I heard such a verbal exchange, it was uttered in jest by two teenagers to the great amusement of their peers, their *barkada*, who had all gathered under the palm-thatched roof of Auntie Diding's porch.

To my inquiries about *gugma*, there were other obstacles. Direct questioning was most unfruitful. To ask *Unsa man ang gugma?* ("what is *gugma?*") could not lead anywhere. It was perceived either as a request for translation (generating a laconic and necessarily disappointing "love" answer) or as a silly and unanswerable question (prompting chuckles or embarrassed giggles).

Because of the respect (*tahud*) that my old, learned, and American persona commanded and because of the general indirectness and soft-spoken modesty considered appropriate behavior in the *barangay*, the villagers were not likely to contribute much on this topic on their own initiative. Enlightenment was more likely to emerge from small talk with informants who were prompt to contradict the norms of ideal behavior and ready to gossip.

In this respect, teenagers were good at revealing with some intended mischief who among their peers was going out with whom, who had met whom at the spring, who had shared a ride to town with whom. Many teenagers in the *barangay* had gone to school for years, and those who had not still knew a few words of English they had learned from their peers and from listening to American rock and pop groups on the radio. (Slightly belatedly, the BeeGees were in favor and the Beatles were still a success, but the hit of the year was undoubtedly "Don't Cry for Me, Argentina.") In a way, they were already lost to *gugma*, being more likely to be "in love" and to have a "boyfriend" or a "girlfriend." Of course, although their behavior was still very much within local traditions, they had already and hesitatingly moved some distance from their parents' actions, liking to mimic some town tastes. The pristine sense of *gugma* I was supposed to discover in the *barangay* was obviously not to be found among them.

THE FIRST INTIMATION of what *gugma* was about came indirectly and almost inadvertently from a conversation I had one morning with Tropio. In contrast to many others in the *sitio*, he neither drank nor gambled but was hard-working and fished diligently, even though his efforts were only occasionally rewarded with economic success. Since he was bemoaning his fate, I wondered anew why he did not remarry. His sensible reply was to repeat that it would be difficult to find a woman to marry a widower with such progeny. But the most important argument was yet to come, and it was a lament: *walay gugma.*

The distressing expression was full of ambiguities, since several translations were conceivable. Literally, it could be translated as "there is no love," but it meant as well "no one loves me" or "I am not in love with anyone" or both.

He elaborated on this feeling by explaining that he still dreamed of his wife, who, in the dream, would call him from the beach as he returned from the sea. In the undoubtedly idealized recollection that he had of his relationship with his wife, they had been so, in his words, *sandurot* ("intimate") *usa sa usa* ("toward each other") *sa among panagtiayun* ("during our marriage"—from *tiayun,* "to be married to each other," itself from *ayun,* "to be in harmony with"). He added, *Nag-ayun ang among pagtiayun,* i.e., "we got along fine as a couple."

From this conversation alone, I would have concluded that intimacy and harmony were the two most important components of *gugma.* Although painted through the pain of its absence, the sense of *gugma* Tropio presented was nonetheless positive, a reward that death had snatched from him. Turning from actual experience, one finds a striking parallel in the public expression of *gugma* as displayed in the semantic environment of songs and poems, in the form of what could be called love laments.

Among the many songs performed not only for our benefit at our hut but more importantly on Auntie Diding's porch by young residents of the *sitio,* one was a great favorite. Everyone knew it, but few could sing it with the same perfection as Tropio's nephew, Dadoy. On occasion, Ned and Minay joined him with enthusiasm. Auntie Diding and *manang* Tibay listened with amusement at a distance, while Virgie and her friends pretended to be indifferent and, wrapping themselves in an eternal smile, proceeded ostentatiously to ignore the suggestion that they were being courted. The song was entitled *Usahay,* "Sometimes":

Usahay makadamgo ako	Sometimes I dream
Nga ikaw ug ako	That you and I
Nagkahigugmaay.	Love each other.
Nganong damgohon ko ikaw	Why do I dream of you
Damgohon sa kanunay	Dream always
Sa akong kamingaw?	In my loneliness?
Usahay magamahay ako	Sometimes I feel hurt
Nganong nabuhi pa	Why am I still alive
Ning kalibutan	In this world.

Nganong gitiawtiawan	Why am I teased
Ang gugma ko kanimo	By my love for you
Kanimo da?	Only you?

Even though this song has a beautiful melody, my only concern here lies with its lyrics—two stanzas, each of six rhymed lines. Since gender is not marked in the Cebuano language, the song could be interpreted by men as well as by women, and furthermore its text does not necessarily imply heterosexuality.

The word *gugma* appears in each stanza. As if often, if not always, the case in this sort of song, *gugma* is not triumphant. On the contrary, it is evoked in its suffering and failing aspect, thus inspiring pity. Its absence/presence is underlined by three separate mentions of "dream" (*damgo*), the theme and setting of the first stanza.

This image is compelling because of the double theory of dreams that prevailed on Siquijor. On the one hand, dreams had a fantastic unreality; they were illusions clearly distinguishable from the ordinary experiences of the world. On the other hand, dreams were considered engagements with the spiritual world, whose denizens felt free to come and visit people during their sleep. The visitors could be souls of other still living people, who were presumably asleep at the time of dream. More often, these visitors of someone's subconscience were said to be the souls of dead relatives. On occasion, all sorts of supernatural beings, ranging from *engkanto* spirits to altogether dangerous mermaids (*kataw*), could enchant someone's sleep. Premonitory or mnemonic, dreams were always strongly ambiguous markers, blurred visions and muffled echoes of that which had been as well as of that which could be, or even that which was purely illusory.

Consequently, the first stanza establishes powerfully the separation, intermittently breached in dreams, between the "I" of the song and its "you." This separation is further underlined by the formal pronouns for "you" and "I" (*ikaw* and *ako* rather than *ka* and *ko*) and through the use of these two singular pronouns instead of the unifying, plural inclusive "we" (*kita,* or *ta*). Further reinforcement comes from yet another contrast established between the "sometimes" (*usahay*) of my dream and the "always" (*kanunay*) of my loneliness (*kamingaw*). *Kamingaw,* the word that ends the first stanza, refers to loneliness as well as to homesickness, two concepts considered unbecoming and extremely painful in Visayan culture.

The kind of *gugma* sketched so far in the first stanza is characterized by its incompleteness, by its unachievement. There is something missing, something deficient, something lacking, a feeling admirably expressed by the Cebuano word *kulang,* which English speakers would probably evoke with words like "void" or "emptiness."

The second stanza further develops the negative implications of *gugma* by reasserting and amplifying previous contrasts, between "I" and "you," between "sometimes" and an implied "always," between temporary pain and the permanency of death. It also introduces new contrasts, between "hurt life" and "teasing love," between "pain" and "love." But more importantly, it denies what in the same breath it asserts. When death is evoked indirectly by the questioning of life on the second line—"Why am I still alive?"—it is only the rhetorical pretense of despair. Not only is an actual morbid despair unlikely to be sung about, but this phrase establishes the lowest point emotionally in the lyrics from which, as progressively as indirectly, *gugma* may rise again.

The second stanza indeed reinforces the urgency of "my love for you" as we see *gugma* ultimately triumph in the penultimate line, while the text devotes the last line to the object of all this *gugma*, to the "you" of the song.

The song has—and this may be the whole point—turned the tables, as "you" may have been convinced not to play hard to get anymore since "I" *gugma* "you" and "only you." In order to achieve this, the singer has now reversed all the propositions of the text. In wondering "why am I teased," the "I" of the song demands not to be toyed with anymore, as he/she wants not to be a "love object" but the object of your love, as "you" are the object of his/her love. Furthermore, in this process, the "I" of the song has now been able to slip, to fade away and become embodied by the singing subject, as real person.

If the song functioned—that is, if it stirred some emotion—it was largely due to its rhetorical flexibility, to its very indirectness, since it did not name anyone but only alluded potentially to everyone. In the end , perhaps, the only ones to "have been teased" (*gitiawtiawan*) were the listeners of the song.

Between the performance of two songs, it was not unusual for someone among the listeners to recite *balak*, poetry that is partly or entirely improvised or has just been committed to memory. The following *balak* gives another good example of what *gugma* is all about. Even though the word is not mentioned at all, it is clear that *gugma* is the topic of this quatrain. *Day*, the short form of *Inday*, is the abstract addressee of the text. Such a term is used for any woman younger than or of same age as the speaker. As such, I have refrained from translating it. The two versions of it that I have collected are sufficiently close to each other to be susceptible of a single translation:

> *Dinhi man, Day, sa kapatagan,*   Version I (Tropio Quilicot)
> *Ikaw may bulak nakong pinili*
> *Luha man, Day, hapit matiti*
> *Kahapdos kamingaw kanimo ug pagbati.*

Day, didto bitaw sa kapatagan   Version II (Filemon Lapinig)
Ikaw, Day, akong bulak pinili
Luha ko, Day, hapit na matiti
Kahabdos kamingaw akong gibati.

In the whole plain, *Day,*   Translation
You are the flower I have chosen.
My tears are nearly dried out,
Pain and loneliness is what I feel.

Without going further into the analysis of other songs and poems, the *gugma* lexical environment appears with some clarity. It pertains to the same ensemble as *kasing-kasing* ("heart," derived from *kasing,* "top"), *dughan* ("breast," as seat of emotions), *lusuk sa luha* ("tear drops"), *kinabuhi* ("life"), *kamingaw* ("loneliness"), *kalipay* ("happiness"), *kasakit* ("pain"), *pinangga* ("darling" from *palangga,* "to love and care for someone," itself from *dannga,* "spoiled with affection"), *kapalaran* ("destiny," from *lapad,* "the palm of the hand"), and so on. It is in essence the domain of affection, the domain of *pagbati* ("feelings").

Almost all the Cebuano songs and poems that I heard were lyrical expressions of *gugma,* or more precisely of unhappy or incomplete involvement, of abandonment or failed seduction, the text being always addressed to a "you" whose generality varied from text to text. One would thus expect that at least some of these compositions were used as courting devices, which brings us back to the conditions of their performance.

Whenever I inquired about almost anything in the *barangay,* my informants tended to take refuge in a nostalgic and regrettably disappeared past, almost in the same way as the townspeople discouraged similar inquiries by sending me back to the *barangay* people as the true holders of an authentic tradition. Therefore, when I pursued the topic of courting, I provoked some sighs and heard many *sa una* ("in the past").

And so in this quasi-mythical past of a generation or two ago, people knew poetry, but not anymore. Men and their *barkada* used to go and play on string instruments the *harana* beneath a woman's window, but only the memory of these serenades was left, and everyone now had transistors anyway. As for the *balitaw,* the improvised courtship song between a boy and the girl whose hand he was asking their respective representatives to negotiate, how could it still exist when children barely asked their parents' permission before marrying?

Things had changed, but perhaps not as drastically as my informants represented. Despite all efforts, I could not find anyone but old people who could still remember the witty exchanges of *balitaw,* because marriage negotiations were quicker nowadays and did not always require the intervention of intermediaries. The practice of *harana* serenading continued, even if this was done with tunes more often borrowed from American pop or rock hits than taken from the traditional Cebuano repertoire. A few women still knew some *balak*, and it would have been a rare man who knew none.

What had changed racially, however, were the conditions of performance. *Harana* serenading still took place, but with the playing of more foreign than native tunes on modernized instruments, it had already become less a form of actual courting than of social entertainment. With the tendency for young people to negotiate their marriages without the help of intermediaries, *balitaw* had fallen into the respectable but sterile domain of folklore. Children were still learning to improvise *balak* in front of their families at weekend drinking gatherings of *sitio* members, but now this improvisatory art had added a new venue, appearing as a regular feature on some radio programs from the city of Cebu.

GUGMA IN THE *barangay* was no less idealized than it had been in town. In effect, it resembled "love" like a twin except for the idealization that it entailed, whether in the likely distortion that Tropio's memory had generated or in the expressive elaborations that songs and poems displayed. If "love" in town was established in contradistinction to a folksy *gugma*, *gugma* in the *barangay* was, in turn, similarly constructed in contradistinction less to a new bourgeois "love" than to an ideal, dreamed, and ancient *gugma* where together sexual feelings as well as social life were dominated by both harmony and intimacy.

AND SO, although Auntie Diding at sixty had become disenchanted with, or at least disinterested in, *gugma*, some had found it, or at least said so. Ned and Minay projected an image of harmony that they generously and programmatically extended to the entire island. Fidel Mahinay, who had a knack for play on words, kept making puns about being a better "philanderer" (*palakero*) than "poet" (*balakero*). Filemon Lapinig, young and handsome, and the beautiful Aurelia, Tropio's sister, had found each other. In the gentle breeze that often cooled Auntie Diding's porch, other young men and women, like Virgie Dagatan and Dadoy Quilicot, with songs, with poems, with oblique looks and allusions, were still looking for and perhaps dreaming of the *gugma* they had not yet found. Even children, who were so much involved and who were constantly encouraged to imitate adults in singing and dancing, were drawn in by the attraction of a generalized, idealized, and elusive *gugma* that embraced not just another person but the whole island. But Tropio, like Auntie Diding and a few others, had renounced his claim on *gugma*.

ON AUNTIE DIDING'S PORCH, the last song was sung, the last glass of *tuba* drunk, the last conversation uttered, the last gossip exchanged, and the last laugh shared. Darkness settled in. The day's sounds softly gave way to the rustle of palm fronds in the wind, the lap of waves against the double-outriggers, an occasional pig's grunt, and the furtive steps of one of Ned's fishermen on the shore.

Back in the cool, thatched hut where my wife and I dwelt, I could note impressions and observations for the day, ponder my shortcomings and the misunderstandings that fieldwork entailed. I hummed the Siquijor anthem I had heard so often in Camingawan, on Dadoy's guitar, in Minay's voice, and from others, too. Its faint echo lingered in my head for a while. Two dissonant clusters of mistuned voices seemed to sing through the two different versions of its lyrics. Its burden written with an unease that belied the sentiments it wished to express, a belabored English version read:

Siquijor, Siquijor
Land of beauty, pure, divine
All thy people now and forever
Will be loyal, brave and true.

The Visayan version of the same stanza, graceful and elegant in its very simplicity, was also more poignant in the lyrical sincerity of its evocation:

Siquijor, Siquijor,	Siquijor, Siquijor,
Yutang among gimahal	Beloved land
Sa tanan mga kakulian	In all difficulties
Ikaw among panalipdan	We will defend you.

With this proclaimed, Auntie Diding and Virgie, Ned and Minay, Tropio and *manang* Tibay, Zosing and Soy, and so many others in *sitio* Camingawan, in *barangay* Lapyahan, in the municipality of Lazi, on the island of Siquijor, could all let sleep descend upon them, visit each other in their respective dreams, and perhaps forget the varied intensity of their waking poverty until the following dawn.

19

Epilogue

F ROM THE OUTSET in my fieldwork, I was confronted by a question that was often raised in English by Siquijorians understandably puzzled by my presence on their island:

"And what is the purpose of your visit?"

Early on, I had learned and memorized a one-sentence answer that seemed to me to encapsulate what I thought I was doing:

"I live here because I am writing a book about the fishermen and cultivators of Siquijor" (*Nagpuyo dinhi kay magsulat ug libro bahin sa mga mananagat ug mga magdadaro sa isla sa Siquijor*).

On the spur of the moment, it had seemed an adequate representation of my endeavor. With the benefit of hindsight, I find it less accurate than I had thought at first. For instance, I did not confine my interest to *barangay* residents who fished and farmed, but town dwellers caught and held my attention as well. More to the point, I took notes while I was in the field, but I was certainly not then writing a book. This came much, much later. In between, life went on.

The night before we left, Tropio came down with cholera, but swift medical attention saved his life.

Shortly after our departure, death took away *manong* Andres Sumagang, whose almost silent company I had enjoyed many a time. He had been spending more and more time, almost entire days, smiling to the wind from Auntie Diding's porch.

In October 1982, Tropio married a widow from the town of Maria who brought with her six young children. Whether this has brought them harmony and intimacy, I cannot say, except that so far they have produced four more children.

His daughter Linda and her child have moved to her paternal aunt's in a different *sitio* in Lapyahan. She works there as an agricultural helper. Another daughter, Cindy, moved in with her elder brother's family in Mindanao. Against Tropio's better sense, his wishes, and his plans, none of his children has graduated from high school.

Married since 1981 to Filemon Lapinig, Tropio's sister Aurelia, burdened with a new child every other year or so, takes care of her aging mother, *manang* Tibay, and has abandoned her activity as a fresh fish vendor (*labasera*), forcing Tropio's sister-in-law, Feliza, to find a new partner.

In 1982, Ramon Quilicot's daughter Lisa married Daniel Larot, the drummer in Dadoy's combo, and took up residence in the *payag* my wife and I had occupied in Camingawan. Lisa was Virgie's best friend, in addition to being her cousin (see fig. 13), and the two women could not have lived any closer to each other.

At about the same time, Dadoy moved to somewhere on the northern shore of Mindanao, which offered better fishing opportunities. Soon after, he met a young woman whom he married. Nobody in Camingawan had ever doubted that he would be a *maayong bana* ("good husband"). In the end, Dadoy's strategy worked to his advantage.

Of Auntie Diding's own children, Berto continued fathering a new child every other year.

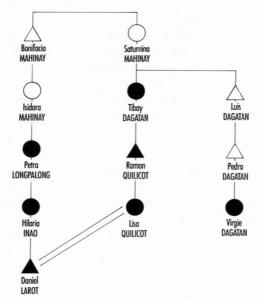

FIG. 13. The marriage of Lisa Quilicot and Daniel Larot

Oyo's wife, Cording, suffering from diabetes for years, died in March 1986—according to some, of that disease, according to others, of "high blood."

In January 1983, Virgie married Sitoy Calibo, a young man from northern Mindanao. His father was dead, and therefore the expenses of the wedding, celebrated in Lazi, were paid by Auntie Diding. She decidedly approved of a son-in-law who neither drank nor smoked nor gambled. At Auntie Diding's express request, the new couple established their residence in Camingawan. Auntie Diding refused to move to Mindanao; neither did she want to remain alone. Virgie and her husband thus reside in Auntie Diding's home. Sitoy wanted to live in his own house, but he had to give in to Auntie Diding's demands. The house has been refurbished. The porch has disappeared, and a new back extension has been built.

With a resident son-in-law at Auntie Diding's, Soy's presence became unnecessary. Still unattached, the young man moved back to his mother's house in Misamis Occidental. In September 1985, Soy was diving off the island of Cuyo, northeast of Palawan, when the compressor that fed his air line failed. He became entangled at the bottom of the sea, and his body was never recovered.

By 1986, Zosing had four children, and they all lived still in the same tiny dwelling.

Victor Saplot finished his term as *barangay* captain and was then replaced by someone else. "A lot of work without money," he had said. There was, however, one advantage to the position, for the *barangay* official's children were entitled to receive free tuition in high schools and in state colleges, as long as their father was in office.

In town, Father Valentin arrived at the end of his tenure as parish priest of Lazi and was reassigned to a parish in the province of Negros Oriental.

An entrepreneur with a privately owned generator and a VCR began to run videos on Saturday evenings. By 1986, electricity had reached the *municipio*, but it was not yet widely used.

Minay received the promotion she expected. As for Ned, he "got tired of the unreliability of [his] fishermen. Except for Tropio, they drank too much and strolled too much instead of working." Berto, Fidel, and Loloy had a fight with Ned at one point in 1983 over circumstances that I have been unable to discover.

"Ned had these three arrested (*gipadakop*) as drunkards (*palahubog*). They did not go to jail. He just wanted to frighten them. 'With me,' Tropio said, 'there is no problem because I do not drink.'"

Ned thus folded his operation in Lapyahan and decided to cast his net and fish-traps in a different *barangay*.

The last time I saw Auntie Diding, she was strong as ever, alive and cracking jokes about her cow being too scrawny and her piglets too tiny to make a proper funeral meal. According to her, she was not ready yet to have her coffin (*lungon*) built; by way of derision, she kept calling it her "wooden mosquito-net" (*muskitiru nga tabla*) and thought this was hilarious.

When I visited Camingawan for the last time in September of 1986, the Marcos regime had collapsed and been replaced a few months before by the Aquino presidency. Political personnel had changed throughout the province of Siquijor, but the conditions that created the poverty of most Siquijorians had not. As Auntie Diding put it, "I am still poor, I am still hungry" (*pinobre pa, gigutum pa*).

Every few months, Virgie struggles with her English to write a letter that my wife and I always find moving. On January 15, 1990, she wrote:

Dearest Auntie & Uncle,
    Before I begin the first of my main topic of my letter, may I greet you (with) a pleasant and a wonderful hello! How are you, Auntie & Uncle, are you in a good health or in a good body condition? About your regarding me and my family together with Auntie Diding, same as usual with the help of our Loving God Creature. . . .

On April 2, 1990, she wrote again:

Dearest Auntie & Uncle,
    We received your letter here last February 16. Thank you very much for your very nice letter and specially to your regarding the people here in Lapyahan and specially my family. I'm sorry that you told me to stop at three children, but we have another one. Now I'm stop this four children because we had no money for educating my children.
    Now Arvin is one year old and my oldest is Analisa is seven years old and the next is Albert five years old and the other one is Arnold three years old. . . .
    About the news her(e) in Camingawan it is very nice Auntie & Uncle because every Saturday (we) have so many people to visit her(e) in Camingawan in the house of Auntie Diding because we have a *ripa* [i.e., a raffle] for borrowing the money, we have 74 members every Saturday and also we have plenty of games, basketball and also volleyball, and others. About your regarding Auntie Diding she well be here, *siging balhin sa baka tabacco sa hunsoy* [i.e., she keeps moving her cow and smoking her pipe].
    About your regarding Sitoy [i.e., Virgie's husband] *siging daro sa ba-ol* [i.e., he keeps plowing the field] all the time very busy to cultivating the land and every Sunday she went to the sea for catching the fish. About Tropio now she is a cwak [i.e., quack] doctor [i.e., a healer] and also his wife. About

Leon Isoy [the neighbor married to one of Virgie's first cousins] *sigi pod daro sa baka sa ba-ol* [i.e., he too keeps plowing the field with the cow].

I (have) forgotten, thank you very much for you to give me a little money for my *penaskohan* [i.e., as Christmas gift].

So I'm stop here because it's to(o) long for you to read my poor letter.

Please response my letter immediately

Sisterly yours,
Virgie & Sitoy Calibo

BIBLIOGRAPHY

Abella, Domingo
1973   Introduction. *Catálogo Alfabético de Apellidos*, vii–xvi.

Agoncillo, Teodoro A., and Milagros C. Guerrero
1978 [1960] *History of the Filipino people*. 5th ed. Quezon City: R.P. Garcia Publishing Co.

Amor, Adlai J.
1977   Siquijor: Isle of sorcery. *Philippines Daily Express* (Manila November 14) 6(191):28.

B.C.S.   See Philippines (Republic of the), Bureau of the Census and Statistics.

Blair, Emma Helen, and James Alexander Robertson, eds. (abbr. BR)
1903–1909   *The Philippine Islands 1493–1898: Explorations by early navigators, descriptions of the islands and their peoples, their history and records of the catholic missions, as related in contemporaneous books and manuscripts, showing the political, economic, commercial and religious conditions of those islands from their earliest relations with European nations to the beginning of the nineteenth century, translated from the originals.* 55 vols. Cleveland: A. H. Clark Co.

Boorstin, Daniel J.
1961   *The Image: A guide to pseudo-events in America.* New York: Harper & Row.

B.R.   See Blair, Emma Helen and James Alexander Robertson, eds.

Buzeta, Manuel, and Felipe Bravo
1850   *Diccionario geográfico, estadístico, histórico, de las Islas Fili-*

pinas. . . . 2 vols. Madrid: [Imprenta de D. José C. de la Peña].

C.A.A.   See *Catálogo Alfabético de Apellidos.*

Carrithers, Michael et al.
1990   On ethnography without tears. *Current Anthropology* 31(1):53–58.

Catálogo Alfabético de Apellidos (abbr. C.A.A.)
1973 [1849] Manila: Government Printing Office, National Archives Publication No.D-3.

Census of 1903.
              See United States, Bureau of the Census

Census of 1918.
              See Philippine Islands, Census Office.

Census of 1939.
              See Philippines (Commonwealth), Commission of the Census.

Clifford, James, and George E. Marcus
1986   *Writing Culture: The poetics and politics of ethnography.* Berkeley and Los Angeles: University of California Press.

Condominas, Georges
1965   *L'Exotique est quotidien: Sar Luk, Viet-nam central.* Paris: Plon.

Del la Costa, Horacio
1967   *The Jesuits in the Philippines, 1581–1768.* Cambridge, Mass.: Harvard University Press.

De la Peña, Apol B.
1968   Needed: New horizons in Siquijor. *Philippine Country Life* (May) 4(4):10, 12, 16–17.
1970   Siquijorians have reached the crossroads. *Philippine Country Life* (February) 12–15.

Derrida, Jacques
1976 [1967] *Of grammatology.* Translated by G. Chakravorty Spivak. Baltimore: Johns Hopkins University Press.

Dorst, John D.
1989   *The written suburb: An American site, an ethnographic dilemma.* Philadelphia: University of Pennsylvania Press.

Dumont, Jean-Paul
1981   Lost relatives: Social amnesia in a Visayan setting. *Philippine Quarterly of Culture and Society* 9(1):9–16.

1984   A matter of touristic "indifférance." *American Ethnologist*
            11(1):139–51.
1985a   Who are the *bricoleurs*? *American Journal of Semiotics*
            3(3):29–48.
1985b   Prologue to ethnography or prolegomena to anthro-
            pography. *Ethos* 14(4):344–67.
1987   Quels Tasaday? De la découverte et de l'invention d'au-
            trui. *L'Homme* 27(3):27–42.
1988a   The Tasaday, which and whose? Toward the political
            economy of an ethnographic sign. *Cultural Anthropology*
            3(3):261–75.
1988b   Dialogue de mythes: Etiologie plurielle d'une île des
            Philippines. *Poétique* 75:325–45.
1992 [1978] *The headman and I: Ambiguity and ambivalence in the field-
            working experience*. Prospect Heights (Ill.): Waveland
            Press.

Echaúz, Robustiano.
1978 [1894] *Sketches of the Island of Negros*. Translated and annotated
            by Donn V. Hart. Athens, Ohio: Ohio University Cen-
            ter for International Studies, Papers in International
            Studies, Southeast Asia Series no.50.

Enciclopedia Universal Ilustrada Europeo-Americana.
1907?–1930 70 vols. in 72. Madrid: Espasa-Calpe.

Espedido, Henry C.
1963   The pump boat comes to Siquijor. *Weekly Graphic* (Jan-
            uary 16) 29(30):24.
1972   Siquijor: The Philippines newest province. *Weekly
            Graphic* (Manila, February 23) 42–43.

Fowler, H. W., and F. G. Fowler (eds.)
1956 [1911] *The Concise Oxford Dictionary of Current English based on
            The Oxford Dictionary*. 4th ed. Oxford: Clarendon Press.

Fussell, Paul
1980   *Abroad: British literary traveling between the wars*. New
            York and Oxford: Oxford University Press.

Hernaez Romero, M[ari]a Fe
1974   *Negros Occidental between two foreign powers (1888–1909)*.
            Bacolod: Negros Occidental Historical Commission.

Inauguration Souvenir Program: Siquijor, Siquijor; Jan.8, 1972.
n.d. [1972] [Place of publication and publisher unknown].

Kondo, Dorinne K.
1990   *Crafting selves: Power, gender, and discourses of identity in a
            Japanese workplace*. Chicago: University of Chicago
            Press.

Larkin, John A.
1978   Negros: An historical perspective. *In* Echauz 1978:xii–
              xxiv.

Lévi-Strauss, Claude
1971   *Mythologiques IV: L'homme nu.* Paris: Plon.
1981 [1971]   *The naked man: Introduction to a science of mythology.* Vol.
              4. Translated by John & Doreen Weightman. New
              York: Harper & Row.

Lieban, Richard W.
1977 [1967]   *Cebuano sorcery: Malign magic in the Philippines.* Berkeley
              and Los Angeles: University of California Press.

Maghanoy, Lois L.
1977   Health and healing in a social setting: Siquijor island,
              Philippines. Ph.D. dissertation, Monash University.

Malinowski, Bronislaw
1967   *A diary in the strict sense of the term.* New York: Harcourt,
              Brace & World.

Manganaro, Marc, ed.
1990   *Modernist anthropology: From fieldwork to text.* Princeton:
              Princeton University Press.

Martínez Cuesta, Angel
1974   *Historia de la isla de Negros, Filipinas, 1565–1898.* Ma-
              drid: Pontificia Universitas Gregoriana, Facultas Histo-
              riae Ecclesiasticae.
1980 [1974]   *History of Negros.* Translated by Alfonso Felix Jr. and
              Sor Caritas Sevilla. Manila: Historical Conservation So-
              ciety, no.32.

Martínez de Zuñiga, Joaquín
1893   *Estadismo de las Islas Filipinas; ó, Mis viajes por este país.* 2
              vols. Illustrated by W. E. Retana. Madrid Vda. de M.
              Minuesa de los Rios.

Maypa, Ulysses F.
1960   Government projects on Siquijor island. *Technical-
              Statistical Review* (Manila, Department of Public Works
              and Communication, November–December 1960)
              4(6):24–25, 41–42, 43–45.

Montero y Vidal, José.
1887–1895   *Historia general de Filipinas desde el descubrimiento de di-
              chas Islas hasta nuestros días.* 3 vols. Madrid: M. Tello.

N.C.S.O.   See Philippines (Republic of the), National Census and
               Statistics Office.

Nowell, Charles E., ed.
1962   *Magellan's voyage around the world: Three contemporary ac-
               counts.* Evanston: Northwestern University Press.

Philippine Commission
               See United States, Bureau of the Census.

Philippine Islands, Census Office
1920–1921   *Census of the Philippine Islands, taken under the direction of
               the Philippine legislature in the year 1918.* 4 vols. in 6. Ma-
               nila: Bureau of Printing.

Philippines (Commonwealth), Commission of the Census
1940–1943   *Census of the Philippines: 1939.* 5 vols. in 8. Manila: Bu-
               reau of Printing.

Philippines (Republic of the), Bureau of the Census and Statistics
(abbr. B.C.S.)
1956   *Census of the Philippines: 1948. Summary of population and
               agriculture.* Vol. 3, part 1. Population.

Philippines (Republic of the), National Census and Statistics Office
(abbr. N.C.S.O.)
1974   *1971 census of agriculture. Negros Oriental.* Manila: Na-
               tional Economic and Development Authority, National
               Census and Statistics Office.
1975   *1975 integrated census of the population and its economic ac-
               tivities. Population Siquijor.* Manila: National Economic
               and Development Authority, National Census and Sta-
               tistics Office.
1981   *1980 census of fisheries. National summary.* Vol. 1. Munici-
               pal, commercial fishing. Manila: National Economic
               and Development Authority, National Census and Sta-
               tistics Office.
1982a   *1980 census of population: Special report no.1.* Manila: Na-
               tional Economic and Development Authority, National
               Census and Statistics Office.
1982b   *Philippines 1980: Special report no.3. Population, land area,
               and density: 1970, 1975, and 1980.* Manila: National
               Economic and Development Authority.
1983   *1980 census of the population and housing, Siquijor.* Ma-
               nila: National Economic and Development Authority,
               National Census and Statistics Office.

1985   *1980 census of agriculture, Siquijor.* Manila: National Economic and Development Authority, National Census and Statistics Office.

Putong, Cecilio
1965   *Bohol and its people.* Manila: [no publ.]

Quilicot, Diosdado Y.
1968   The island of fire. *Philippine Country Life* (May) 4(4):11, 15, 17.

Rabinow, Paul
1977   *Reflections on fieldwork in Morocco.* Berkeley and Los Angeles: University of California Press.
1979   Masked I go forward. *Philosophy and Social Criticism* 6(2):229–42.

Rafael, Vicente L.
1988   *Contracting colonialism: Translation and Christian conversion in Tagalog society under early Spanish rule.* Ithaca and London: Cornell University Press.

Richardson, Laurel
1990   Narrative and sociology. *Journal of Contemporary Ethnography* 19(1):116–35.

Robles, Eliodoro G.
1969   *The Philippines in the nineteenth century.* Quezon City: Malaya Books.

Rosell, Dominador Z.
1938   Siquijor island: Random notes of a student of soil geography. *Philippine Magazine* (September) 35(9):418, 436.

Roth, Paul A.
1989a   How narratives explain? *Social Research* 56(2):449–78.
1989b   "Ethnography without tears" *Current Anthropology* 30(5):555–561.

Said, Edward W.
1978   *Orientalism.* New York: Random House, Pantheon Books.

San Antonio, Juan Francisco de
1977 [1738]   *The Philippine Chronicles of Fray San Antonio.* Translated by Pedro Picornell. Manila: Historical Conservation Society, no.29.

Sanjek, Roger, ed.
1990   *Fieldnotes: The makings of anthropology.* Ithaca and London: Cornell University Press.

Scott, William Henry
1984 [1968] *A critical study of the prehispanic source materials for the*
             study of Philippine history. Rev. ed. Quezon City: New
             Day Publishers.

Siquijor Municipal Development Staff (abbr. S.M.D.S.)
1976   *Comprehensive plan for Siquijor, Siquijor.* Cebu City: De-
             partment of Local Government and Community Devel-
             opment, Direct Technical Assistance Program.

Siquijor Provincial Development Staff (abbr. S.P.D.S.)
1983   *Siquijor Province 1983: Socio-economic profile.* Cebu City:
             National Media Production Center, Region VII.

S.M.D.S.   See Siquijor Municipal Development Staff.

Spate, Oskar Hermann K.
1979   *The Spanish Lake.* Minneapolis: University of Minnesota
             Press.

S.P.D.S.   See Siquijor Provincial Development Staff.

Spoehr, Alexander
1980   *Protein from the sea: Technological change in Philippine cap-*
             ture fisheries. Pittsburgh: University of Pittsburgh, De-
             partment of Anthropology, Ethnology Monographs,
             no. 3.

Stoller, Paul
1989   *Fusion of the worlds: An ethnography of possession among the*
             Songhay of Niger. Chicago: University of Chicago Press.

Toulmin, Stephen
1990   *Cosmopolis: The hidden agenda of modernity.* New York:
             Free Press.

Tumapon, Cipriana B.
n.d.[1972]   Siquijor in retrospect and prospect. *In Inauguration*
             Souvenir Program, 37–44.

Tyler, Stephen A.
1987   *The unspeakable: Discourse, dialogue, and rhetoric in the*
             postmodern world. Madison: University of Wisconsin
             Press.

United States, Bureau of the Census.
1905   *Census of the Philippine Islands, taken under the direction of*
             the Philippine Commission in the year 1903. 4 vols. Wash-
             ington: Government Printing Office.

Wernstedt, Frederick L. and J. E. Spencer
1978 [1967] *The Philippine island world: A physical, cultural, and re-*

gional geography. Berkeley: University of California
Press.

Wolff, John U.
1972   *A dictionary of Cebuano Visayan.* 2 vols. Ithaca: Cornell
            University, Southeast Asia Program and Linguistic So-
            ciety of the Philippines.

Zaide, Gregorio F.
1979   *The pageant of Philippine history.* 2 vols. Manila: Philip-
            pine Education Company.

INDEX

(Visayan family names are denoted by CAPITALS.)

Aglipay, G. (bishop), 19
aglipayanism, 19, 95
agriculture, 10–13, 19, 23–24, 28,
    41, 43–44, 66–67, 70–80, 137,
    171, 173–74, 177, 179, 205,
    208–9
Agustina. *See* MONTUYA, Agustina
Albert. *See* QUILICOT, Albert
Albo, F. (Greek pilot), 57
Algeria, 125
Alvin. *See* DAGATAN, Alvin
Americans, 26–34, 198
amnesia (social), 146–56, 163
amor. See gugma
Ana. *See* DAGATAN, Ana
Andres (*manong*). *See* SUMAGANG,
    Andres
Anong (*Tan*). *See* PAGLINAWAN,
    Mariano
anthem (of Siquijor), 204
Antonio. *See* PASCO, Antonio; QUILI-
    COT, Antonio
Aquino regime, 208
Arturo. *See* QUILICOT, Arturo
Auntie Diding, xi, xvii, xviii, 9–15,
    24, 26, 34, 43–51, 66–80, 93–
    94, 101, 104, 108–9, 120, 124–
    28, 131–40, 143–48, 156–58,
    160, 173–75, 181, 184–86, 196,
    198, 199, 203, 204, 206–8
Aurelia. *See* QUILICOT, Aurelia

Baclayon (municipality), 62–63
Bacolod (city), 36
BACSAL, Matea, 177
BAGUIO, Vicenta, 166
balak (poetry), 186, 201–3
balbal, 13–14
Baliangao (municipality), 190–91
Balicasag (island), 63
balikbayan, 30, 133
balitaw, 202–3
Bandilaan (mount), 62, 67
Bantayan (island), 35
barangay, xvii, 9, 20, 24, 27, 28, 31,
    40, 42, 48, 87–90, 97, 145, 154,
    156–57, 174
barangay captain. *See* SAPLOT, Victor
barangay peasants, 9–14, 27–28, 43–
    51, 66–80, 81–90, 93, 98, 100–
    104, 117, 119–35, 140, 143–50,
    164, 195, 197–98, 202–3, 205
barkada, 47, 144, 149, 198, 202
barrio, 87. See also *barangay*
BATBAT, Bonifacio, 171
BATBAT, Nicolasa, 171
BATO, Santas, xvii, 187–88, 190,
    192, 199
Benigna. *See* PASCO, Benigna
Berto. *See* DAGATAN, Berto
Birhen sa Barangay, 122
Blair, E. H., and J. A. Robertson,
    56–57, 59–60